Of Building

Roger North's
Writings on Architecture

The Honourable
Roger North Esq.
Ætatis cir: 30.

P. Lely. pinx. 1680. Geo. Vertue sculp 1740.

Lely's portrait of Roger North, painted in 1680, from an engraving by George Vertue

Of Building

—

Roger North's Writings on Architecture

Edited by

HOWARD COLVIN

and

JOHN NEWMAN

CLARENDON PRESS · OXFORD
1981

Oxford University Press, Walton Street, Oxford OX2 6DP

London   Glasgow   New York   Toronto
Delhi   Bombay   Calcutta   Madras   Karachi
Kuala Lumpur   Singapore   Hong Kong   Tokyo
Nairobi   Dar es Salaam   Cape Town
Melbourne   Wellington
and associate companies in
Beirut   Berlin   Ibadan   Mexico City

© *Howard Colvin and John Newman 1981*

Published in the United States by
Oxford University Press, New York

British Library Cataloguing in Publication Data
North, Roger, b. 1653
Of building, Roger North's writings on architecture
1. Architecture—Early works to 1800
I. Title   II. Colvin, Howard Montagu
III. Newman, John
720   NA2516   79–40670
ISBN 0–19–817325–3

Set by BAS Printers Ltd
Over Wallop, Hants
and printed in Great Britain
at the University Press, Oxford
by Eric Buckley
Printer to the University

Acknowledgements

The editors wish to acknowledge the kindness of Mr Roger North in permitting them to print the manuscript of his ancestor's essay on architecture, and to express their gratitude for the hospitality extended to them both at Rougham Hall. They are also much indebted to Mrs Margaret Newman for typing the entire manuscript of this book, to Mr James Austin for photographing portions of the Rougham manuscript, and to Dr David Robey for his help in elucidating one of Roger North's more obscure literary references. The editor of the *Architectural Review* has kindly allowed portions of H. M. Colvin's article on 'Roger North and Sir Christopher Wren', published in that journal in October 1951, to be reprinted in the Introduction. Extracts from the British Library text of North's essay and reproductions of some of his drawings are published by permission of the British Library Board.

Contents

List of Illustrations

Frontispiece
Lely's portrait of Roger North, painted in 1680, from an engraving by
George Vertue

Plans (pp. xxviii, xxix)
Rougham Hall, showing the rooms mentioned in Roger North's text.
Based on an eighteenth-century survey at Rougham

Plates (at end)

Introduction

Roger North was the youngest member of a remarkable family of brothers. Their father was Dudley, later 4th Lord North (d. 1677), an accomplished gentleman of intellectual tastes who had a varied career as a soldier, member of parliament, and author. At the time of Roger's birth, the 3rd of September 1653, his father was living at Tostock in Suffolk, but the family spent much of its time at Kirtling in Cambridgeshire, the seat of Roger's grandfather the 3rd Lord North, an old impoverished courtier who died in 1666 at the age of eighty-five. Even after he had inherited the family estates the 4th Lord North was by no means well off, and (with the exception of Charles, the eldest) all his sons were obliged to make their own way in the world. Francis (1637–85) did well at the Common Law, becoming first Attorney-General, then Chief Justice of the Common Pleas, and finally (December 1682) Lord Chancellor and Keeper of the Great Seal, with the title of Lord Guilford. Dudley (1641–91) was a successful merchant who before he was forty had amassed a large fortune at Smyrna and Constantinople and returned to England to become a Sheriff of London, a Commissioner of Customs, and a Lord of the Treasury. John (1645–83) was a scholar who attained the professorship of Greek at Cambridge and the mastership of Trinity College there before his early death in his thirty-eighth year. Montagu, the fifth son, was a London merchant whose career was disrupted by war when he was captured by the French and kept a prisoner at Toulon for three years.

Roger himself was destined for the law. After two years as a fellow commoner at Jesus College, Cambridge, he was entered at the Middle Temple in 1669 and called to the bar in 1675. His own ability and the influence of his elder brother Francis brought him many briefs. He became in due course a King's Counsel and a Bencher of his Inn, steward to Archbishop Sancroft, and Solicitor-General to the Duke of York. Lord Clarendon regarded him as one of the only two honest lawyers whom he had ever met. After the Duke's accession to the throne in 1685 he was appointed Attorney-General to the Queen and was elected to Parliament as member for Dunwich. But with the death of his 'best brother' Francis later in the same year his career began to falter.

George Jeffreys, his brother's rival and successor, proved to be an inveterate enemy who did his best to damage Roger's reputation as a lawyer. And in 1688 the Revolution destroyed the whole Tory interest of which the brotherhood of the Norths had formed part. Refusing to take the oath to the new monarchs, Roger gave up his practice and retired to the country. In 1691 he 'cast anchor in Norfolk', where he had purchased an estate at Rougham, a village some 7 miles north of Swaffham. In 1696, at the age of forty-three, he married the daughter of a fellow non-juror, Sir Robert Gayer of Stoke Poges, and founded a family which still flourishes at Rougham. Here, on 1 March 1733/4, Roger died in his eighty-first year, having survived all his brothers and become the patriarch of his family.

It was, however, neither as the squire of Rougham nor as a successful lawyer that Roger North achieved his posthumous celebrity, but as a writer, and more particularly as the biographer of his three better-known brothers. Brisk, lively, and entertainingly anecdotal, *The Lives of the Norths* are as readable as Aubrey's *Brief Lives* and as revealing of seventeenth-century *mores* and habits of mind. To them, in Jessopp's edition of 1890, is appended Roger's own *Autobiography*, first printed by subscription in 1887. Unfinished, and less polished than the lives of his brothers, it was probably his earliest literary effort.[1] Frank, pithy, and discursive, it reveals its author as a man of an active and inquiring mind, whose intellectual energies were by no means monopolized by the law. In the course of a long life he found time to study optics and mathematics, to edit and publish a seminal treatise on economics written by his brother Dudley,[2] to write manuals on pisciculture, accountancy, and farming,[3] to listen to, and to theorize about, music,[4] to collect pictures, to plant—and to build.

Although never a member of the Royal Society, Roger North was nevertheless in touch with the intellectual and scientific ideas of his time. He had read Descartes at Cambridge at a time when 'the new philosophy

---

[1] As argued by R. W. Ketton-Cremer in *Essays and Studies of the English Association* (1959), p. 77, and confirmed by John Wilson, *Roger North on Music* (1959), p. 361.

[2] See W. Letwin, *The Origins of Scientific Economics* (1963), pp. 189–90 and Appendix IV for evidence that the Preface to Dudley North's *Discourses upon Trade* (1691) was written by Roger North.

[3] *A Discourse of Fish and Fish Ponds*, 'Done by a Person of Honour' (1713), *The Gentleman Accomptant*, 'Done by a Person of Honour' (1714), *The Gentleman Farmer*, 'Done by a Person of Honour in the County of Norfolk' (1726). The manuscript of *The Gentleman Accomptant* is BL Add. MS 32528.

[4] See *Roger North on Music*, ed. John Wilson (1959).

was a sort of heresy', he had attempted to arrive 'at a system of nature, upon the Cartesian, or rather mechanical principles', he was an expert at dialling, and as a 'dabbler in mechanics . . . fell into that disease that all tyros in that art do, a conceit of having found a perpetual movement'. For a person of these tastes the transition from science to architecture was an easy one, as it had been for Robert Hooke and Sir Christopher Wren before him. For was not architecture, in Evelyn's words, 'the flower and crown as it were of all the sciences mathematical', the supreme employment for a man with a mechanical hand and a philosophical mind? But a young lawyer has few opportunities to develop a latent talent for architecture, and but for the fire which destroyed the Temple in 1678, Roger North might never have counted architecture among his 'mechanical entertainments'. As it was, he played a prominent part in the negotiations between the gentlemen of the Middle Temple and Nicholas Barbon, the undertaker of their new buildings, and it was in 'drawing the model of my little chamber, and making patterns for the wainscot', that he learned the use of a scale and tasted for the first time 'the joys of designing and executing known only to such as practise or have practised it'.

This, however, was 'but a beginning'. Soon North was buying the architectural textbooks of the day, Palladio, Scamozzi, and Evelyn's translation of Fréart's invaluable *Parallel of the Antient Architecture with the Modern*. He taught himself the principles of perspective, and spent many happy hours in drawing 'which might have been better and more profitably employed'. As North's ruling passion, architecture took second place only to music, and his active mind delighted in the technicalities of building just as it did in the niceties of draughtsmanship. At a time when architecture was a polite accomplishment rather than a professional qualification, he was soon as well equipped to design a building as any of his better-known contemporaries, not excluding 'the great Sir Christopher Wren' himself. We do not know how long Wren and North had been acquainted when, in 1680, the former was called in by the Benchers to provide a design for their new Cloisters, and to pass the workmen's accounts, some of which North had to settle when in 1683–4 he held office as Treasurer of his Inn. But North's own interest in the buildings was more than merely a financial one, for it was he who designed the Great Gateway which still gives access to the Temple from Fleet Street (Pl. 3). It was built in 1683–4, the year of his treasurership and when it was finished the uppermost chamber was assigned to him as a perquisite.[5] An original elevation for the gateway in North's hand survives among his papers at Rougham (Pl. 2), and the problems that the design presented are explained in a characteristic passage.

When I built the Temple gate [he tells us], I designed 4 pilaster columes, and a frontoon [i.e. a pediment]. But it being necessary for preserving the dignity of such a fabrick, between very high houses to raise the frontoon eves, above the cornish of the houses, which would not addmitt such a distribution, taken from the bottom, and 2 columes had bin too imense for our materiall as well as room, not to mention the purse, therefore I raised the first story with rustick stone, and made a flatt arch for the coaches to pass, whereby I gained the greatest passage height I could; and compass [i.e. round-headed] ones for the shopps, lower so as to lay the thrust of the other upon the solid, clear of the void, and set ballconys over these compass arches. Then a fillett of stone, and above that a deep plane, which served as stylobate, or foundation for the columnes, being more in height than ordinary, and upon that sett the bases, by which means the collumnes were brought into due proportion to the height, and alltogether hath no ill aspect.[6]

That North discussed the design with Wren—but did not feel obliged to take his advice—emerges from a later passage in which he records that Wren tried to persuade him to employ wood and plaster in the pediment and entablature in order to save expense, 'but out of a proud high spirit I declined it, and made the whole intablature and frontoon of stone, and it is as lusty, as most are'.[7]

Roger North's own contribution to English architecture was not large, for unlike his friend Hugh May or that other gentleman surveyor Sir Roger Pratt, he never became 'a profest architect', and did not 'pretend either to great publik designes, nor new models of great howses'.[8] Early in the 1680s he carried out various works at Wroxton Abbey in Oxfordshire, the seat of his brother Lord Guilford. A new stable-block was the principal addition. It still stands to the south of the house, and is a simple building of almost vernacular character with a plain pediment to mark its centre. To the house itself a new drawing-room and back-stairs were added and the 'rooms of state' were fitted up. The work was supervised by one Watson, whom North described as

[5] *Middle Temple Records*, ed. C. H. Hopwood, iii (1905), 1363, 1364, 1365, 1367. The master mason was John Shorthose, the master bricklayer Joseph Lem.

[6] BL MS, fo. 37ᵛ. For a more extended analysis of his design for the Middle Temple gate see pp. 51–2 below.

[7] Below, p. 52.

[8] He did, however, leave rough notes of a 'Project of Rebuilding' Whitehall Palace after the fire of January 1697/8, for which see p. 150 below.

'very fitt for the buissness', but (he tells us), 'I took upon me the honour of being prime architect'.[9] In 1690 the purchase of Rougham gave him a large but old-fashioned house of his own, which he proceeded to remodel gradually, as his means allowed, adding a gallery at the back and an Ionic portico in front (see Pl. 1 and the plans on pp. xxviii, xxix). Later he altered or enlarged the north aisle of Rougham church, in order to accommodate a parish library which he established for the use both of future incumbents and of his own successors at the Hall. But within fifty years of North's death in 1734 all his careful provisions for the future had been set at naught. Already in his lifetime his son and heir Roger 'occasioned him some little trouble and anxiety'.[10] To his own children Roger II was harsh and overbearing. He flogged his elder son Fountain so unmercifully that the boy ran away to sea, and did not return until he learned of his father's death in 1771. Hating Rougham and all its associations, he pulled the house down and lived for the rest of his life at Hastings.[11] At the same time the parish library was destroyed and its contents dispersed.[12] Today nothing remains of Roger North's works at Rougham except an octagonal dovecote, a solitary Ionic capital (Pl. 15), and the avenues that he planted.

The destruction of Rougham Hall leaves the Middle Temple Gate and the treatise on Architecture as the principal memorials of Roger North's architectural activities. The treatise was the direct outcome of his experience in rebuilding his own house, and culminates in what is probably the most detailed account of the planning and building of a seventeenth-century house in English architectural literature. But it is more than just the record of one man's activity as an amateur architect. For North was, in his own words, one who 'loved to drive [whatever he had in hand] to some originall source of reason'.[13] So although the allusions to Rougham are numerous they are introduced in such a way as to illustrate general principles, and the result is a treatise that invites comparison with Wotton's *Elements of Architecture* (1624), Gerbier's

---

[9] BL Add. MS 32510, fos. 137–9; cf. *Victoria County History of Oxfordshire*, ix. 172–3 and plate.

[10] *The Autobiography of the Hon. Roger North*, ed. Jessopp (1887), p. xxxviii.

[11] Marianne North, *Recollections of a Happy Life*, ed. Symonds (1892), i. 2.

[12] A catalogue of the library, however, survives among the Norwich Episcopal Records. It is dated 1714, and lists some 1,150 volumes, of which over 800 were theological. See notes thereon in Bodleian Library MS Eng. Misc. c. 360, fos. 259–61. A receipt for a legacy of £20 left to 'the parochiall library here' in 1722 is signed by a churchwarden and by 'Roger North, founder' (Bodleian MS North b. 17, no. 94).

[13] Quoted from p. 19 below.

Counsel and Advice to all Builders (1663), and the materials left by Sir Roger Pratt and edited by Gunther.[14] All these, like North, offer advice to the prospective builders of gentlemen's houses. Wotton's prose is elegant, Gerbier's pretentious, Pratt's practical and straightforward. Informal and almost conversational in style, North's book is by far the most readable of them all: indeed, it is hardly going too far to claim it as the most entertaining treatise on its subject in the English language.

Though informal in its language, and happily free from the pedantry that makes Evelyn's *Account of Architects and Architecture* so tedious to read, North's treatise follows an intelligible plan, and that plan can be set out as follows:

1. Prefatory remarks (pp. 1–2).
2. Defence of 'the vanity of building' against various criticisms (pp. 3–6).
3. How houses reflect the characters of their builders (pp. 7–9).
4. The nature and perception of beauty in architecture (pp. 10–20).
5. Aesthetic faults in architecture (pp. 21–22).
6. Problems of architectural supervision: the disadvantages of employing professional surveyors (pp. 23–25).
7. Whether to repair an old house or to build a new one (pp. 26–30).
8. How to proceed in improving an old house (including the use of drawings and models) (pp. 31–35).
9. Materials (bricks, timber, lime, stone, roofing) (pp. 36–39).
10. Water and drainage (pp. 40–41).
11. Vaults and arches (pp. 41–44).
12. Walls and foundations (pp. 45–47).
13. Chimneys (pp. 48–50).
14. The use of the Orders (pp. 51–52).
15. Windows (pp. 53–55).
16. Of unity and variety in architectural composition (pp. 56–59).
17. Types of house plans (pp. 60–77).
18. His own experience in remodelling Rougham Hall (pp. 77–88).
19. Additional matters relating to the building of country houses (situation and siting, cisterns, offices, stables, barns, brewhouses, dairies, dovecotes) (pp. 89–103).

Although it was the experience of rebuilding Rougham Hall that induced Roger North to write about architecture, his interest in the

---

[14] *The Architecture of Sir Roger Pratt*, ed. R. T. Gunther (1928).

subject was, of course, of long standing. Twenty years had elapsed since the fire at the Temple had led him to purchase his first drawing instruments, and since then he had not only designed the Temple Gate but planned the alterations to his brother's house at Wroxton. He was familiar with the royal palaces at Whitehall, Windsor, Winchester, Hampton Court, and Audley End; and he observed buildings critically as he travelled round the country, whether on circuit as a lawyer (Salisbury, Gloucester and Durham Cathedrals, Euston, Badminton, Appleby, Belvoir), or visiting his relatives (Kirtling, Chevening, Balmes), his Norfolk neighbours (Melton Constable, Raynham, Felbrigg), or the great men with whom he and his brothers were acquainted (Ham House, Tring). In London he had even talked on equal terms with Wren about matters architectural, and had watched the building of St. Paul's with an eye open both to the aesthetic problems inherent in designing a great cathedral and to the refinements of building technology that it called forth. In the *Lives of the Norths* he tells us how he and his brother Dudley used to go to St. Paul's on Saturdays, 'which were Sir Christopher Wren's days, who was the surveyor, and we commonly got a snatch of discourse with him, who, like a true philosopher, was always obliging and communicative and, in every matter we inquired about, gave short but satisfactory answers'.[15] These conversations are not without an interest of their own, for North asked leading questions, and Wren gave characteristic answers. Why, for instance, in the exterior of the cathedral did the Surveyor break his entablatures out over the pilasters, contrary to classical propriety and (in North's opinion) with unfortunate aesthetic effect? For the reason which compelled Inigo Jones to do the same in the exterior of the Banqueting House.

For they could not have materialls to make good single columnes nor to project the entabletures so farr as to range strait over the heads of the columnes but were forc't in the one to double the orders, and in the other to double both columnes and the orders, and in both to break the entablements without; which shift Sir Christopher Wren informed me of when I observed to him the exility of his columnes, with respect to the grandure of his fabrick at Paulls.[16]

[15] *The Lives of the Norths*, ii. 238.

[16] Below, p. 22. This confirms the statement in *Parentalia* (1750), p. 288, that the lack of sufficiently large stones was a crucial consideration in the decision to split the west portico into two orders of double columns rather than to use a single giant order as shown in several of Wren's drawings. We are indebted to Mr R. Crayford for pointing out that there are structural indications that the west front was designed with a giant order in mind, and that the tremendous weight of the pediment would almost certainly have disrupted the masonry of composite

More amusing, and more revealing in its suggestion of Wren's essentially intellectual approach to architecture, is his reply to North's question about the design of the Queen's Apartment at Whitehall.

In exceeding high rooms [North writes] it is best for them and us to have high windoes square above the others to light the roof, which else will be too dark, and consequently dull. These were not made in my Queen's appartment by the water side in Whitehall altho' I thought that sort of building had required it. I ask't Sir Christopher Wren the reason of it, and he answered that the reflexion of the sky from the water would be light enough to the roof, which was an ingenious thought, and fully satisfied me.[17]

But the most precious of these fragments of Wren's conversation, casually introduced by North into the text of his treatise, is on the subject of aesthetics.

In the next place [he says] I thinck to discours a litle of Beauty, and the true principle on which it depends, for I doe not thinck any thing is less studdy'd, knowne, or more mistaken than that is. I had once some discourse with Sir Christopher Wren on this subject, who for argument sake, held that there was that distinction in Nature, of gracefull and ugly; and that it must be so to all creatures that had vision. I maintained that there was no such distinction in Nature but it arose from the judgement and use of things. He alledged, that of triangules, an equilater was more agreable than a scalene, and some other such instances, as the stated demensions of columnes, which I shall consider anon.[18]

Now in maintaining this proposition, Wren was not striking out a new theory just 'for argument sake'. For in his own considered summary of aesthetic theory, printed in *Parentalia*, he adopts precisely the same standpoint, laying it down as an axiom that

There are two Causes of Beauty, natural and customary. Natural is from *Geometry*, consisting in Uniformity (that is Equality) and Proportion. Customary Beauty is begotten by the Use of our Senses to those Objects which are usually pleasing to us for other Causes, as Familiarity ... breeds a Love to Things not in themselves lovely. Here lies the great occasion of Errors; here is

---

columns made up of smaller stones, however carefully jointed. Those (e.g. Margaret Whinney, *Wren*, 1971, p. 112) who have seen the problem in terms of the lack of sufficiently large stones to span the *intercolumniations* are mistaken, for each intercolumnar section of architrave in the existing portico has in the middle a stone which appears to have no support and is in fact suspended from a secret arch bearing on its neighbours. This was a structural difficulty that Wren knew how to solve, but giant columns and overhanging cornices presented an insuperable problem.

[17]Below, p. 55.
[18]BL MS, fo. 11, and see p. 10 below.

tried the Architect's judgment: but always the true Test is natural or geometrical Beauty.[19]

North's own standpoint was less dogmatic and more in accordance with the philosophical ideas of his favourite Descartes, whom he admired 'for his principles, the shaking off qualitys, which terme confesseth ignorance, and reducing all things to *longum, latum & profundum*'.[20] Among contemporary architectural writers he had something in common with Perrault (whose *Ordonnance des cinq espèces de colonnes*, 1683, he may well have read). Like Perrault he believes in common sense and judgement rather than in the absolute authority of geometrical proportion. Thus, while agreeing with Wren that an equilateral triangle is more pleasing than a scalene, he attributes this to the fact that the former suggests stability to the beholder while the latter 'is in a posture of falling'—in other words to rational deduction allied with experience rather than to any inherent perfection in the form. One of his guiding principles was that 'knowledge pleaseth and ignorance, or surprise, the contrary'. 'Now to apply this speculation to our subject, building. First uniformity is pleasant. For that consists of intelligible parts layd out in due proportions so that the whole is better comprehended, than if it were of discordant and disorderly parts without relation to each other.' From this it follows that classical architecture is superior to Gothic, in so far as the former is based on recognized rules, embodied in 'the doctrine of the 5 orders', while the latter is a capricious mode of building 'introduct by a barbarous sort of people that first distrest then dissolved the Roman Empire'.[21]

Another of Roger North's architectural maxims was 'that nothing is handsome which does not appear to the eye strong'.[22] Thus the corners of a building should be emphasized by 'stones set clasp-wise called coyne stones', because it is there that strength is needed. Solids should be placed over solids, and voids over voids. Nothing suggesting instability can be allowed, whether it is a top-heavy cornice or a mass of masonry poised on Gothic arches. In the last resort the Orders themselves are subject to this rule. For North will have none of the anthropomorphic analogies which see columns as related to the human

[19] *Parentalia* (1750), p. 351. See also J. A. Bennett, 'Christopher Wren: the natural causes of Beauty', *Architectural History*, xv (1972).

[20] BL Add. MS 32506, fo. 19ᵛ, a passage not printed in Jessopp's edition of North's Autobiography.

[21] BL MS, fos 13ᵛ, 16, 31.

[22] BL MS, fo. 70.

figure: for him a column is correctly proportioned if it looks right in relation to its load and material and badly proportioned if it does not. It is all a matter of 'reason and experience', not of principle and authority. However the logic of this argument drove him to further conclusions of a much more radical character than anything implied by Wren's theory of the inherent beauty of geometry. For if an Order suggests to the mind the support of a heavy weight, it follows that it is inappropriate to use it to decorate such things as cabinets, chimney-pieces, or small funerary monuments. Indeed, since it is associated with the idea of protection from the elements, an Order cannot properly be used merely to embellish the interior of a room. Even on the outside of a building North would not admit the propriety of applied columns unless they actually support an overhanging cornice designed to keep off the rain, and it followed that the entablature must be continuous and ought not to be broken back to the wall in between the columns. Finally, since 'an Order of columnes with the entableture doe properly note an intire structure, whereof the columnes are the support, and the entableture, the frame or eaves of the roof', it is wrong to place one order over another, for this is 'like setting one house above another, and besides makes the whole appear litle'.[23] It is fair to ask how far Roger North observed these principles in his own architectural works. At Rougham a pediment carried on a giant Ionic order was the only external embellishment. The shafts of the columns were made of flint faced with brick, and the stone capitals and bases were clumsily cut by some country mason (Pl. 15), but these were (so North assures us) defects that were noticed by few, and from a little distance the whole had a 'a very good aspect'.[24] Otherwise the symmetrical façade that he contrived out of the old irregular house that he had bought was perfectly plain and unassuming, and was saved from many-windowed monotony only by the high-shouldered pavilions which divided its length into three clearly articulated portions (Pl. 1). Within, North was induced by the poor proportions of the hall to introduce a vertical element in the form of 'pilaster work' in the wainscot and screen. Though this was contrary to one of the principles expounded in the treatise, we have his assurance that it was remarkably successful in disguising the lowness of the ceiling.[25]

When he designed the Temple Gate Roger North likewise found that

[23]BL MS, fo. 42 (below, p. 52).
[24]Below, p. 83.
[25]Below, p. 79.

in practice architecture is a compromise between the ideal and the practicable. The narrow space between the adjoining houses and the need to provide an adequate carriage-way made anything in the nature of a triumphal arch impossible and obliged him to set his order of pilasters on a podium which was rather awkwardly pierced by a wide flat arch flanked by two round ones. 'I could not compass the midle arch', he tells us, 'and flatt the side ones, because the story above must be preserved, but that [would have] bin much more proper.'[26] A drawing in his hand shows an alternative treatment of the central opening as a segmental arch, but this was no doubt rejected because it provided insufficient headroom for wheeled traffic (Pl. 2).

That the faults of the Temple Gate were due to its circumscribed site is clear both from North's own remarks and from his sketch for a monumental gateway in Whitehall, intended to form a central feature between the Banqueting House on the south and a replica of the latter to be built immediately to the north of the gateway (p. 150). Here the relationship between entry and façade is solved without violence either to architectural propriety or to convenience.

It remains to consider the original drawings in Roger North's hand that survive at Rougham and in the British Library.[27] Several of these are plans of Wroxton or surveys of the old house at Rougham. Another is a design for a London town-house with a subterranean carriage-entrance (Pl. 11). Only eight or nine are drawings with any architectural pretensions, and most of these are concerned with an attempt to design a compact villa-like house with a central hall lit by a hidden cupola (Pl. 7). The elevations are plain and astylar, except on the main front, where Ionic pilasters support a pediment whose base is interrupted by a round-headed window. The effect is neat and the internal arrangements are ingenious, but in one version the cornice is in direct contact with the capitals precisely in the manner censured by North at St. Paul's (Pl. 6). And when, in another drawing (Pl. 13), we find a chimney-piece flanked by two Ionic pilasters, we may conclude that the author of the treatise was no dogmatic purist, but an architectural latitudinarian whose practice was not always in accordance with his precept.

Neither as a theorist nor as a practising architect did Roger North have any discernible influence on his contemporaries. His writings on architecture were probably unknown outside his family circle, and with

[26]BL MS, fo. 37ᵛ, and see below, p. 51.
[27]See below, pp. 153–5.

the exception of the Temple Gate (long supposed to be the work of Wren) his executed buildings were little noticed. As a commentary on seventeenth-century architecture by a man endowed with unusual intelligence and literary ability the treatise on building is, however, a document of the greatest interest. In its informal way, it treats of matters that must often have occupied the minds of others who were either too lazy, or (like Wren and Hooke) too busy to follow his example, and its lively style is such that it can be read with pleasure by others besides the professed architectural historian.

The Manuscripts

Roger North left all his papers and manuscripts to his second son Montagu, who entered the Church and died a Canon of Windsor in 1779.[1] From Montagu's successors they passed into the possession, first of the Norfolk antiquary Dawson Turner (d. 1858), and then of James Crossley, a well-known literary figure of the nineteenth century. After Crossley's death in 1883 his library was dispersed at Sotheby's. Most of the North manuscripts were acquired by the British Museum, where they now form British Library Additional MSS 32500 to 32551, but one lot, comprising several volumes, was bought by Marianne North, the maiden sister of the then owner of Rougham, Charles North.[2] North's writings on architecture are contained in two volumes, one at Rougham, the other British Library Additional MS 32540. Both are written throughout in his own hand and occasionally illustrated by marginal diagrams.

The Rougham volume 'Of Building', although, as its full title indicates, not intended for publication, is clearly North's finished work on the subject, and is therefore printed here in its entirety. It is written in a stout, vellum-bound volume measuring 23.5 cm. × 18 cm. and occupies 158 pages according to North's, not entirely accurate, pagination.[3] The essay was composed at the completion of his building works at Rougham and can be dated almost certainly to the year 1698. This is the date in the margin of fo. 14; and internal evidence suggests that North wrote his essay in the first half of that year. Thus the fire which destroyed Whitehall Palace on 4 January 1698 is mentioned on fo. 114, while his reference to Chevening, the house of his aunt, Dorothy, Lady Dacre, on fo. 104 as 'My lady Dacre's' suggests that this passage was written before her death, at the age of ninety-three, in the summer of the same year.[4]

[1] Roger North's will, PCC 223 OCKHAM (PRO, PROB 11/667, fo. 242).

[2] Marianne North recorded the purchase on the flyleaves. Sotheby's Catalogue shows that they formed lot 3055 in the sale of 11–20 June 1885.

[3] Previously North had written in the volume, starting at the other end, an essay entitled 'Cursory Notes of Musicke'. This occupies 224 pages and concludes with a full stop, a flourish, and 'fin'. By contrast, the essay on building finishes at a semicolon, on the verso of the last page of the musical essay.

[4] Lady Dacre's will (PRO, PROB 11/446, fo. 160) was proved on 8 July 1698.

British Library Additional MS 32540 contains five essays in North's hand, of which the first two are devoted to our subject. Fos. 1–68^v are entitled 'Of Building', fos. 69–80^v 'Architecture', and it is clear from the slight discoloration of the first and last leaves of both that they were originally separate and probably without covers.

Of these two the fragment 'Architecture' must be the earlier, dating from before the death of North's brother Dudley in December 1691. The evidence for this is on fo. 78^v, where an account of the method of Turkish timber-framing, 'nailing all together with long spikes' (also recounted in the Life of Sir Dudley, *Lives*, ii. 139) is introduced with the phrase 'My worthy and curious freind at Stambole hath informed me ...', wording that North would hardly have used after his brother's death. A *terminus post quem* is provided by the reference to arching over the transept doorways at St. Paul's Cathedral, work carried out in the latter part of 1687.

The much longer essay 'Of Building', on the other hand, is a first draft for the Rougham treatise. North did not consider it a finished piece: 'if I should ... be idle enough to review these papers, correct the order and stile, and make decent draughts to them ...' (fo. 29). At the time of writing the remodelling of Rougham was 'neither finisht, nor doe I know, whether it will ever be so or not' (fo. 29). It appears, furthermore, that North was writing before his marriage in May 1696, for in discussing provisions for a numerous family he adds 'But where is not that call, (which is my chance, whether good or bad I doe not determine,) diversion and action is best directed, to procure conveniences for ourselves and freinds ...' (fo. 22).

The British Library essay 'Of Building', though it covers roughly the same ground as the finished treatise, and often refers to the same buildings by way of example, is constructed on a somewhat different plan and treats some matters barely touched on in the later work. There is even less overlap between the short early piece 'Architecture' and the treatise. Nevertheless it would be repetitive to print both the treatise itself and the complete text of the British Library manuscript; so all passages from the latter containing significant material lacking in the final version are printed here, either as footnotes to the main text, or in appendices, or, in the case of a few passages, as quotations in the introduction. The structure of the two British Library essays is as follows.

'ARCHITECTURE' (*c.*1690)

fo. 69	Proportions of the Orders. Their basis in utility.
fos. 70–1	Utility not the basis of Gothic architectural design.
fos. 71ᵛ–72ᵛ	Strength, convenience, and uniformity the causes of beauty in buildings.
fos. 73–4	Gothic disregard of these principles.
fos. 74ᵛ–80	Origin ·and development of Regular (i.e. classical) architecture.

'OF BUILDING' (*c.* 1695–6)

fos. 1–3ᵛ	Introductory. Reasons for writing.
fos. 4–10ᵛ	Preliminary comments on the dangers in embarking on building with insufficient forethought.
fos. 11–18	Principles of beauty, (*1*) use, (*2*) conformity to expectations.
fos. 18ᵛ–30ᵛ	Whether to build anew or to repair. The latter recommended.
fos. 31–9	On public buildings, with various comments on Gothic and Regular architecture.
fos. 39ᵛ–44	Principles of architectural composition.
fos. 45–6	The development of house types.
fos. 46ᵛ–68ᵛ	On planning a country house.

Two further brief passages are printed here in appendices, 1. The description in North's autobiography (BL Add. MS 32506, fos. 60ᵛ–62ᵛ) of the sector which he devised to facilitate the drawing of the parts of the Orders according to Palladio, omitted by Jessopp; and 2. North's project for rebuilding Whitehall Palace (BL Add. MS 32504, fos. 54–6).

Editorial Note

Roger North's essays on architecture were not prepared by him for publication. It has therefore been necessary to make certain editorial changes to the text of the manuscript, and for this John Wilson's *Roger North on Music* (1959) has been taken as a general guide.

The abbreviations y^e; y^t; y^r; *&*; wch have been expanded, as have most other abbreviations and proper names, e.g. p^{r}sent, retire͞mt, K.Ch.2., D. Lauderdale, Sr Chr. Wren. A few spellings that may mislead the reader have been revised, namely *whither* and *then* when they mean *whether* and *than*, *to* and *too* when they mean respectively *too* and *to*, and *of* and *off* when they mean *off* and *of*.

A final *e* has been added to a number of words which without it would now appear distracting. These mostly end with *s, g, t,* or *v*; e.g. *hous, imens, rang, strang, wast, receiv*.

North's use of capitals cannot be followed. Initial *g, i, n,* and *r* he regularly capitalizes in mid sentence, even in such words as *in, it, not,* etc. Other letters, *h, l, p,* for instance, are hardly ever used in the form of capitals, even to begin a proper name or a sentence. Still others, *c, e, m,* are written in a form indeterminate between capital and lower case.

North's punctuation has been retained as far as possible; but here again idiosyncrasies such as his frequent omission of a necessary punctuation mark at the end of a line has meant that many small alterations have been made, for the sake of sense and clarity. The paragraphs follow North's.

Pointed brackets, $\langle \ \rangle$, are occasionally placed round letters or words supplied, (*a*) where letters written by North have been lost in the binding and trimming of the manuscript, and (*b*) to correct his accidental omission of letters or words necessary for the sense.

Square brackets, [ ], are used to indicate omissions required by the sense. Foreign words and phrases have been italicized here, although North does not so indicate them.

Gallery

Chamber

Dressing Room

Mrs North's Closet

Mr and Mrs North's Bed Chamber

Bed Chamber

Ser-vant

Ser-vant

Ante-room

Balcony

Bed Chamber

Library

Chamber

Closet

FIRST FLOOR PLAN OF ROUGHAM HALL

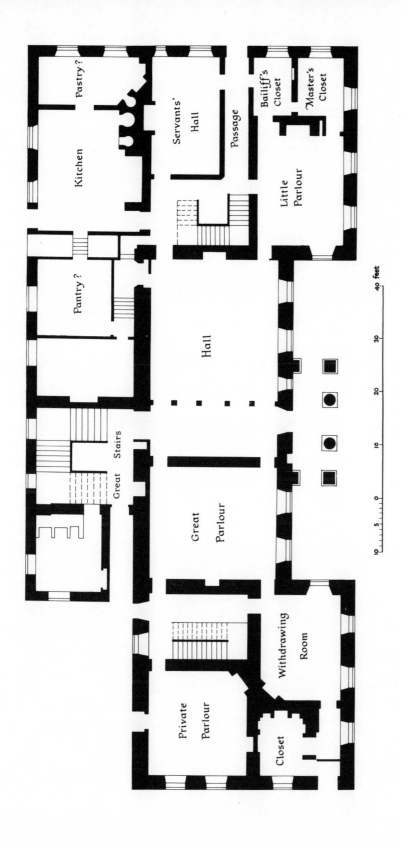

GROUND FLOOR PLAN OF ROUGHAM HALL

*Cursory Notes of Building
occasioned by the Repair, or rather
Metamorfosis, of an old house in
The Country*

*Reserved for private Reflection,
if not Instruction, to such as succeed in it.*

Premise

If it be ask't what comes here? it is hard to answer in a just description; it is concerning what? Building, or rather one person's fancy? The latter is the truer. It is a noble subject, and hath engaged the greatest spirits to act, and describe, and also the poorest of workmen; it is like a stately fruit tree, that grows out of a foul soil, that is beautyfull, and the fruit delicious; they are the hands and it is the sweat of the poorest of labouring men, who out of the slime and filth of the earth, present us with all the magnificence, security, and ease wee have in the way of building.

I remember a story of a grand signore, who was minded to erect a massif fabrick upon a bogg, but could find no workmen to undertake it, despairing that the charge would ever be supplyed. At length one sayd If his majestie pleased to make one experiment, he could tell certeinly whether it could be done or not, which was to be present at the wharf by the sea, at a time appointed, and there to have ready a vast sume of all sorts of gold and silver mony. This was done, and at the time the master appeared with 200 ragged durty workmen and comanded all the mony to be powred out, and then sett his men to turne and mix it with shovells, and all the while he observed his grand signore, who sat wondring what the man meant. At length he ordered this man, and then another, and more successively to toss shovel-fulls into the sea, and still eyed his majestie who sate as amased, but not discomposed, nor started when the mony flew. And seeing him very firme in that point, declared that he found the work feasible, and it should be done; the grand signore asked how he knew? Said he, since you can sitt with patience, and endure the sight of these durty fellows toss your mony into the sea, you may doe any thing.[1]

Another story was this; the state of Venice would build also upon a bogg; and treated with workmen to undertake it at their price; all refused saying it was not enough, to lay the foundation. At last one, at the perill of his neck, took it, and imployed the mony and made a good foundation, and then run away, and sent 'em word, that for as much

[1] This story was doubtless one of the fruits of his brother Dudley's sojourn in Turkey (above, p. xi).

I

more, and pardon, he would finish the building, else they might let it lye, if they pleased; he was as safe and as rich, as when he undertook it, and intended to keep himself so. The state considered this wisely, and approved the man's proceeding, excused, and imployd him, and the work was done.

These are instructive storys, so serve for *avant-propos*; as for my scribling, I have sayd, the greatest and least of dealers in it have wrote their conceipts, which have bin usefull to the order they are of; then why not I, that have had so long to doe with it. And it is not to be expected my wrighting should soar above my practise, or that my descriptions, and examples shoud be from other models than my owne, which I know, if I know any thing, well. I seek my diversion and *passa tempo*. And that I am sure of, I wish any sequel[2] of mine have as much profit as I have had pleasure, *indefessus agendo*.[3]

> [2]Descendants.
> [3]'In my busy activity (as a builder)' (Ovid, *Metamorphoses* ix. 199).

Of Building

This title leads forth an expectation that I should discourse at large of Architecture and the rules or laws derived from antiquity, for creating beauty as well as strength in fabricks to be undertaken. But this hath bin so copiously effected by authors especially of Italy, whose just works have long since bin deniz'd in English,[4] that it is a fondness to pretend to add or much inlarge them. Nor are the termes, as in other sciences, abstruse, so that it might be worth while to open the science of building by explaining them. Therefore it is not my aim to treat the subject in a formall way but onely hint some observations I have made, as much to refresh my owne memory, as to advise my freinds, if any such happen on these papers, and thinck them worth their perusall.

It may be inquired, what should make me so much a pretender, as above, considering my small beginnings, and imployment another way, demanding as much time as life can spare to attend duely. To which I must answer, that inclination hath bin too hard for prudence; and made me robb my profession, for pleasure, which was ever to me very great in the speculation, as well as the practise of mechanicks; and the consummate use of them is had by building. I name not other arts, all of which that I have knowledge of, and indeed all the force of humane understanding and conduct have their share in that buissness; so that it may well be sayd, that nothing more shews a man, than his building; as I may demonstrate hereafter.

But in the mean time, let me owne it a weakness to be propence, as I am, to building; the nicety of which is litle or no improvement to life; say luxury what it will, a retirement to warmth and safety, is all that nature cares for. Pomp and ornament, are but fancy and chimera of the imagination, and lean on pride, ambition, and envyous comparison. Ostentation draws company and that vice; and the monster devours familys, by the enormous charges, that are before, in, and after it. So much for blame.

[4]e.g. Serlio's *Book of Architecture*, 'translated out of Italian into Dutch, and out of Dutch into English' by Robert Peake in 1611, and Palladio's *First Book of Architecture*, translated by Godfrey Richards (1663).

It is a bad cause which cannot be palliated, therefore let us see if the vanity of building will be defended.

1. Whatever vanity it is, it doth not terminate in our persons, nor draw the censure of self conceipt, as dressing, discoursing, &c. doth. That boast it hath, is of the judgment, and contrivance, whereof it is lawfull to boast. And the end or aim is, the accomodation of freinds with ease and delight. And if envy and vicious comparison be absent, litle or no immorality remaines.

2. It is a sober enterteinement, and doth not impeach but defend health. Other pleasures which are less despised, as wine, weomen, gaming, &c. have a sting, which this hath not. And it is also an exercise of the mind, as well as of the body, and a pratique of manage and conduct greatly usefull in all civil life. For what habits ought to be imprest with more efficacy than those of providing materialls, foreseeing occasions, snatching opportunities, waylaying prises, and making bargaines? Then for the forme, conceiving in your mind things not existent but *in potentia*; and comparing them with your occasions, and your scituation; and after bringing them to a more permanent idea, by draught, so as to take further deliberation, alteration and amendment. And in doing this, which a builder should doe, or want great part of his pleasure, he practiseth, and under that, learneth geometry; and after all making workmen understand, laying out the ground, perpetuall overseeing, ordering, and resolving doubdts and querys, setting right, and amending the beginnings of error; are a full imploy, and fill the mind. These exercises goe alone, inclination actuates them, and are much beyond assumed diversions or exercises as by prescription for health sake, while the intervening doubdts and fears of success knaw and deprave nature, more than the formall exercise helps it. A builder is so full, it must be an inundation, and not a flood, that concernes him.

3. Building is very beneficiall to the publik, and in truth the best sort of charity, for much the greater part of the charge is mony paid to poor people. The very materialls, except timber, are the product of men's labour. And the publick hath not a more effectuall means of maintaining the lower order of men, out of rich men's purses, than this. I am sure superfluous mony cannot be better imployed. To maintaine idly mean men and their familys, is to nourish vice and imorality, as will happen if their time be not filled with drudgery for a lively hood. Nay the master himself, not having some diversion that is agreable, and harmless, seeks company and finds his ruin. What then is it, to maintaine men, not onely

idly, but as ministers or at least partakers of gluttony and sottishness, to say no worse, such as wee mean when wee talk of living well. So farr mistaken are comon notions of things, for better it were that the mony were hurled into the sea, that nothing might succeed from it, rather than a pestilence. But when it falls to labouring men and their familys, they are kept in order, maintained, and the product of their labour remains for the comfort of the present age and posterity.

It may be objected, that these men may be better imployed in husbandry, planting, and other real improvements. I answer, it is possible, that wee have more than may be so imployed, but grant it other wise, that the riches of the nation would be so increast. I demand, what is the end of riches? Not gluttony, lust, and drunkenness, but plenty without excess, neatness and elegancy of living, charity to the poor, and liberality to inferiors. Mony hoarded is not riches, but earth, and barren earth, sent abroad and imployed, is wealth,[5] which is either for increase or injoyment. The former is not to be endless, but tends to and terminates in the other. And surely of all injoyments, in the way of magnificence, building, with its appendage furniture, gardens, &c. are the most great and usefull; for the owner is honestly exhalted, and injoys a plenty with vertue, and the exercise of buisness and arts, and the poorer sort participate in their way a competent share. Which is an ordonnance of affairs in the world, that God and nature intends; and the wicked onely labour to prevent or destroy. And this point I may conclude with an observation, that in most countrys and ages, the prime and most exalted spirits, have bin declared lovers of building. And the greatest statesmen, and favorites of fortune, after proof of all the envyed grandure upon earth, have chosen, either upon disgrace or voluntary retiredment, to imploy their time, in designing fabricks and executing them.

4. I shall add, that designing and executing is not onely a lawfull, but a very great pleasure; and hath somewhat I cannot describe, but is more lofty and aspiring than any other injoyment upon earth, and savours of creation, the knowne act of an almighty power. This ambition is not discouraged, but excited by religion; for wee ought to follow devine example, as farr as our groveling state will allow. But to abate these flights, and come to the matter, that is the pleasure that builders have. I read not that wee are sent into the world to be tormented, and to encrease

[5]This is a succinct statement of the advanced theory of trade set out in Dudley North's *Discourses upon Trade*, posthumously published in 1691 with a preface by Roger North (cf. W. Letwin, *The Origins of Scientific Economics*, 1963, pp. 191–2).

the paines of life, but on the contrary, to be joyous and happy, as farr as wee can contrive, by our owne regiment.† This all agree in; but wee differ in methods. Some are for the sences, and mistake their way thro vice and intemperance. Others, and so our religion engageth, seek comfort by doing reall good to themselves, and their fellow mortalls. The pressing arguments, wee often hear against pleasure, mean the vicious and unlawfull; not that which is had from the best use of fortunes with respect to our health, private and nationall, such as among other ways, comes by peace, justice, charity and temperance. Perhaps some lawfull injoyments, in strictness of rule, may be disswaded, (they cannot be forbid,) it is on account of danger, and flattery tending to worse, and in prudence, though lawfull, not to be used. Otherwise lawfull pleasures are the guift of heaven, and intended to be used as expedients to releive the meer paines of life, which at best is bitter enough, and it is enthusiasme and madness to decline them.

5. Lastly wee must consider the real usefullness of building, which furnisheth a true plenty of what is good, that is safety from force and fraude, by the orderly disposition, receipt in, and delivery out of our goods; latitude of place, for accomodating ourselves, freinds and family, variety and ornament, for the diversion of all. Releif from the clamour, occasioned from the want of fitting convenience, which often is a perpetuall rack to a master of a family; nay all disorders and abuses, though moving from stupidity, carelessness or perfidy, shall be charged upon that. It is not a litle, that things are not onely sufficient for use, but pleasant and aggreable to the eye, rather than abrupt and deformed. In short he that hath no relish of the grandure and joy of building, is a stupid ox and wants that vivacity of sence and spirit, that seasons humane life, and make⟨s⟩ it less insipid. And if there be high and low in honest injoyment of pleasure, that by building is the supream. Which concludes this appology, (as I must stile the foregoing excuses for my owne vanity,) and I proceed next to some matters relating, tho but circumstantially, to the present subject.

1. It is a manifest infelicity that happens to building; all men pretend to judge, and thinck themselves masters of it, and very few have an idea so just as to satisfie either themselves or others, with what is done. And I know not which sort is most dissappointed, those who invent and execute for themselves, or such as, (for invention at least) imploy

†of life *erased*.

others. It is not amiss to inquire the reason of this unhappyness. No man is a stranger to habitation, or structures; but every one is well aquainted with some sort or other. So none is without prejudice, and you cannot charge any with ignorance, or unacquaintedness with the matter, as if there were an art to be acquired, such as geometry or algebra; but the way of living every man hath, gives him a *gusto* to what he hath by use happened to approve of, and that he calls well and others he calls not well. And this sort of prejudice once attach't, is hard to be removed, and tho some are inquisitive and curious, the generality goe on in an assurance of their owne understanding, hate to be corrected even by themselves, but shoot their bolts, determine, and declare themselves wise; and as the errors or prejudices in the mind proceed and are seen more or less in all the outward actions, nothing more exposeth them than building. I can shew you a man's caracter in his house. If he hath bin given to parsimony or profusion, to judge rightly or superficially, to deal in great matters or small, high or low; his edifices shall be tincted accordingly, and the justness or imperfection of his mind will appear in them.

It is diverting to observe instances of this. I knew one bredd a servant, and by accident grew rich. His caracter was industrious and servile, and from a walking surveyor of the excise was taken into a revenew-farme, and so by others' braines got his estate. He built an house in Norfolk, and adorned it with a park, gardens, and planting without, and curiosity (as he thought) of finishing and furniture within.[6] But in truth nothing was well done, but what related to servants. The capitall part of his house was paltry, but kitchen, dairey, brewhouse, &c., for a duke, supposing he delighted often to visit them; but his rooms of enterteinement, as also the face and profile of the whole house abroad, such as a citisen would contrive at Hackney. A framed lanthorne upon the roof, shass windoes, and an elegant court yard, and within some right

[6] Identified in BL MS, fo. 4ᵛ, as Buckenham Hall, Norfolk, built *c.* 1680 by Samuel Vincent (d. 1690). 'Mr. Vincent', says Blomefield, 'built the hall that is now (1738) standing, and is a neat pile of brick, on the summit whereof is a lofty lantern or turret, and on the top of this house he (being a very great humorist) erected a fish-pond, with a bason of lead to contain the water, and had pipes of lead which brought water by an engine from a canal in the gardens, into every room (it is said) of the house; he also built an elegant stable, and other offices, and made a park' (*History of Norfolk*, ii, 1805, 268). The house was demolished in 1946 (except for the stables), but a plan made by C. R. Cockerell in 1827 (*Architectural History*, xiv, 1971, Fig. 6b) shows extensive offices almost equal in area to the house itself. Vincent had been a close associate of Nicholas Barbon, 1675–85, and purchased the Essex Street development. North probably encountered him first in this connection. (Information from Mr Frank Kelsall.)

wainscote, which from the native plainness was the best, and frequent carving, but that mean; much of painting, and pretended guilding, but in truth laker, which in time grew pale, and despicable; and the painting for most part of various affected colours, which please the ignorant, but nauseate the knowing; windoe plans[7] and chimnys all marble. But the rooms low, windoes broad, which increast that defect; no back stairs to the cheif apartments; in the gardens, much fountaine work, but spoiled by a monster of a wooden tower in sight, which raised the water; and that water conveyed not onely to the offices, but most rooms in the house to moisten and mould every thing. Nor was his way of living various, being all vain and ostentatious, without judgment, and extended principally in things which servants rather than masters admire: that is, profusion in dyet and wine, such as he used to comend, hoping to partake, and whereby he sought that which in his course of life and fortune went for great and glorious. One pasage was diverting when I saw the house, the servant took out a pannell of wainscot and said there my master hangs his old hatts, then lifted up a board of the floor, here my master sets his old shoos. And yet this man had spent 20,000 in his building, and thought of nothing, but the out-doing a neighbour nobleman who had built, and, being a court favorite, lived in splendor.[8] In short, in spight of all this pretension, the servant stared you in the face; and had he bin but the bailif, and his wife cook laundry and daiery woman, his house had not bin amiss. It was hard to suggest any thing for ease and saving of servants which was not there done; and if it had bin told him, an engin was contrived to make brooms sweep of themselves, he had endeavoured to procure it. And in the end, so much folly was not without reward; for he broke first his fortune, then his heart, and dying his house is sold, and held by a stranger, and these are the instances which hold up the saying: fools build houses, and wise men live in them.

Another instance is of that peer touch't before, who took an old seat neer Thetford,[9] and being a man of pleasure, sharp wit, but withall arrogant and severe, sought to make nature bow to his will, and without either tollerable soil to plant in, must have pompous gardens, avenews, &c., and without using due method, and taking that thought and paines as is requisite in regulating an old house, and I shall touch afterwards, he

---

[7]Presumably the internal cills of the windows are meant.

[8]Henry Bennet, Earl of Arlington (1618–85), the builder of Euston Hall (see below).

[9]Identified in BL MS, fo. 4^v, as Henry Bennet, Earl of Arlington (see pp. 142–3 below for North's more detailed critique of the enlargement of Euston).

expected to have a seat equall to or beyond any in our clime; and had success accordingly, for he was alwais doing, and as the perfection of one thing, betrayed the vility of another, that must be altered, and so perpetually, till he had spent more than would have made a compleat new house. Here you might see a courtier, that in confidence of his owne universall skill, and immortality of purse, run on into vast expences, to produce a perpetuall repentance. *Qui non cavet ante post dolebit*; of this more anon.

98.   A knight of the shire having had 30 years since 10,000 for the porpose of building an house sett his heart upon doing it in the best manner, and to the best advantage;[10] and for that end, traveled with his bricklayer, whome he used also as surveyor, to most eminent houses in England, to take patternes, and observe the modes of great houses. His caracter is avaritious, and mean spirited, and the bricklayer, for such a person, ingenious. The house they built was a new fabrick intire, of which a model was made and coloured, in great perfection.[11] Now the marks of this man's humour were, first the model was as for a suburbian house, neer a square with a lanthorne, and small courtyard, which is a citty-humour, and litle; and pleaseth on account of thrift, because the square figure hath most room for least walls, excepting onely the sphericall, which is not for houses. And this brings all inconveniences together, as want of light in the midle; the case is not the same, in great and small pyles, for a square will doe for the latter, but not the former, which must be spread for air and light. Here the back staires open to the great staires, and those have no light, but from above the cornish, which looks like a steeple.[12] So here was a mixture of the gentleman, usurer, and bricklayer, and the project proves accordingly.

Nothing is more discernable, than an upstart citisen, or mechanick in his house. All fall to building, and constantly retein their native litleness, even when they aim at, and spend to obtein grandure. They can not raise themselves to be above trifles, and to understand the vanity of gaudyness. The grand maniere, none can reach, but such as have seen many men and cittys; and knowing all, can distinguish and choose the best. Beauty doth not consist in small embelishments, but in the outline

---

[10]Identified in BL MS, fo. 9ᵛ, as Sir Jacob Astley (*c.* 1639–1729), for many years MP for Norfolk, and the builder of Melton Constable, Norfolk, *c.* 1665–70. The name of his master-builder is not known. The house is illustrated in *Country Life*, 15–22 Sept. 1928. See below, pp. 74–6, 123, for North's analysis in greater detail of the faults in this house.

[11]This model survives and is now in the Norwich Museum.

[12]A reference to the semicircular roof light contrived to light the staircase (see p. 75 below).

or disposition of a fabrick, which well contrived will be fine, whatever the materiall be. And since beauty is what is generally aimed at and pleaseth; before I come to consider it in building I shall spend a line or two of its nature and source.

⟨2.⟩ In discourse with . . .* upon the subject of beauty, I urged, that in nature, the distinction of handsome and ugly had no place, but arose by use and the reason of things. He (for argument sake), held the contrary, that there were things naturally handsome or deformed, which were so to all eys, learned or unlearned. And instanc't in tryangles, that all approved an equilater, and disliked a scalene; and so the comon demensions of columes, which were aggreable to all. I thought even those instances proved my side, as may appear anon; but first I would know why wee are pleased, or displeased with any thing. And here I medle with no appetites nor gross sensations, for that which gratifies or hurts us corporally cannot be thought aggreable, but in things more indifferent as objects of sight, which touch us but lightly.

Wee find by effect that things which conforme and agree together please, and such as thwart and clash, the contrary. This holds in most things, especially sounds. For now it is proved to the eye it self, that discord is from opposed and crossing movements, and concord from such as co-operate and agree. It is found also, that movements in unequall and uncertein periods, as the clapping of a door, and any sound, not a musicall tone, which consists of equall timed pulses, are intollerable; but any regular movement, as the sound of a bell, pendlum clock, dropping of water, and the like, are not unpleasant, but so much the contrary, as to induce repose, and sleep. There is some cause in nature of these differences, which I take lys in this.

That which is most understood, or brings more to our knowledge, and comprehension, is pleasing, and things not understood nor compre-hended are painefull, that is ugly and offensive. Againe things understood, or appearing to be just and fitt for the use intended are handsome, and others unfitt or unequall for the occasion, are blameable, and therefore ugly. These 2 rules, will determine all questions of beauty and ornament.

1. As to the former, I have no proof but an universall assent of mankind. The effect springs from a sence of imperfection all of us have,

*In BL MS, fo. 11, North identifies his interlocutor: 'I had once some discourse with Sir Christopher Wren on this subject, who for argument sake, held that there was that distinction in Nature, of gracefull and ugly; and that it must be so to all creatures that had vision.'

and cannot avoid; wee dayly find novelty, which speaks our ignorance, and that is a trouble; so wee, desiring to have ease, makes us† ambitious to know, and comprehend more than wee doe, and thence is curiosity and inquisitiveness, the gratifiing which is ever a pleasure. For the perception that wee have of the least advance towards perfection, must needs be gratefull; and this is so setled in our natures, that as in other instances, wee are often pleased, when there is this reason for it, tho wee doe not immediately reflect upon it; wee are not so much philosofers to understand the causes of our passions and opinions, it's enough that they are, and wee discover them by signes, which are an approbation with joy at some things, and aversion with paine at others; and such as no naturall appetite is concerned with, as musick, building &c.

Granting then that whatever is comprehended is pleasing, and the contrary offensive; and that altho wee doe not advert to that reason but onely find the effect in ourselves, I shall apply it to some instances; as first that of regular or equall timed movements, as a clock, water dropping, and, (most eminently) musicall sounds. These are aggreable, because by the past wee know the future, and are not surprised or doubdtfull what follows, and imediately the movement⟨s⟩ of our parts fall in with the measure, as the keeping time with a drum, or musick, and all jog on in harmony together. On the contrary, uncertein movements are uneasy, because every stroke is various, and depends not on the past, nor the future on that; and nothing of the measure is understood. Such is the claping of a door by the wind, which comes sometimes faster and then slower, so that wee know not when to expect the stroke, or expect it in vain, or it comes before it is expected. This makes that movement or sound insupportable. It was one of the complaints against the wind-mill 1682. raised on a tower for lifting water at York buildings, that the sailes made an uncertein light in the neighbouring houses.[13] I need not insist more on this; which is manifest. The greatest wonder is that the same should hold, when the inequality is imperceptible and that is concerning musick. For there is no reasonable account from nature to be given of the gratefull reception of concord, which is diversified by regular mixtures

---

†*Thus in MS.*

[13]This windmill provided the motive power for the waterworks established on the south side of the Strand by the York Buildings Waterworks Company set up in 1675. The original buildings were destroyed by fire in 1690, and in the eighteenth century a steam-pump took the place of the windmill (cf. *Survey of London* xviii. 48–9).

of pulses, and the aversion to discord, but this principle, that the regular is understood, and the irregular not; the soul is wrought upon, allwais alike, and all impressions from sence have their effect, but our bodys are weak, and have a limited power. Wee can move no part so swift, as strings, or bells sounding vibrate; those vibrations thro sence touch the soul, tho the body cannot by any voluntary action imitate them, and wee cannot distinguish pulses, that are quicker, than wee can move some part of our bodys, where by wee indicate that distinction. And wee cannot know the nature of pulses, or strokes upon our sence, which are not in our power to distinguish. But in generall wee know the effect they have upon our soul by the pleasure or displeasure they give and by our examination of things distinguishable and discoverys art hath afforded, of things indistinguishable, such as musicall tones, and accords, found to be regular and symetricall mixtures of pulses in time, wee conclude that all regularity and symmetry is pleasant and disorder the contrary. I sayd it hath helped us to this discovery of sounds, but it is wanted of colours, which doubdtless please and displease upon the same principle. For nature acts by single and uniforme means. It is not to be wondered at that sounds, made of distinct strokes, and colours (probably) by distinct specks of variegated light, should to our sences, which are not able to observe that distinction, appear continued; when the best modern philosofers esteem the duration of time it self to be composed, by repetition of sensations, too quick for our observation, and that the intervalls between one perception and another (suppose it of any duration), is as nothing to the creature perceiving; therefore the time seems continued.[14] And according as those perceptions are easy, wee are contented, when uneasy, as to sikly people, wee are querolous and weary of time, altho wee cannot see the nature of those perceptions and how they please or hurt us. This (by the way) proves a distinction between the soul and body. Nothing is lost to the former, but all graines have their effect, as in weight, but the body looseth all things, which the senses by action of our parts cannot catch, and that is much the greater part of naturall impressions, which all work upon the soul, tho hidd from the scrutiny of sence. So this concludes the first rule of beauty, derived from the understanding and comprehension of things.

[14] In his *Essay concerning Human Understanding* (1690), John Locke discusses the concept of time in terms of the succession of ideas in the mind and was doubtless one of the 'best modern philosofers' whom North had in mind. See G. J. Whitrow, *The Natural Philosophy of Time* (1961), p. 49.

2. Usefullness without defect, or superfluity, this will not spend much of our time, because it is self-evident, that there ought to be enough, whatever the occasion is, and too much is impertinent; either of these, defect or superfluity, is ugly, because unreasonable. And as the former, this also works upon the soul, altho the sence hath no nice distinction of the reason, nor is it at all adverted to, but upon view, the soul pronounces handsome or ugly, without staying for a scrutiny. This will farther be cleared when I come to apply these rules to our porpose. In the mean time let us not wonder that men approve or dissapprove things and know not why.

Now to apply this speculation. All wrighting and discourses about building harp upon symmetry, as if that implyed beauty, without more; not reflecting why symmetry should produce beauty. Symetry is when all the parts are measured by some scale, which conteines the measure of all the parts. And some fabricks so set out, however symmetricall, are ugly, therefore it must be a particular symmetry and accompany'd with reason and usefullness which must please. And I cannot allow symmetry to contribute to beauty further than as it is manifest to the sence; nor hath it that effect on the soul as distinct pulses, seeming a continued prolation of sound. For if an height be 9. 10. 12. &c. of the breadth, it is neither perceived (having no marks) nor hath it any effect good or bad in the mind, and I thinck I may pronounce that nothing in symmetry is perceived, as having marks, but equallity. The mind can lay one space to another and (a litle more or less) judge it equall, but $1\frac{1}{2}$ or other measure the mind takes not.*

Now in building there is order, uniformity and strength.

1. Order is a beauty, as in trees, planting which is done usually in equall spaces, and strait ranges. For the mind instantly takes the designe, and is satisfied. And when such things are out of order, it is not displeasing, because the objects doe not much importune the sence, and wee conceive them good things and profitable; therefore approves them in any order. But other things out of order which are evil, or at least not

---

*In his early piece, 'Architecture', BL MS, fo. 69[v], North had observed: 'And concerning the proportion of a man, wherein there hath bin much redicolous observation, as if there were any real beauty in his symmetry, more than in that of a horse or a stagg &c. I can easily allow, that because wee converse together frequently, and nothing is so familiar with us as our selves, for which wee have a naturall flattery, wee find no fault with what is like us.[15] But still the true foundation is use, and without that there is no naturall ornament.'

---

[15] For systems of architectural proportion based on the human body see R. Wittkower, *Architectural Principles in the Age of Humanism* (1952), pp. 13–15.

good, as weeds, spiders webbs, and the like, have no beauty, but the contrary; yet of those, such as are regular are pleasing and admired; but wee must not take the content we have from conceived profit, which makes us be pleased with woods, and waters, and other things very disorderly, to be caused by any native beauty in them.[16] Riches, and beauty are two things; wee have not the like pleasure in the variety of barrenness, as of fertility. And wee are neither to understand such things as by novelty or variety seise, and detein our attention, and so please by way of diversion, to have beauty; because many things please accidentally as our humours and fancys are prepared, which cannot for that reason be said to have a native beauty. Things of a bizzarr and burlesque sort, please, not from beauty, but extravagance and novelty, and excite laughter rather from contempt than value of them. But levell-ranges, strait-courses, and equall-spaces, or such as intermix regularly, have an innate decorum, because at first view wee thinck wee shall comprehend and at next reflection perfectly understand them.

2. Uniformity; that is a word grassant[17] in all discourses of building; it is what all expect to find, and blame if not observed, and scarce any know why, but it is hansome, say they, because it is uniforme. I observed how comon it is for many to be pleased with a fair front, and none know why; I add that the most knowing injoys no more, onely he may give a better account. It is possible the vulgar, who admire more than understand, may be pleased with faults, but not for any efficacy on the sence to please, and tho the reason be such as might well, and doth, displease the knowing, yet as new or as trick or some odd device, their fancys and not their senses are caught. And nothing insnares weak judgments like ignorance pretending to art. And of this sort the Gothick way hath much, and shall be noted afterwards. But uniformity is the same to all, ever aggreable, and springs from severall causes. 1. Most productions of nature have it, and it is monstrous, when wanting. A bird hath two equall wings, a man 2 armes, and most creatures parity of eyes, and leggs; therefore wee expect the same from art. 2. An uniformity helps the understanding and the memory. Wee can better take an

---

[16] 'And sometimes disorder itself, in things that are not importunate to our sence, as landscape is, is pleasant' (BL MS, fo. 13). North's observation that 'disorder' might be agreeable in landscape deserves notice as an early admission of the attractions of informality in landscape, though he attributes them to an extraneous cause, and certainly appears to have made no concessions to the picturesque in his own planting. For the beginnings of picturesque theory in English writings on landscape see E. Malins, *English Landscape and Literature 1660–1840* (1966).

[17] Implicit.

account of a front uniforme, than not so and easyer retein the idea of it, and are therefore more pleased. Some ages have affected variety to a fault, and particularly it is in chimnys of wrought brickwork. In Henry VIII's time and some time after, if 40 were raised, they shoud all vary. According to what is sayd meer variety is offensive, because every instance is new work for the understanding and memory. But a regular mixture of severall things, which comprehends uniformity, is artfull, and a grace.* But the cheif ground of beauty in uniformity is usefullness, of which next.

3. And whatever share the other matters have in the constitution of a comendable fabrick I am sure, usefullness, is the most considerable and fundamentall cause of all its vertues.** It is to be observed, that when a fabrick is look't upon by divers; wee hear the words, fine, good, stately, well, and the opposites, according to the suggestion of every one's caprice; but all mean the same thing, which is that it pleaseth the sence, or the contrary. And if wee look into these men's heads, wee shall find, that they are acquainted with habitation, and the uses of fabricks, and with the materialls they are done with; and out of all this in each man's prejudice the judgment is made, and things are not of such stated and determinate vertues as to be judged alike by all, and men shall *toto celo* differ either in thing, manner, or use. But some things have bin by ancient authority establish't and approved in succeeding ages, and are not controverted by any, as uniformity, level tables, or ranges, solids upon solids and void on voids; and the like. All or most of which, have not foundation in nature, but the experience of the materialls imployed, and the occasion and use of them, of which wee have a foreknowledge and thereupon calculate our approbation.

1. It is necessary a fabrick should be strong, and where ever weakness appears, there is a fault; and that was so much affected by the Gothick architects in shew that it carryed them into the worst of faults, real weakness. Wee see in our ancient churches, a world of contrivance in leading the ribbs of a massy roof into one threadd, and so in vast length,

---

*Compare BL MS, fo 72ᵛ: 'Whereas when there is such an ordinance of the parts, so as some answere others and things are set in straits, and paralells, curves also being regular, you comprehend the whole, which gives an acquiescen⟨ce⟩ of thought, and there is so much of perfection, that nothing can be added or taken away; whereas in case of incoherent variety, take away what you will, the matter not mended, nor by adding any thing, therefore imperfect.'

**'*Utile dulci*[18] ought to stand (tho not wrote) in the front of every fabrick' (BL MS, fo. 14).

---

[18]Horace, *Ars Poetica* 343, 'Omne tulit punctum, qui miscuit utile dulci'.

and strange smallness downe to the bottom; as if the whole should seem to stand upon knitting pins or so as every one should conclude impossible to stand on the seeming support.[19] This, if the gimcrack were not discerned to be a meer shew, and not the true support of the fabrick, must instead of secure injoyment terrifie the people, least it should fall on their heads; and security without the least fear in a structure is so necessary, as the very apparance of an infirmity is a great mistake in decorum. Yet some ignorant people will say, a fine peice of architecture, when there is some odd projecture, that is not understood, how it is made fast. Whereas the true censure is, Naught, for it looks as if it would fall. And for the same reason, all overhanging the foundation, is bad, because it is in that weak, and cannot be handsome; nor would the most barbarous age endure it but in strait cittys on pretence of gaining room. That this is not from nature but experience, appears by other things, which by such overhanging are ornamentall, as clock cases, cupps with feet, &c., which need not such a bottom and support as an house doth; so not tollerable in that.

2. To head a building with a cornish is a great beauty. For injurys fall by weight from above, so it is reasonable every thing valued, should not be exposed but covered, especially a building, which is to defend the inhabitants from falling wett and is to be defended it self. And being not weight but the foreading of the roof, may overhang the walls, and is so much the better as it defends them and all the appertures from falling and driving wett; besides it appears a bandage of the whole fabrick at the summit, as fascias are in the middle; wherefore such settings off have a great grace; and no wonder being so very usefull.

3. Decent abbutments are very great ornaments; wherein wee must distinguish between such as speak defect, as if put there to prevent falling; and such as being part of the fabrick appears reasonably plac't to render it firme, and out of danger of swerving. The former are seen in most ancient cathedrall churches, where the thrust of the roof being of weighty stone, is taken, (as by propps,) and borne away in half arches, to butteresses at a distance. Which looks as post-nate, and not an originall member of the fabrick, or at least that the walls are weak, and need such

---

[19]Wren too censures 'the affectation in the Gothic way of making weight seem to rest upon Nothing' (Bodleian Library, MS Bodley 907, fo. 17ᵛ, 1700), and similar criticisms were a commonplace of eighteenth-century writings on Gothic architecture, e.g. James Essex, writing in 1764: 'the Gothick Architects endeavoured in all their works to surprise by an apparent weakness' (BL Add. MS 6772, fo. 272).

helps.* The other of shewing forth the proper support and abbuttment, is the usage of the regular way of building now approved and in use. And for this reason midles are made to rise higher than the sides, because those, by abbutting, warrant the height. And here uniformity comes in, for whatever is needed to hold up one side is as reasonable to be applyed on the other, that the fabrick may appear not apter to swerve one way more than the other. And for this reason it is not so well, if the fabrick be of great length all in one range; but breaking it in parts, either by lifting the midle, or adding pavilions at the corners, which shew a composure for strength. Hamton-Court, as now built, hath this fault: it hath a flatt balustered head, and rangeth all alike, 2 sides of a square, which are the principall views of it, and having no breaks nor risings, to shew somewhat of compacted frame, is dull, and insipid.**

4. It is ornamentall to midle all places with a void, and not with a solid. For folk are apt to seek entrance in the middest, and, which is more reasonable, the void there weakens a building less, than on either side. If an entrance be broke thro a wall, it is done with most security in the midle, for then equall solid on each side is left to support the whole remaining. It is for this reason that a portico of 3 columns or of 5 columns, or 7 &c., cannot be handsome, because they carry solid and not void in the midle as one of 4, 6 or 8 doth, which is a rule well knowne to builders; and it extends to all manner of devision, as well as

*The parallel passage in BL MS, fo. 18, has: 'But to set an affected, gross, or (if I may say so of propps or undersetters used to keep up decaying fabricks) deformed strength, as on the outside of Westminster abby church, and many others of that time, and within leave you in fear the whole shall fall about your ears, is far from judgment or beauty, and must be pas't upon the account of humour or fashion of those ages, from them to be endured, but not from a moderne artist.'

**North had elaborated his criticism of Hampton Court in BL MS, fo. 39ᵛ: 'If you were to designe a long walk, fenc't on both sides, you would not continue the fence without interruption, but at certein periods open into cross walks, which gives a refreshment, and new life to the *promenoir*. It is the same thing in the heading of a building, which is the crowne of all. If it be all of one height and flatt, as some are, it is a meer barne, and hath not the most requisit ornament, variety. And this fault Hampton court new-sett-up by the present Government hath most egregiously, for it is towards the garden and park of a square forme, pink't full of holes, some round, and some oblong, other square; that were it not for the angles, which hinders the rotundity of view, one would take it rather for an amphitheater, than an habitation. And the order of round windoes, which are sett between those of the great appartments and the upper story, seem port holes in a royall cittadell, and would give one a conceipt as if gunns peept out there. But that which is worst of all, there is nothing rising at the angles, as pavilions, or ayering chambers above the comon range of the roof, nor no large rising frontoon with a grand order in the midle, but a small one, having short columns, like the midle door within of an old fashioned cabinett. And the whole line of the roof flatt and strait, but balustred, which look⟨s⟩ like the teeth of a comb, and doth in no sort answer the grandure of a royall palace.'

columniation; such as wainscote, which in every side of a room if possible, should have a pannell in the midle. So for plantations of trees, 4 rows not 3 &c., and churches have their nave, and 2 isles, not unlike a man, and his 2 armes, which shews how nature and reason, or the use of things conforme.

I should have noted in the former paragraff, that strength and firmeness is the true reason, why an equilater is more agreeable than a scalene tryangle. For one stands true with equall foot and abuttment, with respect to its center of gravity, and so wee are satisfied it stands secure, whereas the other is in a posture of falling, and a less impulse will bear it over one way than the other, which is not in reason so well, therefore doth not content or please us. The famous *torre cadente* at Pisa, is an architectonick-whim, to make a tale for travelers but much unfitt for the purpose, a weighty fabrick, which should have no semblance of faling.

4. When one upright riseth from another it is handsome to set off the angle with some slope, or cartouse, as in the margin, for so much higher the fabrick riseth, the weaker it is, and it is reasonable to apply an abbuttment, from the lower wall, when it is there ready to be so made use of. And it is loss of place and opportunity to neglect it, therefore ornamentall to imploy it. The case is the same, when a basement trencheth on precipice or low ground, to scarp it, as the way of fortifying by ramparts is. For that gives a broad abutted foot, and renders the superstructure manifestly secure; and therefore is approved and truely ornamentall, observe a small description in the margin.

5. The securing a corner by stones set clasp-wise, called coyne stones, is most agreable, because most safe and strong to a coyne; and as a cornish becomes a house for the sake of weathering, so the same at doors and windoes are beautyfull, the reason of which, and divers other ordinary members in fabricks, are manifest, and need not be inlarged.

6. The last and most eminent instance of beauty in buildings, is the proportions usuall⟨y⟩ assigned to columns, and their appendages; the discription of which I decline as extant in all writers of architecture, and pass on to shew that, such have not their beauty from any thing naturall and instrinsick, but from our knowledge and experience of their use. The ancients, as Vitruve, write in a positive stile, as dictators or masters, rather than philosofers; the former give the laws and rules of their matter, without inlarging with the inducements and reasons; the latter seek to bring the judgment, as well as memory to work, and would have

learners understand as well as remember. Therefore in authors, wee hear onely that such and such are the measures of the severall orders, and the modernes entertein themselves more in finding out the meaning of the ancients, than improving any thing, taking their prescripts as laws; and neither enter into the originall reason of what they define. Where doe wee find any that tell us that more models[20] in a columne make it too small and fewer too gross and lumpish, and why so many, neither more, nor less? Wee can find nothing beyond this, that the Ancients have bin pleased to fix and approve such proportions, and we are to beleeve, they tryed and proved as stricktly as they could for finding out the best. This is sufficient to serve the occasion of most builders, who have not leisure, or experience, supposing they had witt enough to setle fitting proportions from their owne heads. And more especially, because all new inventions are exposed to caption, whereas ancient patternes are far from envy, and the artist is screened by authority they bear. Therefore as a safty against erring, and indemnity against spight and petulant captiousness, they walk upon old authenticated experience, and erre (if at all) *cum patribus.* But wee that divert ourselves with the speculation, more than the practice of this art, love to drive it to some originall source of reason.

And as to the orders, since the world is agreed upon them, and therefore admitt no variation (considerable), I judge their decorum to be thus founded. Wee have a previous gage of weight, by owr owne strength, by which wee estimate the force that all bodys have to descend, according to their sort and magnitude; wee know the postures of rest to be a level, and of falling, a declive. Wee know what stone, wood, iron &c. are; that iron will bear more than stone (quantity for quantity,) and stone more than wood. And with these experiences wee come to the view or judgment of a fabrick. And if wee thinck the propps not sufficient, according to the nerve of the materiall to bear so great a weight as is lay'd upon it, wee say it is too litle, or too high, or the superstructure lumpish and heavy. If wee thinck the support able to carry more, we say the pillars are too short, and too gross, or the superstructure too light. For a superfluous addition of materiall for strength, displeaseth, as much as too litle; for it deprives room, and space to no, or to ill porpose. If a roof could be carryed by no support att all, wee should be glad, having

---

[20]i.e. 'module', that is the dimension (usually the diameter or semi-diameter of a column) from which the proportional system of classical architecture was calculated. The larger the module the thicker the column will be in proportion to its height.

assurance of its not falling, and pillars set under, the less the better, but such as are must be such as will carry the weight, and endure the injurys of weather and time, so as to give us content, and then wee say it is well, that is putt together in reasonable proportion of stuff above and below, proper for the occasion, and not too litle or too much, in either. This judgment is gross, and condescends not to minutes, but comes near enough to determine as there is need. Tho stone and wood differ, wee make litle account of it, and judge of fit bulk much alike; yet some distinction is made, as the Tuscan intercolumnes are allow'd to be much wider than the Corinthian, because the architrave may be of wood. And in our new built churches, finisht with plaister, arches are all brought to single columnes within, and being wood, are endured; but could not be handsome in stone, because such in that forme could not stand. And many will blame them as they are, because counterfeting stone, they should be in such forme as, if reall as the semblance is, would stand. It is for good reason that the greater the columne the less the intercolumne may be; because spaces for men to pass, will be great respecting the bigness of a man, in a great order, tho the pillars have not so many models between. And also, the architrave must be long, and will not hang so well, unless such great pillars are brought closer.

And to draw this discourse of beauty to a conclusion, I shall observe one thing more, which is that fashion, and usage or custome that makes an object familiar, holds in building as well as in dress and courtship. There is much of indifference in many things, much examined, and critiscised upon. And that which wee are conversant most with, and have bin bredd to like, wee shall call handsome, and well, and novelty otherwise; tho perhaps, a litle acquaintance, shall make that better approved. Therefore if any spirit would be advanc't above the vulgar, which approve and dissapprove most by custome, or example, and neither know, nor care to know why, must apply all its industry to discover the true reason and efficacy of things, and holding to that, and having cognizances of antiquity and knowne patternes, may vary, and defy censure. However, since following approved patternes screens, and varying exposeth him, and in a monumentall concerne that is not transient but lasting, and once done, not to be altered or corrected, it is prudence to vary as litle as may be, and to doe it with good reason, and not for ostentation of skill, for tho well, it bears a mark of arrogance to pretend outdoing antiquity; and wee have not many Michel Angelos, to pretend to that. From henceforeward wee will take it for granted, that in building, right reason, that is judgment of usefullness, is the criterium of all ornament and decorum. And having shewne some excellencys on that foot, I will add some faults; *contraria juxta se posita magis elucescunt*.[21]

1. The perpetuall breaking a surface, with carving, sett offs, and small members, this is conspicuous in Henry VII's chappell, Westminster, which is so full of it as to be spoyled, and it is as easy to examine the parts of a mist as of that.[22] In all things plain and ready-intelligible parts are best. A clutter is alwais faulty, because it torments the sence to comprehend it. The use of carving is to make distinction of parts, or members. The settings out, or in, doe not alwais doe it; but if an edge or selvedge, be inricht (as they call it) by carving, the border is conspicuous. But carving for carving sake, without such use, is an impertinence, like babble in company, of no profit. More cost more worship, is not a law in architecture, but rather the contrary, to cost little, and be truely great, is an excellence of soveraigne perfection. If one will comend a work, say it is great and lasting, and not costly, but yet suitable to the occasion.

2. It is a fault too much in use, to break the strait course of an order; as at the Banquetting house, where the intableture rangeth with the wall, but at the columnes breaks foreward. The columnes are ranged to support the entabliture, which they doe not if it breaks back against the interstices; the intableture ought to run strait, as the true burthen of the columnes, and not of the wall, the rather because so the projection is a defence to the walls and foundation, as they ought to be. And it intrencheth also upon the plaineness, and easy intelligence of the profile, which in a strait course, is no sooner seen than understood.

3. Another comon failing is to double orders, one over the other, which I esteem ever amiss; because the entableture is supposed to be the setting off the frame of the rooff, and the cornish for weathering the wall, and these 2 piled up, is house upon house. But I grant that this, and some other faults, as setting columnes by pairs, and not at equall distances, and also the next foregoing instance, are excused on account that materialls are not to be had for any large structure, that will hold for magnitude and strength, in such a way as shall not break &c., but they

---

[21] This was an old rule of logic which was already proverbial in England in the sixteenth century and may be translated as 'Contraries appear more evident when they are set one against the other' (cf. *The Oxford Dictionary of English Proverbs*, 1970, p. 142).

[22] John Evelyn found the 'sharp angles, jetties, narrow lights ... and other cut-work and crinkle-crankle' of Henry VII's Chapel equally displeasing (*Account of Architects and Architecture*, 1696 ed., p. 10).

are fain to shift as well as they can. This was said to me, when I inquired why such things were in Pauls, and wee must pass them on that account.*

4. Another cheif ornament of a fabrick, is the manifest reason of the whole, so as no part appears to want or abound in strength, but every where *quantum sufficit* and no more. Therefore the gothick way of making wonderment at the stupendious weight borne upon thredds of which I took occasion to speak before, is one of the worst of faults. Magick and trick will not serve in building, where lives depend; those are fitter for theater, and puppet-show, where men come to be cheated a few hours with a vain shew of what is not.

In intend next to discourse of the conduct of a building-designe; and recommend principally that a man be his owne surveyor; especially if it be a limited designe, either for the use of a private family, or reforming an old house. If a palace is to be built intirely new, or any publick edifice, as church, townehouse or the like, it is a work proper for a surveyor and hath too much drudgery for a man of quality, tho such will regulate the *gousto* of a surveyor's invention, which doth often fall short of true greatness; as I shall shew in time. But where a man builds for his owne use, none can contrive well but himself. I exclude not councell, and of the prime artists is best, but the owner must pronounce; and if he leaves the affair to his surveyor, and is not at the beginning and end of all things himself, he shall be miserably dissappointed in charge as well as convenience. And for this reason few dable in building, without much repentance, unless they deal for themselves. And this will not be done, unless they are skilled in draught and can invent and judge, as well as make modells and paternes for guiding workmen; and so have a full idea of their buissness, and be able to answer the numerous questions workmen will come with. If a man be so great and rich, that he hath no need of restreint in expence, and neither cares to thinck nor to act, (if he

---

*North treats this point more fully in BL MS, fos. 42ᵛ–43; 'A third observation is, that breaking the entablement over the columnes is not good. But if possibly it can be contrived, lett the cornish &c. run strait. I know neither this nor the other decorum is observed in the great fabrick of Inigo Jones, called the Banquetting house, nor in Paul's, neither of which impeacheth my opinion. For they could not have materialls to make good single columnes nor to project the entabletures so farr as to range strait over the heads of the columnes, but were forc't in the one to double the orders, and in the other to double both columnes and the orders, and in both to break the entablements without; which shift Sir Christopher Wren informed me of when I observed to him the exility of his columnes, with respect to the grandure of his fabrick at Paulls.'[23]

---

[23] See Introduction, p. xvii.

were fitt for either) he may leave all to some that are wiser, and pay well for their ayd. But without this opulence, I would advise such unactive persons, not to medle with building, but in very ordinary amendments, for reason mentioned, and more fully to be displayed hereafter.

The faults of surveyors and workmen, when left too much to themselves, are to be noted. As, 1. Supposing a capitall surveyer, which by the way is not knowne in every age,* he is very costly, and must be payd like a king's serjeant, or will contemne you and your work. 2. He will be so very buisy, that you shall not get him to attend your affair, or not so frequently as is requisite, and so shall leave you either to yourself, or some underworkman. You shall have nothing from him but a draught or model, in the execution of which multitudes of occurrences will fall for advice and improvement, which will not at first be thought of; and many alterations will be made with advantage, which you cannot venture upon, for fear of somewhat evil emerging in another place, or for altering the contract with workmen; and you shall be pestered with your owne fancy, and suggestions of others, (for all are wise in building, or thinck themselves so,) especially workmen, that you shall be at your witt's ends, if you are not a master of your designe, and can judge of, and governe it, without any one's help. If it be reforming an old house, I pronounce none can doe it tollerably, without long and perfect acquaintance, which a surveyor will not give himself time to have, and it must be the owner or none that doth it to content. It is another intollerable fault of surveyors, 3. To practise their owne whims, at your cost. They having viewed many fabricks, in life, and in draught, with the ornaments of the antique and moderne invention, have a world of crotchetts of their owne, occasioned or built upon them; all which they have an itch to put in execution, and it is miracolous if they doe it not the first opportunity of building they are imployed in. And lett a man arme himself what he can, they will argue and perswade him beyond his intentions. 4. They will also doe things in a different way than you prescribe. I have made draughts, and given them to be executed by an

---

*In BL MS, fos. 7ᵛ–8, North lists those of his age: 'To touch these againe, few ages can bragg of a good surveyor of building, or such as wee call architects. Inigo Jones was one, who did all things well and great. But since there has bin Pratt for Clarendon hous, Webb for Greenwich gallery, and Gonnersbury, and at present Sir Christopher Wren; dexterous men, especially the latter, as to accounts and computation, but have not the grand maniere of Jones. His plaineness, seen in the repair of Pauls, Convent Garden, and the Banquetting house, hath more majesty then any thing done since. There must be a peculiar soul, to inspire a good builder; it is not daubing on of ornament which graceth, but a good disposition or profile.'

under surveyor imployed by a nobleman late deceased; and he varyed all the proportions and for the worse.[24] 5. Lastly he will right downe deceive you in his estimates of charges, and will not have thrift, (however necessary to you,) obtruded upon him. And so he will ingulf you in charges, to your bitter repentance; and you will be much mistaken, if you thinck to check your work under him, for there is no mean, between using him in all or laying him wholly aside; because he will not bear contradiction, but is an animall allwais opiniative, and for the most part capricious and fantasticall.*

It will be sayd, that if not a prime surveyor, you may use a head workman, and such there are who have good skill. I answer, then you must be content with deminutive low invention, aggreable to the spirit and education of a mechanick workman, and it shall neither credit nor please you; and altho such a one is servile and obsequious, (which by the way doth not allwais happen, but they will be as pardie[25] as the best) and so give you no trouble; yet that work shall taste of his servility, in many meannesses and trifles which a gentleman cannot approve. I here exclude not councell, which even of the lowest workman, or servant, is usefull, and may hint bluntly to your fancy some things you had overseen, and you'ld not have neglected for any thing; but it is a resignation to them which I blame.

Here I cannot but digress in complaint of this age, for laying aside the care of building for themselves, and familys; but leaving it to workmen,

---

*North concludes the passage on surveyors in BL MS thus (fo. 8ᵛ): 'But for the rest, that is the disposition for accomodation of the family, it must be set out by the master, and the least servant he hath will informe him of what apperteins to their station better than Mr Surveyor himself. But be the artist compleat, and let him espouse the buissness. Either you must interpose, and contradict him, or else he must proceed after his owne way, and doe as he thincks fitt. If you contradict him, he puffs and snuffs, grows weary of the work, and unless highly oblidged, leave⟨s⟩ you in the mortar. If you give up the reins, he will be so fond of new compositions and ornaments of his owne framing and invention, that for the letchery of putting them in execution your purse shall be martirized. And then the end is malencholly in stead of cheerfull, and that which should be a delight is hatefull to the eye. Therefore working by surveyors is for princes, and great men, and not for private gentlemen, who have neither the purse nor interest to purchase such costly councell as theirs is, so that if they are not their owne surveyors, and that well also, it's better to sitt still, and be content with their great grandfather's old mansion.'

---

[24] Evidently at Wroxton Abbey, the seat of Roger's brother Lord Guilford (d. 1685), where one Watson was employed to superintend the execution of Roger's designs (above, p. xiv).

[25] A word in contemporary use as an oath, with the sense of 'certainly' or 'assuredly', and here used by Roger North to mean 'assertive' or 'self-assured'.

such as bricklayers, carpenters, glaziers, &c.* It is scarce knowne that a person of quality hath built in or neer London for himself; but all is done by profest builders, and the gentry hire or buy of them. It is manifest from what I have urged, that their pinching spirits will infect all their works, and whatever they pretend to for accomodating great men, there is allwais some scantyness that spoyles all. They pay for ground, and then cutt it out to the advantage of their trade. They sell by feet-front, which is the ordinary way of estimating the ground rents, and therefore will have enough there, whatever is wanted in other places. I will not exaggerate this which is so plaine, but onely observe that this humour hath vitiated all our modes, as well of furniture as of houses. For to bring two windoes into a room, which is not bigg enough for one with convenient jaums, they make them narrow and the peer small; and a peer being the fit place for glass, and they not receiving one tollerably large, the whole must be lined with glass, that what is wanting in breadth may be made good in height. Nay it hath brought into fasshion narrow frames to looking-glasses, just a border, which is not great; for a glass hath the property of a windoe or door, and requires a border, as the jaums are, a 5th or 6th of the width, else it is not well. Then because there must be the parade this litle room must be broke into dining room, bedchamber and closet; which the lady is content with being small, and so furnish't rich (or seeming so) with less cost, that is with cabbinetts, china, sconces &c., meer trifles. And this hath added to the mode, round stools like small drumms they call taburets;[27] and many other ways, aggreable to litleness, whereby all the grandure proper to quality is layd aside; large rooms, great tables and glasses, capacious chimnys, spacious

---

*In his draft North had reported a conversation with Dr Nicholas Barbon[26] on this point (BL MS, fo. 10ᵛ): 'I was once pleased with an observation of a London-undertaker, Dr Barbon, That one might know by the visage of the city houses in the cheif streets, of what calling the cheif contriver was. As some being set out with fine brick-work rubb'd and gaged, were the issue of a master bricklayer; if stone coyned, jamb'd, and fascia'd, of a stone mason; if full of windoe, with much glass in compass, and relieve, a glazier; if full of balcone and balustring, a carpenter; and so others. Which on reflection I have noted, and one may, in the face of most houses, discerne the calling of some builder or other most conspicuously. And as a camelion is participant of the colours neer her, so all sorts of spirits give a tincture to the actions that come from them.'

---

[26]Barbon was, among other things, active as a speculative builder in London after the Great Fire. Roger North knew him well (see *Lives of the Norths*, iii. 53 ff.).

[27]'A low, upholstered seat or stool, originating in France in the second half of the 17th century, where it played a part in the rigid etiquette of Louis XIV's court; a few privileged ladies being allowed to sit on a tabouret in the royal presence' (John Gloag, *A Short Dictionary of Furniture*, 1969, p. 660).

hangings, are not to be found, as when the nobility built their owne house. Nay the evil spreads, so that country gentlemen of value and fortune, in their new erected seats, creep after the meanness of these town builders and order their houses in squares like suburb dwellings, than which nothing is more unfitt for a country seat, as may be shewed more fully in proper place. It were to be wish't that the gentry and nobility would look farther for their invention, than suburb models, which may serve a family, in a London expedition, but not in country living, which requires somewhat more like a court. But enough of this.*

The first point which offers first to gentlemen who are inclined to build, is whether he shall begin a designe new from the ground or repair his old house. And this will not trouble him much, unless the old house be of a good materiall, that will either stand as it is or endure battering, and after all alterations, be considerable in saving of charge, and have full proportions, so as not to spoil what you add of new to it. And if a person can judge so well of his house to know, whether all, or any, and which of it is worth keeping, he may be trusted with the following menage, for that judgment is nice. Many out of avarice in keeping an old stair or stack of chimneys, spoyl a good model; which shall be tainted with some deminutive cast or other, to humour an old scrap. Others neglect wholly very substantiall old houses, which are convertible with litle charge to good and moderne use and forme, and out of an humour affecting novelty, pull all downe. The mean between these two, is the subject for a just understanding to determine, and depends upon a skill in generall, and thro acquaintance with that particular house, and its condition; but no rules can be lay'd downe for direction; therefore I must leave this point to discretion and suppose an old house convertible to good forme and use, before the question comes, whether it be best to work upon that, or one wholly new. And this can be no question neither, but with regard to men's abilitys, and circumstances; for abstracting them, it is

---

*In BL MS, fo. 9, North had dismissed such builders more pithily: 'Pinching for room to increase the sale of houses, is the first and greatest point with them, next to deck a dining room, withdrawing room, and perhaps a closet with some new fingle fangle, to tempt her gay ladyship. And then they are fitt to receive a family of the nobility or cheif quality, who as soon as they enter shall find their house like a campaigne tent, with all the nusances of it in their nose, and no sort of latitude, as a raised fortune would expect. And as I say'd before, the soul of the arkiteckt will be seen in the work, be it base or noble. And using such men in the designing part of a country seat shall succeed much worse. For they cannot depart from the citty way of compacting rooms into as litle wall as is possible; and punching the walls full of windoes like pidgeon holes; and if they doe venture at any thing great in the way of beauty, it shall be so trite and comon, as to be seen in every bake house. This is the end of building gentlemen that use workmen for cheif architects.'

indubitable, that all new is best. But perhaps it may fall out, that a man cannot conveniently take that course, and the other he may, or he may have more for his mony in so doing. If a wish were to decide, doubdtless that which is all done originally to your mind, with that strength and firmeness, as well as compleat mode and order, is the favorite; for really there is scarce an old house, but alter it as you will, shall leave some staine of obsolete antiquity upon the model, either by low floors, beams appearing, or walls patch't; and such faults shall be insuperable. And many goe farther and say, it is better cheap, to build new using old materialls, than to patch or alter old. For many chargeable members must be new, as floors, ceilings, windoes, &c. which are but the same, and perhaps not so large, in a new model. And the charge of these alterations amount⟨s⟩ to the price of new work. So that I must yield the point for the new, but in particular cases, as my owne was, to make the other way more reasonable.

And that is my next undertaking to shew, and falls upon this difference, vizt. where the master hath all his mony ready and to spare out of his capitall, for payment of builders and for materialls, so fast, as if it were issued almost at once; and that he values not time for providing, and forecasting advantages, and hath no need of an habitation, or to be present at the work, while it is doing; and in the end, hath his house built, and his estate deminish't so much as the charge is; then he may build new. But this is not every man's case, and many must have some habitation, which an old house will afford even while it is altering, the family removing before the workmen, and at length fixing in their destined apartements. And so the master is ever at hand to conduct and order what is fitt, which will be dayly and hourly needfull. And he may proceed, or stop, and whenever he leaves, the house is bettered so much, or he may move slow, and work out of the gro⟨w⟩ing profits of his estate, and not sink his capitall, which makes a vast difference; he that builds out of interest shall break a builder out of principall. Besides, the new is an engagement to goe thro whatever happens, which men will strain to doe, and mortally wound their estates rather than leave a monument of their folly, and as the use is, to be so called after their names, when an house is left imperfect. But in mending an old house, it may, as was sayd, be carryed on no further, than the owner sees convenient; and he may set up his staff when he pleaseth, and injoy so far as he hath done with content, altho not so happy as if he could have finish't his designe. And the more desirous a man is of large accomodation, the more reason he hath to decline the new, and take to the reforming part. For an old house, will have much room convertible to uses, which a man will not allow him self in new, where extent multiplys charge intollerably; and it may fall out that a man may compass his designe in this way, that cannot undertake the other, and therefore in prudence, ought to steer the safest and surest course.

I have touch't this plenty of room gained by the stragling lines of an old house; which may fall out for the best, at least for waste uses, as necessary to a family as any other. I cannot but add, that a new fabrick is so chargeable, that it is usually for thrift pinch't in the demensions so as to be very inconvenient; rooms are small, staires publik and noisy, offices offensive, and the like. And yet from mode, this is called a pretty-box, and is very fitt for a citizen's or a family that have onely a small pension to subsist by, but not for an English gentleman, that hath buissness and managery, and desires splendor, and elbow room as well as aire within his walls. And whoever knows the humour of most old houses, will find in them so much extent, as shall give a surprising plenty of road† to him that will undertake to new-model them. And men cannot foresee all their wants, and if they have not a superfluity of room, to be apply'd as they shall find occasion, they will repent of doing so much, or of not doing more. Besides, old houses are often prudently plac't by waters, and wood, for use and defence, and have many barnes stables and outhouses, at convenient distance. Whoever thincks he hath done, after finishing his pyle, he is mistaken one half. For besides furnishing, there must be erected such conveniences; and if this new be set neer for their sakes, there is danger, the fancy should be hurt by their deformity, whereas by an house that speaks it self old any thing of that nature is passable. And yet wee find, that men are so fond of lofty scituations of houses, to leave all manner of convenience for the sake of them; and as often repent for this, among other reasons, that the being exposed to the fierceness of winds and weather, is a worse mischeif than all their prospect will pay for. In regard the former displeaseth perpetually more, and the latter pleaseth perpetually less; nay to the possessor, the finest prospect is like a ded wall, and not such a pleasure as it is to traveller or stranger. It is a never failing experience gained by living in the world, that care and management of husbandry, is the onely laudable means for a country family to live in plenty. There it is insanity,

---

†road *crossed out*; of *not crossed out, no doubt by accident.*

for such to affect the citty way of living, and consequently building, in the country, as for visits, not thincking of accomodations for buissness.

Another inducement to mend an old, rather than build a new house, is the diversion it affords, and that is not to be slighted. Why else are hunting, &c. so esteemed and reputable? Living without some designe is dull even to a torment, especially for minds active and healthfull bodys. As for such as live onely to eat, drink, and sleep, ⟨they⟩ are at home in a prison, or it matters not where they are. Action and buissness are the emolument of liberty, and that which setts its price. Where need requires, it is best imploved to gaine, but where men are not so much prest, how can it be better directed than in contriving and executing benefits or improvements of living, in which all a family, freinds, and strangers participate, and the poor are releived? And this is done, by imploying our spare time and mony, in mending and adding to our habitation, as wee find may be agreable and usefull. And the slow process is so farr from vexation, as the *beau-mond*, who would injoy *per saltum*,[28] thinck, that it is one of the greatest benefits the designe affords. For to say truth, it is almost indifferent how men of estates pass their time, and where they ly or abide. It is the enterteinement of the mind that consummates pleasure.

The last convenience, I shall mention as to mending an old house, and not the least, is that it avoids censure, and screens against envy. A fine house is like fine cloaths, with the foolish, pride; and with the wise, a distinction of quality and fortunes. To affect the former, is secure (not of honour but) of contempt. And that of fine building is an impression that holds longest, and therefore, when the mistakes of it are capitall, they are the greatest mortification, for a man lives in the midst of obvious memorialls of them. All pretension to exactness usually proves a misfortune, for nothing is so sure as failings and miscarriages, and such a critick cannot bear, and is much more afflicted than any that neither have nor pretend to any thing extraordinary. When men delight in making treats, what a creveceur[29] is a prime dish ill drest. No dinner were a choice, before such fretting and fuming as I have seen on such occasion. When a man aimes at setting himself forth in building a fine house, it is more than probable, he hath swallowed an high conceipt of his model, and shall as much dislike it when put in practise. What else can be the

[28]'By a leap or jump', i.e. in a hurry.
[29]'Sinking of the heart', i.e. disappointment.

meaning of so much altering and pulling downe, as wee find building-gentlemen are pleased to be condemned for. According to the vigor of their haughtyness, so is their paine, at any dislike of what is done. And who are so arrogant, as builders of houses? Are they not, for most part, citts,[30] attorneys, and such upstarts? And such as cannot thinck any thing fine, great, or pompous enough for them. This is demonstrated by their wonderfull nicety in trifles, to gain which they neglect true greatness of ornament, so that the publik is unhappy in their mistaken greatness and looseth what from generous hands, would add great splendor to the nation. To lett these pass, who are ordinarily the builders of new houses, I come to observe what a benefit a reformer of his old family seat hath. He can after all call it an old house, which by the force of modesty sets it off, and if any thing be good it is better accepted for it. Then he is screened from blame, as well as envie; for what is more required of a man than to repair his old house? And if there be any faults, as ceilings low, beams seen, or the like, the old house appologiseth. And much charge of decoration is well spared, for it is a vanity, to pretend that new, which will of absolute necessity discover it self old. And this shews a frequent error in judging such works. They will say this and that ought to have bin better embellish't, or made look like new; which often is most ignorantly or else malitiously suggested; for a daub in one place, shall make a worse defect appear in another; and the prudent will lett an old house be patch't, and look upon it as a thing made for use and convenience and thinck much it should be so well as it is. It hath less of vanity, and pretence to superiority above our neighbours, than new fabricks, which most of all excite envy; more modesty, and less arrogance, and consequently more of security and less spight and censure. That this is not a meer fancy, I appeal to the knowne observation, that nothing is so sure a forerunner of a statesman's downfall, as his building a superb fabrick.[31] For on the one side, his arrogance and overweening, hath gat the better of his hypocrisy and caution, and envy takes the advantage, and falls to wo⟨u⟩nding him incessantly.

One thing more is not to be slip't. If a man be his owne contriver, he shall have great diversion, in hearing the judgments of others. He shall find all shall harp on the same points, finding faults, or proposing amendments, and scarce any shall ever touch the true and reall faults of

[30]'Citizens', e.g. merchants and other self-made men.
[31]The outstanding example of this, in Roger North's time, was Clarendon House, Piccadilly, built by the Earl of Clarendon and barely finished before his fall in 1667.

the work. You shall know all the failings that have bin either by your owne oversight, or the workmen's mistakes, but strangers shall not penetrate so deep; and instead of a true judgment of the reasonableness of the whole, they shall stik at some outside superficiall thing, as new and old distinguish't and not alike, &c., all which is both a comfort and pleasure, that the true faults are not found out.

Having spent so much paper, about preferring the repairing, and mending old houses, before that of building from the ground new, I shall next discourse of mending well.

It is often found that miserable penitence attends builders for want of firme judgment upon their subject matter at first, and then want of good order and method of proceeding, either of which creates perpetuall emerging difficultys and dissappointments, not with⟨out⟩ a repeated torture by alterations, than which nothing is greater disgrace to a builder, for it is a gross symptom of error, and punish't with vaine charge. For prevention of which observe:

1. Consider well your owne ambition, that is what sort of housing you desire, which I must allwais allow to be more than is strick⟨t⟩ly needfull according to your circumstances, else a farme is equall to the best. But the distinction of well borne and bredd, is by elegant and neat living. And then consider your estate if it hath such luxuriant spare branches as may be lopt off to render the rest more flourishing. If the latter be a plaine case, you may venture on any thing. If not, have great care of engaging beyond a power to stop, in case the times or any other accident proves cross to your porpose. And this was one of my cheif invitations to mend old, rather than build new, which I shall not repeat, but add, that if your aim be low, and at moderate things, you may the better build new, than if you aim at somewhat great and relieve. For that is purchas't cheaper and safer in the mending, than the building projects.

2. When you are sure of your owne mind and aim, consider well your old house, if that be in the case; if it be very narrow, and low, so as not capable of taking good formes within as well as without, or if it be of a materiall, that is either rotten, or not fitt for breaking, as many times the case is, it is a vanity to bestow more upon it than is called necessary repairs, and ordinary decorums, to take away offence, while you use it. And if the dwelling be fixed to your† ground or near it, it is much better to pull all downe, than to pretend to alter, which ma⟨n⟩y are satisfied of

†*MS not clear.*

by experience, and too late repentance. In such case either all new, or if that may not quadrate with your affairs, then rest contented with your gransire's old house, whereof the antiquity hath both excuse and reverence; and so vain expence is prevented, as that is allwais which fails of its end, credit, purchasing in lieu of that, censure as well as charge; and this *premio* is seldome wanting.

3. Then you have to consider next what qualifications, or assistances you will have wherewith to manage your work. It is much best, as I have shewed, to be architect and designer yourself, at least so farr as may serve your owne porpose. If not, it is very needfull to have some builder (if not a surveyor) at hand allwais to be at the head of the buissness, so that you leave nothing to the discretion of workmen; else their errors, or numerous questions will confound you. And without some apposite means of this kind it is better to sitt still, than doe much in building or altering.

I would willingly add some examples of formes of houses amendable, with the nearest and best method of doing it. But the sorts of houses in England are so various, and hard to describe in words, that I cannot without much time and paines attempt it with any satisfaction. One sort I will venture to touch upon, and that is both frequent in England and very troublesome to mend. And that is what they call the half H, a front and 2 wings all single building. This forme is fit for a colledge or hospitall, to be devided into cells, and chambers independent of each other; but not for a dwelling house, that ought to have a connexion, and unity, without crossing to and fro from one part to the other, thro the air, and abroad; and that cannot be aforded in such houses. And it falls out that the singleness of the building makes the wings look narrow. Such inventions were for want of the art, of disposing lights, and roofing comodiously any broader fabrick, which are now of ordinary practice, but not knowne in former times. It is usuall to make the parade rooms in the midle or front, and the apartements in the wings, so you have bredth and height, which much accomodes the new designe. And that I thinck is best cast, by doubling the front, within from wing to wing. This gives a range of rooms with vistos from side to side and you may make this range either your principall, or secondary, as you find fittest. And as for the wings, such as are left, if any be still prominent, they fall well to represent pavilions, and will be of use and service in the designe of the house, for closets, inner rooms, or the like, and may be ornamentally distinguisht in the roof.[32]

[32] What Roger North advocates is (to adopt the vocabulary of the time) converting a 'single-

There may be houses of this sort, that will need less alteration, and some more; the conditions of the fabrick, and the builder's aim and purse, are the ingredients composing his designe.

The last and principall advice I have to give a reformer of an old house, is in the first place to be well acquainted with the place, and then settle your contrivance, putt it in draught so as it may be considered and reflected on from time to time by your self, and made intelligible in order to have the opinion and advice of others. And after this draught hath bin made and altered, as will happen many times, you may begin to thinck it is neer its perfection in the designe. It is so hard to image to ones self all the occasions and advantages of room, as practise will suggest, that continuall changes of fancy will obtrude, nay even at meals or half asleep, some discoverys will arise, most important, not thought of in all your intention of study, which you would not have overseen. Then your draught is ready to receive and keep in your remembrance what you continually gather by thincking. And this will not fix suddenly; an opiniative artist shall pronounce, and snuff if he be disputed with; he will not take the time, and be instructed as your self will, and these affairs will not want time and deliberation, or be amiss. Therefore I must needs recomend a slow series of thought and continuall reflection, and comitting to draught and then judging and altring, as occasion shall require, and this in order to reasonable content, when things are done. And after all I must prognosticate, that many things will discover themselves in the life, that lay concealed in the pourtrait or image of your building, and you must be prepared aforehand to bear some oversights, and to be satisfied, that they are in things not very materiall or essentiall, as will happen upon precipitating your project. And the best remedy I can propose is this, that notwithstanding all your thincking and drawing, reserve a scope to alter in circumstantialls from time to time, as the work goes on. As in the disposition and partition of rooms, imployment of waste corners, and many litle contrivances; which will be most usefull in practice, and scarce discernable in draught, or obvious to thought beforehand. Let nothing be finally determined but what is done; make no alteration, but where the trouble and charge is small, and the use very great, and not in things that make much appearance.

---

pile' house, i.e. one only one room deep, into a 'double-pile' one. The alteration of Ham House, Surrey (see p. 144 below) for the Duke and Duchess of Lauderdale by William Samwell in 1672–4 was an example (see J. G. Dunbar, 'The Building-activities of the Duke and Duchess of Lauderdale, 1670–82', *Archaeological Journal*, cxxxii, 1975).

After such draughts as these, brought to the utmost perfection you can give them, you may, if you thinck the charge *tanti* have a specie-modell[33] made, exactly to resemble the life, wherein your self, freinds and workmen, may inspect and judge; and many doe not take an idea from draught, but must have the species presented. This will improve your designe, and ease you in direc⟨ting⟩ the workmen who⟨se⟩ *grossiereté* is difficult to be instructed from a draught *in plano*.[34] But if you are by yourself, I thinck the charge of that may be spared. For it is a want of applycation of thought, not to perceive from draught, as well as model, any designe of building, and erect it in your mind sufficiently clear and distinct for your judgment and use. And being continually at your work to observe and direct, the artificers will not run into errors, as when left to themselves. In which case it is almost necessary you should have a specie-image to guide them. It is wonderful what a vivid representation of building may be made *in plano*. I have made the erection, of the uprights; and by the help of perspective, delined a flying prospect of each story, representing the view one hath, that looks into a model, to my intire content,[35] and if farther exactness had bin required I could have as well done it, as sometimes for exercise and tryall, I have drawne the image of a line of rooms as they would appear, if the walls were taken downe and floors onely standing. Those who have proved the pleasure of this exercise know the fullness it hath; and are truely Epicureans in industry.

When this thincking part, and drawing our model is over, I would have our freind sett to provide materialls; but I must not forget to admonish him one thing, which is, that he be sure to make his designe large enough, and up to the height of his present ambition, as well as prospect of ever desiring, according to the circumstances, he shall have clear reason to limit himself by; and not to contract it, for any present humour or fancy that it will be sufficient for him. The reason is that it may happen he may desire some inlargement; and increase of family or buissness may require it. Then if his model be perfect and closed, it is probable he cannot inlarge without deforming the whole. Whereas if he designes large at first, he need build no more than he hath occasion for, and doe the rest when opportunity serves. So he is sure not to deforme his model by any future additions. And he may goe on doing upon his

---

[33] A model 'in kind', that is a three-dimensional wooden model.
[34] i.e. an architectural drawing representing two dimensions in one plane.
[35] Cf. Pl. 12 for a drawing of this sort by Roger North.

model, taking onely care that whatever he doth be a part of it, tho perhaps occasion break the direct order of proceeding. If all your structure be part of your model, you may joyne and close it, and add the embellishment when you please; and in the end, if you live and have means to accomplish it, you are sure of content. And in this method you shall walk safe, and by steddy perseverance in your porpose, at length attaine much more than you would have thought possible ever for you to compass.

It is observable, that this work of mending old requires much more art and invention, than designing new houses. I mean not here, comon repairs, but the thro reforme of an old house so as to make it moderne and elegant in its face and use. In a new designe some one thought governes the whole; as the placing the grand rooms and apartements are layd out, and the order of the storys and roof setled, other rooms and conveniences must take their places accordingly, and giving way to their betters, be disposed where they will fall with most accomodation to the family. This occasions much cobling about the inferior members, whose appertures must conforme to decorum without, however deforme within. And in this after the principalls fixed, the rest is no pain to the invention, the maine lines governe and there's an end. But in regulating the old, every corner and place demands a distinct consideration, how the best conversion and application may be. And it is not easy to imagine how a dexterous contriver shall improve a place to useful ornamentall porposes, and so aptly fitted as if such had bin the originall designe of it; and bring 1000 of ordinary judgments to bear, few or none shall discover it. And farther, there is more art to cover faults, than to compose perfections. The latter may be done by authentick patterns and rules; but the other hath no patterne nor rule, but is the product of originall skill. Old houses will have, to the present esteem, gross faults; and an artist by disposing the adjacent parts, both hide⟨s⟩, and with small additions render⟨s⟩ them ornamentall; at least to such eyes as are not very nice, or who have no hints of the defect given to draw the observation that way. A jugler, to conceal the action of one hand, points with the other earnestly to the roof. This draws away the spectators' eyes. The like is done in building; when faults cannot be taken away, they must be disguised, and covered, or the eye averted by some more engaging part.

⟨*Materials*⟩

I shall next sett downe some notes of what I have observed touching materialls. And first

OF BRICK

It is best husbandry to make it, for if nothing else be saved, neerness of carriage is gain enough. But there is farther to ease the charge, the clearing of foul grounds of bushes, brush, or whinns, and the making a larger brick which will rise in your work faster than sale brick.[36] In burning a clamp and coal is good, for the bricks are piled, and may be taken or let stand. But in taking observe alwais to clear to the ground, and shovel the dust away clean to the bottom, before new breaches are made, else much brick will be buryed in dust. If by kilne and light fire, the firing must be fresh and dry. It hath most force when just dry; if it be in any sort decayed, the fire is weakened. The bricks must be well whited, that is dryed, before setting, and not be sett too close. And slow burning and long is best, and leave not off, till the fire and flame come out freely at the top thro all the brick. A small kilne and 1 pipe is best, without your building eats very fast, as, if it be all new brick, then the kilne must be large and many hands imployed. But the small burnes oftner, surer, and wastes not fire so much.

The brikmakers are a bad, and theevish sort of men, so are not to be trusted with advance. If the earth be stony, they will scarce ever pick it well enough, and, if not well followed, doe their work very ill, and lay the fault on your side. They will burne too fast, and leave off too soon, steal all they can find, and run away on the first trust worth breaking.[37] You contract by the 1000 — I give 5.6d in a stony earth, and 4d for drawing

---

[36]Bought bricks as opposed to bricks made on the site.

[37]This passage reflects Roger North's own experience. On 16 Nov. 1691 Richard Musselbrook of Fulham, brickmaker, contracted with him to come to Rougham and make 60,000 rough bricks 'of the usuall London size', that is $9 \times 4\frac{1}{4} \times 3\frac{1}{4}$ in., and 60,000 'good stock brick of the same size', both at 4s. 6d. a thousand, together with 50,000 bricks $12\frac{1}{2} \times 6\frac{1}{4} \times 4\frac{1}{4}$ in. 'without core or samell', at 5s. a thousand. However, after some months' work Roger North found that the earth was bad for brick-making and that the bricks were consequently of poor quality 'and therefore judg'd not contract-ware and upon refusall to advance beyond the contract

out of the kilne. Bricks are either sandy, or clay. The former hold weather well, and doe not scale in frost; they burne rotten, and doe not glaze or melt, therefore a slack burning is better with them than others, and the fire must be slow. Of the clay some weather well, being very hard like sinders; others scale with frost intollerably, but are fine and hard in the hand. And were I to chose, I would have the sandy brick rather than any, but the sindery clay. And in brickmaking, if the charge will availe, nothing better than covering the stakes, or rows of bricks for drying and covering the kilne. If wett comes during setting, it much hurts the ware, unless covered. Earth dugg in early winter to take the frost is best, because it makes and moulders with less labour. And of all things avoid marle or chalk stones, which spoyl all. Bricks rub'd and gaged are a fine but a weak and decaying work, much worse than plain.

TIMBER

In London and the coast northward deal is of great use; it is equall to any, for inward work, especially beams, because they have a spring, and rise against their weight which no other wood will doe, and if redd and rozeny, serve tollerably in roofs; but nothing but oak will bear the ground. There are some yong deals that are brought over with great timber, they call deal poles, which serve for out housing, where strait sparrs are needfull.[38]

Ash, (if winter-felled) and elme, will also serve in inward work, where no wet comes. Ash is apt to worme if sappy. Elme cutt dry or wett, lasts but not alternately. Pople will last long, kept dry; and, to say truth, almost any wood, except such as wormes. Oake is the proper building timber on which you may depend, saving sapp, which will rott from its company in the least wett.

In buying, oak standing is for timber-masters that can guess at measure as a bucher at the weight of a beast. But lying comon measure is best for a gentleman; for being brought home and contrived by himself

more money weekly . . . . Mussellbrook left his horse cart and tools, and went away, having burnt 2 clamps, one very badd, the other not so badd, and divers of the first, and most of the last fitt for use' (volume at Rougham entitled 'Leases and Contracts'). Sir Roger Pratt gives comparable prices (*The Architecture of Sir Roger Pratt*, ed. Gunther, 1928, p. 29).

[38] The deal timber referred to was imported from Scandinavia and the Baltic. On the price and measurement, etc. of timber see also *The Architecture of Sir Roger Pratt*, ed. Gunther (1928), pp. 236–7.

yeilds advantage by the chipps, and waste, if any be; but building in one place or other usually eats clean. The error of girt measure is the buyer's advantage; but it will be more when the seller is not carefull to cutt off such peices, as according to the rule of girting cast advantage very much from him. Carriage is a weighty article in all building, especially timber, and nothing needs conduct more than that. If you will take timber ready saw'd, and so delivered in scantlings at your work, it will now come for 1.4d or 1.8d foot solid; running measure, without great caution, is a cheat, and will much surprise you. And measure by reducing to feet solid, is subject to this disadvantage; that the sap and the waxes will arise to much, and is all loss. But having great and small, wany[39] and square one with another, it is the best way for such as doe not manage and contrive for themselves. Whatever the timber is, keep it as much from wett as you can, especially if lime be near, or the wett passeth from it.[40]

LIME

The hard stone is incomparably best, but all countrys have it not, and are content with chalk, which with sharp sand makes a good body, but of it self will never harden beyond the stone of which it is made. Walls doe well, with the mortar made fresh and lay'd hott from the slaking. But then the lime must be good, and slack soon. Generally it is the best way to pan up the lime towards winter to be used in building next sumer, and it shall be found that all the unslaked parts will be buttery, and slak't, which is great gaine as well as good for the work. But all persons have not means to conduct for the best, and must doe according to circumstances. The bubbling of ceilings and rendring, as also mortar scaling in walls, is from the lime slaking too late in the work. Therefore where the lime is hardest, it needs most lime and water to slake it well. Quick lime powdered and put in water, is a cement for quick working any thing fine.

STONE

Of stone *equarrè*,[41] or ashler, I have litle to observe, being not used in our country[42] in comon building; but mostly flint; and that is a very good

---

[39]'Waney' or 'wainey' means timber with an irregular edge, usually corresponding to the contours of the tree-trunk from which it was cut.
[40]i.e. the lime transmits wetness to the timber.
[41]Squared.
[42]i.e. Norfolk.

and durable materiall for building, as any whatever, altho it doth not make so fair a shew. It is necessary to mix brick with it for turning the coines and some bandage while the wall is green. It is wrought with a stiff mortar, least the weight above croud out the lower courses and it is not good to rise too fast, but lett the lower part harden somewhat, before the upper presseth too much. There is a sort near the coast called pebble, taken from the sea beach, that is wrought lapping the mortar about each stone, very stiff, so that one would wonder it holds its place, but is very strong. And in all rough flint work there is much of that lapping the mortar, and it is observed that stone never lys well, that doth not swim in mortar, not touching any other. There is in Norfolk of old used a sort of fine flint-work, and some very exquisite; they break the flint, and by breaking the edges, bring it near a square, and so lay it with a black face.[43] And in all flint work it is good to fill the joynts with shivers, thrust in, which makes the mortar sett and binds the wall.

COVERING

Whatever is lay'd on, the timber and lathing should be oak. Stone slatt is a very durable covering. Next that, ely-tile,[44] knowne by the white colour, is best; unless slak-burnt, and then it scales and is stark naught. Of the sandy tile, that in Essex, is best; Norfolk hath none good, but some are made and used, for want of better. Thatch is so ruinous a covering, that it is fitt onely for cottages, and mean outhouses; those of greater account as barns and stables, and granerys, are better covered with Dutch tyle, which will ly flatter than trenchar-tyle,[45] and weather well. They may be lay'd in mortar, or pointed at the back; else the snow will drive in, as abroad; for they will not fitt exactly. Some are made in England, but none so good as in Holland, if tollerable, and in Norfolk not such. If not the best, they are the worst covering. In lathing for flatt tyle, allwais observe to counterlath; that is nail a lath in the midst between every sparr, cross all the lath. This is a strength more than is

---

[43]For flint 'flush-work', characteristic of East Anglian church architecture in the fifteenth and sixteenth centuries, see Alec Clifton-Taylor, *The Pattern of English Building* (1972), pp. 205–7.

[44]No roofing-tile specifically associated with Ely seems to be known, but the tiles made in the Cambridgeshire area were light in colour.

[45]'Trencher-tiles' are not otherwise recorded, but were probably flat in form, as a trencher was a flat board or table. Dutch tiles were S-shaped in section.

easily conceived, but is rarely done unless contracted for. And of coverings next to lead (the charge of which is not for private persons to sustein) reed is most durable, but not being so elegant, is used for the greater outhousing, and none better. It is also used for head farmehouses and without objection, but for danger of fire, nothing catching from a candle readyer than that. And for that reason it is usually spartled,[46] that is plaistered with mortar. Where any sort of tile is used, it is very good to hipp with mill'd lead, but care must be taken to bind it well at fitt spaces, or the wind will raise it. 3lb to the foot will doe, and the binding may be a plate of iron to goe cross it, to keep it downe or else a slipp of cast ledd doubled, which is stiff enough. This mill'd lead is beatable close to the tile, with less hazzard of breaking than other stiffer lead is. If lead be used for guttering, as is most necessary in double roofs,[47] now used, lay one sheet dripping downe upon another, and not strait sodered, for the stretching and warping of the lead will crack it, when there is not scope to yeild. You may soder the dripp, and it will be more secure against overflows. And it is good to let the sheets rise as high under the tiles, as conveniently may be done, for the same reason. If lead is to be sodered on a flatt, let not the soder rise upon the sheets, but cut a grove under in the wood, and after the lipps beaten together into it soder them. Lord Alington's house at Horsheath, hath all the sheets devided by a crevise, and so carrys the water by small gutters under each crevise, to maines, and out at one vent.[48] But this is nice and apt to prove ill.

WATER

The conduct of water from an house, is a matter that deserves care and contrivance as much as any thing whatever. For when it is left to dripp round, and sometimes with short-eaves, it is a great annoyance to the windoes, and walls of the house; and however cast farther off either by long eaves or pipes to the grounds, it is an inundation every showre, and makes the house an island. It is observed that walls of brick will filtrate

[46]Evidently a local Norfolk term for the method of fireproofing thatch described in the text, though not included in W. Rye's *Glossary of Words used in East Anglia* (1895). According to the *English Dialect Dictionary* a 'spartle' was a wooden spatula used by thatchers for raising up old thatch in order to insert fresh wisps when repairing a roof.

[47]i.e. the central gutter created by the parallel roofs of the 'double-pile' house.

[48]Horseheath Hall, Cambs., built by William Lord Alington to the designs of Sir Roger Pratt in 1663–5 and demolished in 1792. These gutters are described in some detail in *The Architecture of Sir Roger Pratt*, ed. Gunther (1928), p. 253.

from the bottom to the top, and wett the very wall plates. Therefore it imports to clear well the water off, that the habitation might be wholesome. And this is done by all sorts of walls more or less.

Either the ground will drein it self, or not. Where the former is, the work is easy, for if there be no fall to carry off the water, there may be cavernes made, and covered with brick, as is done at all the corners of Chelsea Colledge,[49] and the water conveyed in shall sink away, and keep the neer grounds dry. But if there be no such expedient, a fall may be purchast by digging draines to a farther distance, and it is a bad scituation that in so doing will not give a fall. These draines being of brick will last ages, and being arch't and earth't over are no inconvenience, nor eye sore, but open draines are intollerable, because cattell will be ever filling them up, and they will stink most offensively.

It will sometimes happen, that a reasonable fall is had from one side or quarter of an house and not from the other, which, notwithstanding the fall draining one side, shall be anoyed by wett. My advice in that case is, to bring the water all to some comon channell, and so lead it to the lower ground from the body of the house, and not vent it abroad, till it comes to the dreining side. For compassing this, the whole house must be batlemented or cornished; the latter is more in use. And in the midle, neer some waste-wall, where the most recess of the house is, contrive a maine gutter large, to pass along thro the out wall, to vent the water by a sess-pool, and large pipe downe, and so under ground away. And from the cornishes convey the water by some covert gutters to this maine; all which may be done, if thought of in time, and taken into your contrivance. The cautions are to make gutters large and deep enough; and if one passeth into another square, lett a stop be over against it, else a swift current will pass clean over; and let no gutter open and shoot up or against the current of another, for that will swell. It is a very great inconvenience to suffer a dripp about an house, it is not onely foul and unwholsome but hinders plants growing, and whatever the charge is, there is no blame, the use is so great.

VOULTS AND ARCHES

There will be occasion sometimes for arching as for cellars, and grotts, and, if your fancy so directs, a fire-tight room. It is not unreasonable, to

[49]The Royal Military Hospital at Chelsea, built to the designs of Sir Christopher Wren in 1682–92.

desire a place, where any thing may be put, which you would not have subject to the casualty of fire.

As to arches in generall, it is fitt to know, where the pinch and strain of them lys, that they may be sufficiently fortified to stand. I doe not approve flatt arches over windoes, but rather scene-arches,[50] being about a sextant, for those are not indecorous, because reasonable. The flatts are less decorous, because weaker, both to the eye, and in reality. The ancients thought it no disgrace to shew an arcuate discharge in the body of a wall. It look't like care, and governement, and not ignorance in the work; the flatts, if water comes at them, are apt to decay, unless very well wrought. And no flat arch is good that is not massive, and full of visible strength, which ly's most in the deepness of the frame especially at the key; of this observe that I made at the gate of the Midle Temple, and the weaker are seen at the Westminster gates by Whitehall.[51] The latter are so wide to be offensive, and the wonderment at the work, which is much made of, doth not compensate.

The pinch of most sorts of arches, especially the semicircular, ly's in the shoulder; there it is apt to crush within, and rise up. So that if it be fortified there all is safe, and untill it be so done by filling or abuttment, it is not good to strike the centers. The long way of an ellipse pincheth in the shoulder very much, and if you would examine this force, take this rule.

Describe the out and in sweep lines of your arch such as include your compas work, and then draw lines from all (or equidistant) points of the outward tangents to the inward, and where those run together thickest, is the greatest strain of the arch, and where most force bears.

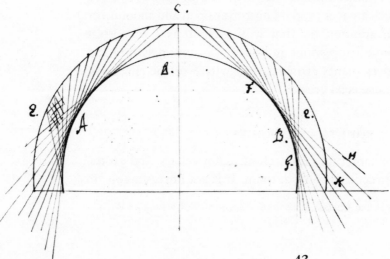

Observe in this arch, the pressure opens the joynts at D, so there no crowd is, and they close at A,[52] but the crowd is onely the weight of the key stones. But at A and B the crowd is most, being of all the superstructed weight, and if the materiall be too weak it crushes there; and at E the arch is apt to yield outwards, or rise, If this rule be applyd to other figures, as the long-oval, it will be found that upon the returne at the shoulder, is vast hudle of force, which the lines discover. And in the scene arch, the thrust ly's all at the impost of the arch; and as the arch is flatter it runns onto the meer abuttment, so that a flatt arch (as it is termed) is no other than a wedge.

The reason of this is, that weight ly's upon that body that most immediately susteines it. That which hath no void, in the perpendicular of it, ly's upon a plaine base. Then as the weight is made to overhang, it⟨s⟩ pressure is by the perpendicular, but cannot be supported there, because it is void. Then it must fall upon the next solid contiguous to it, which is in a strait line, as neer the void as is possible. As what support hath the point C? It cannot be sayd by E which is less under it, but by the line C H, which is the first solid continued from it, and neerest to its tendency by the perpendicular, and so of all other points, in the whole substance of the arch.

Now here observe the crush of the substance, and the abbuttment have each their designations in this sceme. For the crush is made by a contraction of the weight in the arch C E into the lesser arcuate space F G. Wherefore the crush upon that is more, than the weight of the materiall, on its owne substance, without that disadvantage. And if the materiall gives way, it is in that space F G, but the abbuttment, if one perfectly true were to be made in this area, it must be a stopp against the thrust of all the lines between H and I, and altho the line I K be the impost or base of the arch, yet it hath a thrust also upon it to drive it outwards. But K H is meerly thrust outward. Therefore the guard must be a sufficient stopp against the lines H I which secures the arch in all events. And as the arch grows flatter it will be found the thrust leaves the base and goes all upon the abuttment, as it is in the flatt arch.

The same rule that holds for abbutting and securing an arch for carr⟨y⟩ing a wall, holds for volts. For if it be a long vault, it is onely extended in length, from one face to another, all circumstances else alike.

---

[50] A segmental arch whose arc occupies one-sixth of the circumference of a circle struck from a centre in the middle of the window. The heads of the windows at Rougham Hall were segmental (cf. Pl. 1).

[51] The two Tudor gateways, both demolished in the eighteenth century, whose remarkably flat arches can be seen in the engravings reproduced in *Survey of London* xiv, p. 12 and Pl. 66.

[52] *Sic*. For 'A' read 'F'?

If it be cross arches, then the like considerations in the diagonall line take place; if sphericall, all around. But for this latter, a neat way of compiling an arch of brick without center-frames hath bin found out, used at Paul's and I proved to my great satisfaction.[53] And it is done upon this sceme; project a hemisphericall shell upon the diagonall of a square or oblong square space; then suppose the sides to rise up, and abscind 4 segments from the shell. The longer sides shall take out the greater, and the shorter lesser segments. And the shell shall come downe to the diameter at the 4 corners. The arch, when made, is of this forme, and is certainly most beautyfull, and proper for covering any place, which you would have look well within. The method of doing it is this: find the center of the room by the crossing of the diagonalls, and there fix a rodd that shall indifferently turne about, as if it were to describe an intire hemisphere upon that point, and let this be the gage of the work. Build up the sides in sweeps with spring courses tog⟨eth⟩er with the wall; and if the gage rodd be cutt, or have a pin at the length of half the diagonall, build from the ends of the diagonalls, sweep-wise by the guide of your gage rodd or pin, and the walls strait till they terminate in, or cutt the arching; and carry up alltogether with fitt band workman-like. And you shall find that in process of the work, the walls will take a sweep, according as the section would have made; and the sweep of the shortest sides will be finished first, and after that the shell goes gathering over it and then it may be fitt to gage also the thickness of the shell, which is done by another pin or notch in your rodd; but till it is risen to the height of a scene arch, it is good to fill without the shell solid, to make good the abuttment. Then after you begin to gather in your shell over all your walls, and perhaps sooner, the overhanging may make the brick apt to slip; but this is onely untill the whole course is key'd or closed, and then it binds it self, and how neer soever the bricks ly to an upright they will not stirr. And in the working, of a course, it is easy to hold downe 4 or 5 of the last layd bricks with sticks strained downe close from side to side; and so the work will goe on to close in one key, which put in, all is fast, and this exquisitely true to the figure, as well as lying of the brick; for the gage rodd shews them when they poynt to the center, whereas in arches wrought upon frames, that is done by a rude guess; and if the error were

---

[53] For Wren's own account of this form of vaulting see his second Tract on Architecture, printed in *Parentalia* (1750), p. 357, and in *Wren Society*, xix. 131. The main vaults of the nave, choir, and transepts of St. Paul's Cathedral are formed on this principle. For a drawing showing its application to one of the western towers see *Wren Society* iii, Pl. xx.

very materiall no such arch could stand; but a litle more or less, is not of much moment, because after the work is dry, all joynes in one body.[54]

This is a great retrenchment of charge in arching, and more easy, and practicable than one would imagine. It must be a good workman that keeps his courses true levell, because he cannot strait a line, as the use in working brick is, but round he will come, and a litle out of level is not seen underneath, especially if plaistered.

OF WALLS, AND PARTICULARLY FOUNDATIONS

I would not mention things obvious in books however materiall, for I make not a collection of any thing, but my owne observations of things less comon. As to walls, nothing is so materiall, as to draw in the superstructure, that it doth on no account overhang but fall within the base. But this must have bounds; for too much spreading, is usless, and demands a distinct covering to weather it. In Queenstreet, the houses had an order of pilasters, which overhung the wall underneath, and weakened the houses; the lord Conway's was regulated in that, as may be seen; and the rest must follow in line.[55] It is also very imprudent to hang much weight aloft, by massif gables, cornishes, and battlements; if they may be avoided. For those moved by the weather, and other accidents, have force and sway to carry the shake too farr and weaken the wall. Fascias are much used, but between every story is too much, and neither ornamental nor usefull; a man wears but one girdle. Comon builders clap them between every story, they know not why. It is certein they weaken a wall, for they can scarce be so well weathered, but water will insinuate to the wall there, and if not well weathered with lead at least, they expressly spoyl the wall.

The great distress of fence walls is the want of good coping. About Chelsea Colledge, wood painted is the coping, which doubdtless is good, and lasting. Ordinarily, the head overhangs for a dripp, and is then gathered in, by bricks layd aslope flat; and a range of others level a-top.

---

[54] For the construction of brick vaultings without centering with the aid of devices similar to the 'gage-rod' described here see R. Mainstone, 'Brunelleschi's Dome', *Architectural Review*, clxii (Sept. 1977), 157–66.

[55] See *Survey of London*, v, Pls. 16–19, for illustrations of the surviving examples of these well-known houses in Great Queen Street, built *c.*1637–40. Lord Conway's house on the south side of the street was pulled down in 1743, but Roger North would have known it well, for from *c.* 1675 onwards it provided accommodation for the Lord Chancellor, and was therefore the London residence of his elder brother Lord Guilford from *c.* 1682 to 1685 (ibid., pp. 78–82).

If the bricks and mortar be not excellent, this is a bad way, for the mortar decaying with the wett, the bricks slip, and the wall is exposed, for which nothing is worse, than water getting to the center. And some are so foolish, to frame their coping bricks, so that the joynts point inwards, which will lead in the water. A better way is to set the bricks on edge, and so a brick corner makes the point at the sumit of the wall. Mortar is not to be trusted to, in the leading a wall; for in England, rain and frost, will get the better of it. Those who have compass bricks[56] made to set on edge upon the wall, with the round upward, find that the joynts being strait from the top to the bottom of the head, the water hath a strait course downe and will insinuate it self to the wall. Against which I ordered walls, with good effect, thus: after the wall levelled 2 sallying courses; then 2 courses sett off on each side each an inch or better, then a course of brick on edge, which also sett off an inch on each side, and lastly a course of flat brick on length. This defends the wall because the joynts are broke, and no one over another, but solid against joynt to stop the water, and the compage of them is so bound and levell, that, if it were compiled without mortar, or all the mortar fell out, the head would stand. And this is necessary to be done, where brick, as mine is, sucks water; for when frost comes upon them wett, they will, upon thaw, part from the mortar. Stone is the best coping, but of that some, as the Kitton,[57] will pass water, and spoil a wall at first if not prevented; which is done by oyling, and if that be too costly, flett milk[58] and quick lime. In time when a crust gathers it weathers well enough. If walls are such that frost much hurts them, as when done with peble or flint where the mortar is more exposed than the stone, nothing is better than to thatch the first winter with straw or brakes,[59] and cope next spring. For the wett running continually from the head, the frost will never find the wall other than wett, and so hurt it; but if it be thatch't, with eaves overhanging much, then the water of the head as also the slope falling of rain will not annoy it so much. And if one winter be gained without ruin, they are secure for ever, and the more time they stand the stronger they are. Brick walls endure the frost much better than stone, both because the joynts are thin, and not in such massy lumps of mortar as stone walls have, and because they suck the moysture and dry sooner; for this reason it is

Section
a thwart

---

[56]i.e. semicircular bricks, still used for coping walls.
[57]Stone from the well-known quarries at Ketton, near Stamford.
[58]Skimmed milk.
[59]Bracken or fern.

that brickwork is done in some places, as in London all winter, but during hard frosts.

As to foundations, the cheif care is where one side is earth bound, and the other not, as in cellaring. If the materiall be not good, the wall is apt ⟨to⟩ splitt and give way inwards. So at settings off. If it be not done gradually, but all at once, as where it may be done at 2, 3 or 4 courses, it is better than at one. The difference appears in the margin. The la⟨t⟩ter bears the weight upon the whole base, the other upon part, but thrusts out the other.

The cheif imploy of a foundation, is to be a firme, and immovable foot to set an huge weight upon, for long continuance. And this cannot be had, neer the surfase of the earth, because the soil is not so firme, nor is it so abbuted laterally as deeper, but subject to squeeze from under its weight. And the frost and weather hath too much power to dissolve all cement neer the surface, therefore it is necessary to goe downe deep, to have a sound foot, safe, and well abbutted laterally. For this reason also, the trench should be filled with masonry, to the upright of the digging, and that spread no more than is needfull, and not be left to be filled afterwards with mould. But if the soil be not secure from wett, and you would keep the wall underground dry, some have advised to leave a space, and ramm well the void with good clay.

One thing I thinck unusuall I have found out and practised, for retrenchment of charge in foundations where lime is dear. The bulk and coursness of the work there, devours more lime than a whole wall superstructed. And in raising up old foundations I have observed an incredible hardness and bond of the work, from age and continuall moisture, so that I have esteemed such indurate strength superfluous. For when the wall is earth bound on all sides, so that it cannot spreadd, and frost comes not to moulder, it is enough, if the materiall will cohere, and not dissolve from it self. Therefore I used clay, till I came neer the surface, and expect full strength and duration from it. For after each course lay'd ramming brought the clay to fill all the joynts, squeezing into every void; more than this in comon fabricks, is certenly a charge not necessary. Another thing is considerable in laying foundations; most lay the first course in mortar, which is needless, and a considerable loss. Lett the first course by layd upon the gound, and if stone well rammed downe.

CHIMNYS, SMOAKING AND CURES

Nothing about an house is more important to be well executed than chimnys; for they are a beauty within, and (if seen) without, and the carrying smoak, or not, a consequence that either makes an house delightfull, or intollerable.

I shall not medle with the comon rules about chimnys extant in books, but some incidents of newer invention. Corner chimnys are much in use; but for want of right judgment, when proper, and how, often spoil rooms. 1. They warme a room, because it heats the sides, wheras a flat chimny heats onely over against, which is so far off as to be litle warmed. 2. They are a compendium. For 4 rooms on a floor may be served with one stack, but if flatt, but two, without leading the tunnells farr along the wall, which thickens the wall and looseth room. 3. They stand in a waste place, a corner, and destroy not room so much as if flatt, for then the setting forewards, as is necessary, intrencheth on the best room very much. These are the comendations. But after all I must rather recomend flatt chimnys, where your room will fittly receive them. And that distinction is made cheifly by the largeness or smallness of the room. For if a room be large, the corner chimny is a pinch of which there is no need, and is therefore an eysore. 2. It is too farr from the light, and for that reason inconvenient. 3. A flatt chimny is plast in your eye at the entrance and is the best ornament the end of a room is capable of. And after all the striving of artists to sett off angle chimnys, they are not such decorum to a room, as a flatt chimny in true place.

Therefore I confine angle chimnys to small rooms, or where space is strait, so that the fabrick will not receive them in the right place flat wise. And in such rooms as withdrawing rooms, and closets, they are most useful. For there is scarce a side, at least that where the chimny should be, but hath a door, or windoe. And then, if there be a chimny also, there will be no room for the company free about it, but the angle gives that room. And where such chimnys are made, and any thing of ornament extraordinary is sought, let me advise not to carry up the face to the ceiling, so as to cutt off an angle at the ceiling, than which nothing more deformes a room, but run in the tunnell soon to the wall, and let the mantle fall back with decent shape, and cease in a pedistall, and statue or flower pott; and then the upright walls take place, and maintain the square of the cornish, which is ever required, and aggreable to be in view.

The comon faults of angle chimnys, are that of cutting the square of the room, at the ceiling, as well as at the floor, and also the making them too large, which certeinly spoyls a room; for a great cant in a small place is a monster. The invention it self is a pinch, so litleness becomes it. This is much the case of most houses in London, contrived by tradesmen, and builders; for they have a notion that angle chimnys are in fashion, and build them with the same demensions as is usuall for flatt chimnys, which should not be. A corner chimny big enough to roast and boyl, is a strange, but ordinary sight in such houses.

As to the smoaking of chimnys, I conceive it is from 3 causes, 1. litleness of the tunnell, 2. eddys about the fire place, 3. stooping winds without.

1. Litleness of the tunnell will make a chimny smoak, because the quantity of air, which the heat works into a current, cannot pass fast enough out above; and then the superfluity recoyles into the room. 14 inches tunnell is usuall; where the fires are greater, as in kitchens, more room, or rather a double tunnell is necessary. This mischeif is found when folk will carry a tunnell in a wall that is too thin for it, and in the late London houses, where to gratifie the humour of the present time, every closet high and low must have a chimny; and so the tunnells are pinch't into so litle room that they will not carry smoak at all.

2. Eddys. These are very accidentall, for sometimes the pointing of a door shall sweep out the smoak from the chimney, and a great current of air thro a room by opposite doors, shall draw the rest, and draw downe the chimny. And most frequently there is eddy in the waste, and wings of a chimny, which happens when the hollow hath not a due proportion, and is drawn together too suddenly; then the stream of air doth not lick all the walls, but meeting with stop, eddys, and comes forth at the corners. And if a tunnell were sett off at once square without slope, it would not carry the smoak, but that which stops against the flatt above, recoyls into the room. Then if the slope be too sudden, it is all one in its degree.

3. Lastly, a stooping air without is the worst of faults. For that shall drive so violently downe a chimny as to carry the fire from the hearth, and is very hard to cure or releive. It is occasioned by adjacent buildings, and the position of hills. A reflection of some winds from higher building, will sometimes bear downwards into a chimny; and the like of trees or hills. Nothing is wholsomer to chimnys, than a free air, and a plaine country. Houses that stand on the sumitt of a cliff, where the

country on one side is plain, and there a precipice, as Beavoir Castle,[60] Windsor, &c. shall allwais smoak, when the wind comes from the flatt towards the valley. For the wind at the edge, begins to stoop, and so the edge of the hollow tunnell takes it, and drives it downe into it. At Beavoir many inventions have bin, but none effectuall to cure it. At Windsor it is not so bad, because opposite to the cliff the country riseth againe; so the wind doth not stoop so much.

As to cures, the cause knowne points to it. If that can be removed, or enervated, the work is done. As, 1. make a wind store,[61] to cure the litleness of the tunnell. For the strength of the blowing, getts the better, and makes amends in the swiftness of the draught. Other expedients in a less degree may be had in like kind, as a double back with slitts, or making up the cheeks, and the like as occasion shall require. 2. For eddys, changing doors, or the former contractions, may doe. 3. And as to the faults without, by reflexes or stooping, they have screens to turne allwais backing the wind with fanes[62] to governe them. Some cover the flatt, and let out the wind laterally, others lett in pipes into the shaft pointing upwards; and nothing but proof will determine the effect, for sometimes they will make a cure and often not. The securest way is to erect a tunnell, of brick or tin, so as to surmount, if it may be, the inconvenience.

[60]Belvoir Castle, Leicestershire.
[61]A 'wind store' must be some such device as that described by Richard Neve in his *Builders Dictionary* (1726). This was a brass ball hanging in the chimney and containing water which when heated by the fire gave off steam which helped to force the smoke up the chimney.
[62]Vanes.

The Regular Orders

Concerning which I have observed, 1. that it is not well to set one order upon another. I know the authors not onely alow, but give rules, for the doing it, beginning with the Tuscan for the basement, so with the Dorick next, then the Ionick, Corinthian, and Composite to conclude, being light and gay, having deep modilions, which the French call *corbeaux*, and our workmen corbells, in the cornish, which is a coronation of the whole fabrick. I should avoid this heaping house upon house, for each order supposeth an intire fabrick, of which the entableture is the rooff-frame, shewing it self, and sett off ornamentally. Therefore be the height what it will, and whatever shift is made, I would have but one order from base to the covering. If it be too high for the width; help it with pedistalls, or rustick, or attick, which, having the place of a basement, sett off the order.

I was forc't upon such expedients in building the Midle Temple Gate: I designed 4 pilaster columnes and a frontone;[63] and to preserve the dignity of the fabrick, I was forc't to raise it very high, the houses being so on each side. If wee had not topt them, all had bin spoyled, and the building had looked mean. But the width would not bear 4 columes from the bottom. Therefore I raised a table, to sett the order upon so high, that it received all the apertures of entrance; and then grounded the wall with brick rubb'd and gaged, which sett off the stone. If it had bin all stone from bottom to the top, as some gentlemen advised, it had bin like a steeple. But the rustick base, being all stone, and the rest above brick and stone, shewed a lightening of the work, and by making a distinction disguised the height. And thus I gained a just height for the order, and made a fair front. I owne the faults, which I foresaw but could not mend. The flat arch in the midle for the coach-passage, and compass arches on each side, is not proper; for the midle should have bin compass, and the iles flatt. But that had lost a chamber, which could not be. And next the coines are too small. I had not room to make them greater. If it had bin all stone without breaks, it had confounded the corner pilasters, by taking away their profile or shape. The thrust of the

[63] From the French 'fronton', meaning a pediment.

51

flatt arch, falls not upon the hollow of the compass arches, which had bin a fault inexcusable, but upon the solid above them; and therefore there is no reall absurdity in the disposition of those arches. One thing is worth observing; that the flatt arch is made very deep, and the stones rising towards the midle, and the range of them make an handsome stylobate for the columnes, and accord extreamly well. The rest is ordinary; onely the height of the columnes, and the midle intercolumne, exceed the rule of the Ionick order.[64]*

I acknowledge also that pilastering is a defect. Nothing comes up to the grandure of a massy collume. The purse I managed would not reach it. And the publick would not permitt such an incroachment on the street. But if materialls can be had, to make it practicable, especially on the outside of houses, or other fabricks, lett the columnes be solid, and not flatted, or buryed in the wall.

Another thing observable, of the orders in generall, is that they should not be small. The use of them in cabinetts, and chimnys is not well. The grace of them lys in the magnitude, and when small, they look mean as in a model. And they cannot be great enough, for the increase of their grandure, reduplicates the admiration of them, whereof wee know no limits.**

*North provides further details in BL MS, fo. 43: 'This consideration, which draws also vast charges if effectually performed in great works, hath occasioned Sir Christopher Wren in many places to waive stone work above the columnes, and to use wood and plaister. For so it is more secure and, being neer the projecture of the cornish, is preserved from weather, and lasts reasonably well. There is much of this at Chelsey Colledge in some of the frontoons there. And he would have perswaded me to use the same method at the Temple gate; but out of a proud high spirit, I declined it, and made the whole intableture, and frontoon of stone, and it is as lusty, as most are. But I grant, rather than pinch the demensions of the orders, it is better to cover so. For to say truth, in a private house, one man's life, which a plaister will well last, goeth a great way in the reason of adorning, which the bulder doth for the most part to please himself; and it seldom happens that posterity like any thing wee doe.'

**North's views on the use of columns are more fully stated in BL MS, fo. 42: 'My reason for this opinion is, that an order of columnes with the entableture doe⟨s⟩ properly note an intire structure, whereof the columnes are the support, and the entableture the frame or eawes of the roof. Wherefore, one of these above another is like setting one house above another, and besides makes the whole appear litle. But if an order take a basement from the plann of the fabrick, it can neither be too great nor run too high, and there is the greatest vertue of the orders, when they are drawne out to an immense biggness.

This lett in another observation which will be found true in the generall: that the orders never look well in litle. This is matter of fact, and I beleeve few will dispute it, but the reason may be less noted. It is usuall to addorne cabinetts, small monuments and chimnys with columnes, which is a debasing them. The reason is, wee expect house work where wee see collumnes, and in these uses they are not giants, as the case needs, I mean the support of houses, but dwarfs or

---

[64]For the Temple Gate see Introduction, p. xiv, and Pl. 3.

Of Lights

Some things will hold proportion with the bodys of men, and not the grandure of a fabrick, and of that sort is lights. For howsoever great an house is, the windoes must not exceed $4\frac{1}{2}$ or 5 foot wide. Else it is a breach and not a windoe. A man approaching a windoe expects it to be of usuall size, and if it exceed, then he thincks of weakness in the fabrick by such an aperture, and also of needless extent, and that less would serve and be stronger. For he looks not at it, comparing it with the rest of the house, but with himself, who presents himself at it. But in publik building, where the windoes are to light the space, and not to be accessible, as in churches, windoes hold proportion with the fabrick; but it is otherwise, where men dwell and come to ordinarily. A small or ordinary room should not allow above 4 foot to the windoes. I know it is an error, to affect much light, and wee confess it, by darkning o' lights againe with curtaines; it is rare to see a want of light, where the sky appears; it is walls, building, and trees, which taking away the sky's light, darken a room, and not the smallness of the aperture.*

This mistake of over lighting an house, which is both cold, and bad for the eyes, came in upon the reforme of building in Europe after the Gothick arrived at its utmost refinement. The castle-manner used in

children brought out for a jest, or to play with, and not for any thing serious. And the more close cause is that wee know the nature and strength of materialls and consequently that things will cohere and be strong in small quantitys, which will dropp asunder, if not well armed, in greater. So projections will be endured in small works, which in greater were nonsense. And in the former to make an ostentation of strength, such as columnes and their entablement declares, is to give a child a horse's thys, altogether incongruous. Therefore orders should not be sett upon the stage unless they are admirable for their magnitude; and in that beauty (for so I must terme it) there can be no excess, while proportions are maintained.'

*More precise precepts for lighting rooms occur in BL MS, fo. 44^v: 'Now it may be ask't, what is light enough. I can answer, either one 2 or 3 windoes, of moderate size as the rooms are. A room of parade 3 windoes, and not 4 unless it be extraordinary large. Sir Christopher Wren has kept to the order of 3 windoes in Pauls, which is a discretion few will observe. A parlor, chamber, or eating room, should have 2 windoes, and the cheif use of 2 rather than one windoe (which for matter of light might suffice) is for hanging of a lookinglass, which is not well, if a light falls not equally on both sides of the object. And no furniture contributes more to the life and spirit of an apartement, than good and well plac't glasses.

'A closet should have but one windoe, because 2 distracts the light, and objects, as pictures, and curiositys, appear not so well; so for wrighting or reading, one light is better, tho the room be large; besides, there is more room left for shelves &c.'

these countrys in elder time, when warrs forrein or intestine were almost perpetuall, used very small windoes; and those took place even in churches, as may be seen in the eldest modells. Peace and plenty made way for luxury in building as well as in other things, and then they left the castle manner, and fell into a contrary extream, of making an house like a bird cage, all windoe. The French buildings were so, and wee followed, and, as in other foolerys, out-did them. The degrees of change were, whilst all the panells of light were round-headed, to increase the number, and from 2 onely in a windoe as the use was, they came to 4 and 6 and then to have 2 ranges of them one over another. Then the round heads grew strait, but the number of lights increast and multiplyed, so that our great dining rooms for dancing in the reigne of Elizabeth and James I wanted no windoe, where it was possible to have any, and the roof stand. The Itallians allwais kept to their single apertures, vizt the long square, filled with monton and transom. And at one time, such windoes were made in England. I am informed that the Byrse in my lord North's house in Kirtling[65] is the first building in England, where they were used. The Lord Keeper North's house at Wroxton, had great roomes caged by windoing; and being to be finished up, I urged very much, to have above half the lights stopt up, and it made the rooms exceedingly better, and if I had had my will, more had bin served so. Light is a good thing, and illustrious, therefore men are apt to say there cannot be too much of it. The reasonableness of small lights, used in churches built *a la regolare*, is seen by the other extream in our plaister churches in London, where the white walls and much windoe, makes it a pain to sit in them. The best Gothick churches are almost all light, but then they took it downe by painted glass in the windoes, scarce ever found wanting in them. This made the light moderate and solemne; but our churches are for light like amphitheaters built abroad.

The Italians allow to the height of their lights but 2 squares; we desire more. In hot countrys much light is more inconvenient than in cold. The Arabs have but a small hole of one light, at the upper corner of a large room, northwards; because they find, wherever light is, heat will be. The Arab phisitians sayd keep your sick of the small pox from light, that is cool, and wee, following them, shut out light and so kept them hot; a

[65]One wing of the sixteenth-century mansion at Kirtling, in which Roger North was brought up, was demolished in 1748, and the remainder in 1801, leaving only the gatehouse. This is described in *Country Life*, 24 Jan. 1931, where a view of the house before 1801 is illustrated. The 'Byrse' was presumably a counting-house or treasury.

strange mistake practist on the lives of men, for severall ages, and but latly oppugned by Doctor Sydneham,[66] and overturned. Wee that are a cold climate can bear higher lights, and they are decorous, by the procerity of them, and also they light the roof. And for that use the Italians use a freese or small light apart above the other, which is not so stately as tall windoes are, and on the outside look small, like the ports of a ship. In an high room, it is almost necessary to advance light to it some way or other, unless it stand by water, and then the sky reflecting from that will be sufficient.*

Sky lights serve for staires, and servants' rooms, and are but a shift at best; therefore should not appear in principall places; which makes me wonder that the best and newest houses in Norfolk, lord Toundsend's, and Sir Jacob Ashley's, are no better served in their principall staircases;[67] for those should be perfect in all respects, being a place all of notice and observation.

To conclude this discourse of lights, I must needs recomend cupolo-lights, for refectorys and dining rooms. They are very ornamentall in staires, but side lights are better, being brisker. They do well in a grand sale, but no where better than in the eating room. The reason is, that they are indifferent to all the company, and promote society by equall observation to and of all. In a side-light room, those that sitt averse are not observable to those that face the light. And a raised light is an advantage to feature, for it lays the shaddow of the prominencys downewards, and strong, which setts off the lights in each object. And it is not inconsiderable that being well windoed, they evaporate the smell of meat and keep sweetness in the room.

*In BL MS, fo. 38, North records how he was led to this conclusion: 'The Italians allow but moderate height to their windoes, seldome above 2 squares, which the heat of the country, that allwais attends light, excuseth. Here wee endure more, and the height adds not much to the cold of them; but in exceeding high rooms, it is best for them and us to have high windoes square above the others to light the roof, which else will be too dark, and consequently dull. These were not made in my Queen's appartment by the water side in Whitehall, alltho I thought that sort of building had required it.[68] I ask't Sir Christopher Wren the reason of it, and he answered that the reflexion of the sky from the water would be light enough to the roof, which was an ingenious thought, and fully satisfied me.'

---

[66]Thomas Sydenham (1624–89), a leading physician of his day whose *Observationes Medicae* (1676), was a work of European celebrity. He was responsible for the introduction of new methods in the treatment of smallpox.

[67]For a ground-plan of Raynham Hall (Lord Townshend) made *c.* 1672 see *Archaeological Journal*, cxviii (1961), Pl. xvi. For Melton Constable (Sir Jacob Astley) see *Country Life*, 15–22 Sept. 1928.

[68]For the new Queen's Apartment built at Whitehall in 1688–9 see *History of the King's Works*, ed. Colvin, v (1976), 295, Fig. 23 and Pl. 37.

Of unity and variety

These wee hear of in the discourses of plays, poetry, and painting. The first cants it into a devision by time, place, and fable. And in that and the epick poetry, demand unity, yet allow for variety by plotts and episodes, which yet must hang upon the main. So the painters will not have a clutter, but some principall thing, at first view eminently cheif, to which all the other figures must relate. It is the same for building, and, to say truth, all things of delight in the world. The rule is not from men's invention, but from nature, and truth, as it is found the best and most experienc't senses will dictate. The reason is what I hinted at first, that pleasure from without consists in exercising the understanding without pain, and not in tormenting it, without any, or hard-gained satisfaction. If a play be double, that is 2 storys without dependance on each other, the audience is distracted which to attend, and when one comes, it breaks off the attention to the other, and hath the same disturbance at every transition. So 2 pictures in one is unlike nature, for wee cannot look at 2 things at once. So in building, 2 differing manners and ranges in one house, as if two houses came together, and justled, is disagreable.* And yet this doctrine of unity must not exclude variety, but artists must find out such as will divert, and not devide, and that is the consummate height of art.**

*In BL MS, fo. 30, North illustrates this point: 'How well I have conformed ⟨at Rougham⟩ to these propositions I submitt to the crittiqs, and conclude with this one caution, to such coblers as I am; that in what is new they doe not follow some greater or more magnifick order than the old, but to come as neer it as they well can, so as to make all of a peice, as much as is possible. This course I took in perfecting so much as was done of the Lord Keeper's house at Wroxton, where in the new I proposed the same sort of windoes as in the old, tho not the mode, and his lordship like't it well, and persued it. And this mistake I have not seen so conspicuous as in Mr Windham's house at Fellbrigg,[69] where is added to an old house a stately appartment, raised as high in the first floor as the ceiling of the old hall, which hath made an ostentacious stair case, but the flights are so long, and the ascent so high, and the whole so different from the rest of the house, that I am not, tho the generality are, pleased with it.'

**North elaborates this principle in BL MS, fos. 43ᵛ–44: 'And first I observe, that there is in the very shape of a fabrick somewhat, which in a person wee call an air, and falls under no rule, but is studdyed by painters with practise and examples and not precept; this where it happens

[69] For the west wing at Felbrigg Hall, Norfolk, designed by William Samwell for William Windham and completed in 1686, see *Country Life*, 22 Dec. 1934, p. 668, and R. W. Ketton-Cremer, *Felbrigg* (1962).

In the gothick times, structures of great pomp and strength were made, but failed in the way of setting off their fronts and views. They continued ranges of the same heights and order into great length, not breaking the course, or intermixing any thing great in the way of ornament; I say great, for of small ornaments, which I esteem trifles, [of which] they had enough and too many. But those take not the eye at any distance, where a building should be viewed. It may be they made no account of any thing without, so the room within was agreable. As wee see in most cathedralls, Westminster Hall, King's Colledge chappell, of which the latter is much the fairest, and set off with 4 turrets at the corners, but nothing else. It is certein that no true beauty is found in the out-line of a Gothick building, and cheifly because they used no breaks for variety in their ranges. A long building, consisting of bays of the same invention continually repeated, is a dull object. A long walk however well planted, is not compleat without opening, and crosses, to interrupt the sameness of it, by new views. The dullest road I ever saw was a fen-bank, where for 5 or 6 mile the landscape had no change; and was like traveling in a trunck, seing onely a small hole at the end. Of the moderne fabricks, Hampton Court, hath this fault conspicuously. It is new built, but the old had a better view, for that had gate towers, and some risings, but this is all of an height: balustred, flatt, which looks like combs stuck at the topp, and a series of round windoes, like the ports of a ship. Bridewell[70] hath a better face, where is a midle, and 2 ends raised above the rest, and the midle above the others, and all joyned with the lower order; and that, for too much length, is broke uniformly on each side with a setting out, and frontone. So Chelsey Colledge hath an order of collumnes in the midle, and 2 pavilions which terminate the wings. The

(for it is very often casuall, and seldome product't otherwise, than from example or patterne) delights the eye no less at distance, than neer hand, and shall be so conspicuous by the meer tour of the outline, which onely is distinguish't farr off, that however confused, and small it seems, the understanding shall pronounce it great.'

'And first, the pinking of walls with too many apertures, is very opposite to the true relish of greatness. It looks more like a colledge, or inne; where a world of people come for meer accomodation, and it speaks litleness within. It is to be considered that aperture is onely for use, and if there be more than the nature of the building declares needfull, it is a foolish superfetation; whereas there is no greater ornament than plaine walls, if there be a basement, cornish, coyns, and jaumes to the apertures there are, in due forme and order. So thatt all the minute trumpery usually pay'd for to inrich walls is lost in true ornament, which comes out of the generall air of the whole.'

---

[70] In the BL MS North calls this 'Bridewell by Moorfields', making it clear that he was referring to the Bethlehem Hospital, Moorfields, London, built to the designs of Robert Hooke in 1675–6 and demolished in 1815–16.

meer observation of that fabrick, is a sufficient instruction in this matter; for it must needs occurr, that if any range in that building had bin all of the same height and manner, it must have bin very dull.

Of the ancient fabricks, there are 2 sorts, which seem to contradict this doctrine of variety, that is their temples, and amphitheaters, both of which had no variety of parts, but went thro with one and the same order and manner. I must needs grant, that the danger of introducing variety is great, least trifling be the consequence. And singleness and plaineness where the order is great and good, is a vertue, and if a fault, the best of errors. The temples were single things, which spoke but one single use, that is sacrifising. To what end should that be broken? Why should hipps and valleys and gutters be made in a roof, to gaine no good, but onely to make a figure without, and imply no sort of advantage within? So also in a small dwelling house, what needs breaks? One pile and one covering is sufficient; if a porch be in the midle, to wether the door, it is enough and justifies an ornament, as a lofty pediment, to sett it off. And where countrys are warme, an open walk in the midle. This plaineness is without question comendable. But what is that to a greater extent of building, such as Bedlam,[71] Chelsea Colledge, or Hampton Court, which speaks a provision to be made for various and numerous sorts of people; and is rather a compound than a simple fabrick. Wherefore singleness doth not become it, as it doth a church or small house.

The amphitheaters were all of a peice without, and I beleeve they were content with a moderate beauty, where there was such vast magnitude and strength to be provided. I beleeve it will not be controverted, but if those buildings instead of 3 or 4 orders one above another, had bin composed with one order onely, carrying a stately intableture, with fitt apertures, and broke forewards ornamentally on each quadrant, they had bin more beautyfull;* and if prime and perfect beauty had bin the aim, as it was in the building temples of the gods, they had not bin set off as they were, *tale quale*. And this argues for breaking the height into severall orders. The whole was made for seats and staires,

---

*North's discussion here presupposes the general observation he had made in BL MS, fo. 37: 'Setting one order upon another never doth well and should allwais be avoided, if possible; and whatever the height be, lett there be but one order of columnes, and that supporting the roof. If the height be so much that the composition cannot well be so made, raise the bases, by rustik underneath, which may be done, and if it still needs raising, an attique, or work of a finer sort, may be sett upon the rustick, with decency enough; and this is in my opinion better than setting one columne upon another, which hath ever to me seemed heavy and improper.'

---

[71]The Bethlehem Hospital.

which staires were in the hollow under the seats, and it was fitt to make walks and windoes, upon severall landings, for the people to spread and evacuate by. Which severall ranges of windoes, or arches, did not so well consist with one great order, which should have had but one aperture in the height, because more ranges of apertures speak severall storys, and single columnes but one, so that there was reason to break the orders. But the strickt rule of beauty is not to be taken from them; nor is there any thing exquisite in the proportions, however artists have given themselves the trouble to describe them.

The distribution

First the midle is most considerable in every building; and ought to be sett off with a large and massy frontone,[72] that speaks, entrance porch, or covering, all that is necessary to invite persons to approach and enter. This is necessary, whether columned or not, and however a break foreward doth well, it may be without even that, provided the springers of the frontone cornish are over a solid, and not in the upright of a void. This supposeth a range cross the house a thwart; and shews a composition by designe for putting all well together. And nothing is more stately. It was such a grandure, that the Romans granted the priviledge of having *fastigium domus*,[73] as an honnour, or reward of merit.

This very well bears a cupolo to rise in the midle; in great designes, that should not be omitted. But I cannot reccomend it in private houses, being a leaky shaking buisness, and in no sort worth the charge of making and keeping. If there be a prospect, few care to mount so high for the sake of it; and no oven is more insupportably hott than such a place in sumer. In short it is a trifle for shew but important in mischeif, and none but such as know litle of them will care to have to doe with them. It is reported that the lanterne at Lambeth upon the hall, cost 1500 £, before it could be made weather-tight. Chelsea Colledge is a model I must allwais appeal to, for the best forme of this, and other members. And when that lanterne or cuppolo was put up, I was sorry it had no better foundation than wood, but few if any alive will discover that defect by any decay.

After this, an house may have the wings plain or set off with pavilions. The latter is much more beautyfull, for it looks like strength, abbutting both ends of the fabrick, and shews a compact firmeness of the whole. These are called pavilions, and formerly wings. The manner of forming a tabernacle of state, is by joyning single pavilions, by tent-gallerys, and

[72]From the French 'fronton', meaning a pediment.

[73]The word *fastigium* means the ornamental features proper to a temple façade, which were normally restricted to sacred architecture, but might in exceptional circumstances be permitted to a private residence. North would probably be familiar with the case of Julius Caesar, who was privileged in this way (cf. Cicero, *Philippic* ii, 43).

have fronts all ways, being a great pavilion in the midst, and 2 lesser at each corner.[74] They may be made of the same height with the house, and compass by the same running cornish; or they may be made to rise higher, but the pick of the roof must range. And this will fall out well, when the midle onely, and not the wings hath a deep sparr,[75] with lucerne[76] windoes, for then the windoing of the upper story of the pavilions may range with the lucerne windoes of the midle and the cornish with the cornish of them. And then the upper rooms will have square windoes in an upright wall, and may borrow height of the roof space by ceiling joysts well plac't, and be much improved, and no garret. It is to be noted that the cornish of the pavilion will dy against the roof of the midle and the cornish of that against the wall of the pavilion. That this invention will succeed well I know, having practis't it in my owne house, with much content. I found it necessary to use breaks in this manner, to remove the fastidious view of a plain and too great length the house had before. Winchester house, tho unfinish't, shews a very reasonable model;[77] for the vastness of the house is accomodated with lights and entrances, by severall breaks in the front, still opning wider forewards; it's pitty it never was finished.* Building too plain, and deep, will want light and many accomodations, which breaks afford. I doe not allow that pavilions stoop below the fabrick; for then garretts will range with principall rooms, and cannot be well. It is much better to set them full a story higher, and pass the cornish of them over the ridge of the midle. But the portico may stoop. And the point of its frontone may doe

---

*Compare the passage in BL MS, fo. 41 : 'I have many examples of this sort of decoration by breaks; and the cheif, and where it was most necessary, is that of Bridewell by Moorfeilds, where so long a range could not well be better distributed to give the whole a grace, and take off the fastidiousness of its length. The like is done at Chelsey Colledge where both the midle and 2 wings are adorned by like distinctions; so that you see a sort of portall in the midle with its frontoon above, and pavillions at each corner. And the great house began at Winchester, (pitty it is that it hath not its perfection,) is broke in a different manner, but proper, and decent. Clarendone house had a double midle frontoned and four grand pavilions, but that house wanted some rooms of parade which might correspond with the grandure of the whole, and therefore deserves not a place among the well designed fabricks, because also it was new, so no excuse.'[78]

---

[74]By a 'tent-gallery' North presumably means a single-storey, open-sided gallery or covered passage-way.

[75]Sparr appears to mean 'rafter', and here by extension 'eaves'.

[76]An English corruption of the French 'lucarne', meaning a dormer-window.

[77]The unfinished royal palace at Winchester, designed by Wren for King Charles II, and begun in 1683.

[78]Clarendon House, Piccadilly, built to the designs of Sir Roger Pratt in 1664–7 and demolished in 1683.

well, to range under the cornish of the midle; but it is much better to break from that forewards, and the covering coincide with the midle roof, for that will give a magnitude to the collumniation, than which nothing more becomes. And the portico will darken the house less, for its roof being set higher, and the order of the cornish correspond strait, all which quadrates with the decorum of building, that much consists in level ranges.

It hath bin the use of the Italians, and ill imitated in England, by some fond surveyors, to set the portico into the house, as wee find at Greenwich, the Queen's house, which looks towards the Observatory, and Sir John Maynard's house in Gunnersbury, which looks upon Braintford road.[79] This robbs the house of principall room, and interrupts the file of rooms, which is a prime beauty, and which is worse it darkens the best rooms. As at Gunnersbury, the dining-room hath no light but from this portico, which is almost as bad as a secundary light, and certeinly dull and improper. In Italy, this is proper and usefull, because it abates heat, and averts the force of the sun's light, which is offensive; and is also *fresco* and *aieroso*; not so aggreable here as with them, but at few times; wee have generally speaking, too much air, and too litle heat, and therefore need not spoil an order of rooms to obtein one and abate the other.

I have often wish't to see an house built *alla moderna*, composed of greater and smaller orders of rooms compact well together, with regard to use, state, and decorum, but am not so happy. I offered a litle at it in my owne. Mr Guy's house at Tring, is new, of Sir Chr. Wren's invention, and hath many elegant dispositions but wants that.[80] The country model, and that of a suburb villa, are different. The former partakes of the nature of a court, as a lord of a manor doth of regality, and should, like the court, have great rooms to contein numbers, with fires suitable and other conveniences, according to his condition. A villa, is quasy a lodge, for the sake of a garden, to retire to injoy and sleep, without pretence of enterteinement of many persons; and yet in this age, the humour takes after that, and not the other. And the inconveniences are not dreamt of till experience shews them. The ancients, I mean our

[79]The Queen's House designed by Inigo Jones in 1616; Gunnersbury House by his pupil John Webb in *c.* 1658 and illustrated in *Vitruvius Britannicus*, i (1715), Pls. 18–19.

[80]For the house at Tring, Herts., designed by Wren for Henry Guy in *c.* 1670 see the engraving of the front reproduced in *Wren Society*, xix, Pl. lxxiii. The internal arrangements are shown in a drawing recently acquired by the RIBA Drawings Collection.

elder country men, took another course; they built in different orders, so as to accomodate all orders of persons and occasions; of this among many other instances I shall mention Audley Inn house;[81] which hath a court at first entrance, of low building and portico walks, which serves for *passer tiempo* and lodging of officers and servants. The next court is for parade, and a loftyer order. This may be esteemed out of fashion, but is not to be for that disesteemed, when reason justifies it. For what is more necessary to a numerous court, than walks, and numerous apartements; and to dispose in them in order so that you have a pompous walk, from the port to the grand-sall, the building rising as you advance; and no fitting demand of such a family left open and unsupplyed? The house of my father, now my lord North and Grey's at Catlidge,[82] hath this proposition of greater and lesser building nobly performed. I doe not find such an elegance in the outward forme, as latter ages have introduc't; but nothing of lofty and noble, or what indicates such caracter of mind, conjoyned with usefullness within, is wanted there. And if wee observe the buildings from the age of Henry VIII downe to Charles II, wee shall perceive more of the august than in any time before or since. I might point to a great many houses, Burleigh by Stamford, Hampton Court, New hall,[83] &c., not to forget my father's, which demonstrate this judgment; for even there is such a string of rooms, fronting east, and ending north, with 2 turrets, which contein hall, butterys, chappell, great parlor, 2 withdrawing rooms, as are not to be ordinarily matched.

The latter ages have bin more addicted to a citty life, after the French way. And that recourse to London, hath encouraged the trade of building, and that ledd into ways of compendium and thrift for gain sake; and not onely in the cittys and townes, a compact model is used, but in all country seats of late built, the same method is practis't, to the abolishing grandure and statlyness of that sort the former ages affected.

[81] For the great Jacobean house of Audley End near Saffron Walden in Essex, much reduced in size not long after North wrote, see Lord Braybrooke's *History of Audley End* (1836) and P. J. Drury in *Architectural History*, 23 (1980).

[82] Catlidge was an alternative spelling of Kirtling, for which see above, p. 54 n. 65.

[83] For Burleigh House, Northants, see *Country Life*, 3, 10, 17, 24, and 31 Dec. 1953. Engravings of New Hall, Essex, mostly demolished in the eighteenth century, will be found in *Vetusta Monumenta*, ii (1789).

An account of the Severall Modes of Houses

It comes in my mind to recapitulate my observations of housing in England.[84] I suppose wee have followed the patterns of our neighbours, so that bating somewhat of time, and then of smallness, wee may rank ourselves with the French, and collating our housing with theirs find 'em much alike. Their seats are at this day called *chatteaux*, and till Henry VIII ours were most castle fashion, affecting moats and batlements, with angular towers and litle windoes, and afterwards, as hath bin observed, came in larger and square windoes, and as well extravagances as advantages in our lights and other ornaments.

The larger houses before that time, were most court fashion, built round, and all single, which is very inconvenient; for heat and cold are troublesome in a single building, and there is no retiring from either; and the round enclosure dulls the lights, and hinders prospect. It's true, that in great fabricks, it may be needfull to have aierys, or small courtiles, to give light to back stairs, and servants' back rooms; which serves, because there is no great regard to the delight of such persons, but warme and tollerable lodging and light enough to prevent mischeif serves. Wherefore to give this to principall rooms is intollerable. Syon-house by Thistleworth is of this sort, Kerby the lord Hatton's, Hunstone in Norfolk, an ancient seat of the ancient family of the le Stranges,[85] and my father's as to some part, but not the cheif.

Another sort of great house, is that they call an H, or half H thus ⌐⌐ being a front and 2 wings. This is but half as bad as a court inclosed. However if the buildings are double and not single, it may doe tollerably well provided the house be not long wing'd. So also a court inclosed, where one or 2 sides are doubled, is tollerable, because the

---

[84] In the BL version, fo. 45, North observes that he 'could recommend it to the inquiry of some industrious, as well as ingenious person, to take an account of the formes of houses built in England, in severall times and countrys, and note the stepps of changing, and by what marks the age of a fabrick may be knowne.'

[85] Syon House, Isleworth, Middx (see G. R. Batho in *Trans. London & Middlesex Archaeological Soc.* xix, 1958); Kirby Hall, Northants. (see official guidebook by G. H. Chettle); Hunstanton Hall, Norfolk (see *Country Life*, 10–17 Apr. 1926).

better rooms are layd to the best light, and the others postponed to the court.

This of an half H is the most frequent model of English seats, since castle fashion was layd aside, and hath obteined till very latly, that the square piles have come in use. So much for the outsides.

Within, the disposition of English seats, hath followed a mode, but perpetually, as their manners altered, changing. The beginnings were rude, and more after the way of the Germans, (as perhaps even the French, or Normans at least) than since. It is likely the world anciently, being neerer the state of nature, might less vary according to nations, than since arts have taken place, and invention a buissness. A great room for the family, was the cheif of the house, and there with a fire in the midst the family past their time, and probably cook't and eat in the same room; and it may be sleeping there too, was not unusuall; but when at one end of this great room, another was added for kitchen, with a chamber for the lord and lady, it was compleat; and litle more was thought of for divers ages of men. Then negotiation and buissness suggested another room at the other end of the house, called a parloir, which signifies a place to discourse in. This was the lord's withdrawing room, and soon gained a room over, for a stranger to lodge in. And then adding to the kitchen a buttery and pantry, that is offices for the drink and bread, the economy was fully supply'd; and it is not long since this hath bin much refined upon, I cannot allow beyond Henry VII. And since that wee have growne into much variety in disposing our conveniences of habitation, in which the court hath ledd, and the country followed.

One may call for some proofs of this conjecture, which, as much as conjecture needs, I can give. Beyond the Saxons wee have no knowledge, unless it be that probably the Romans may have refined us in our buildings as well as garb and manners, and reduc't our buildings from dirt to stone. For Stow observes that the ancient houses in London were of stone, but with litle windoes, partaking of the castle fashion; but the Romans were frugall, and not much addicted to the superb in private houses, at least not in their colonys. For the soldiery were a moving people; and warmth with safety was all they sought in conquered nations, and such were their *hyberna*.[86] But then the Saxons, that is a German rabble, overcame us, and wee were turned to their manners,

---

[86] Winter quarters.

and after them to the French, dated with the Normans Conquest. And before that time wee have litle or no evidence of housing, or building, but some monasterys, churches, and colledges, which, by what yet appears, were rude and lumpish. But even those have bin so altered and improved in succeding times that it is all wee can doe in an ancient building, to pick out a peice truely so.

There may be some castles, of age before the Norman, but none before the Saxon conquest. But I verily beleeve no house for dwelling so old as the conquest of the Normans, which is not a castle. And that of the Earle of Thanet's at Apleby in Westmorland may be a specimen;[87] which is such a rude heap of stones upon a sumit of a mountaine, as shews the intent was for guard as well as habitation and also the latter to be incidentall the other the principall intention. And there are accordingly some towers odly scituate, which the late Countess of Pembroke, who lived and dyed in those parts, and much given to heraldry and antiquity, was pleased to call by antique names. The fairest was Julias Cesar's, and another she called Pen-dragon's tower. And to leave this antique inquiry, I conclude all the prenorman buildings to be meer heaps of stones, and not worthy a minuter consideration.

In the Norman times wee have a specimen compleat of an house made up to the height of regall pride in that age, so early as William Rufus. It is the pallace at Westminster, of which wee have the hall, chappell, (now the Parliament house,) the anticamera, (now the Court of Requests,) the bedchamber, (now the Painted Chamber,) and the retiredments, where now is the house of Lords. And of this ordonnance, wee may suppose, the gentry made their houses, but in all degrees of lessening. Wee have a tradition, and credible, that the order of the king's family, was to dine and sup all in the great hall; and that the Courts of Justice, were but the tables, where the folk eat, which all stood in a row on the west side of the hall, except the king's tables raised up at the south end; and there the king sat to doe justice, and had his secretary's office, *intra cancellas*, by where his dispatches were made, now the Chancery. The Court of Crowne Causes was the uppermost below, where the king also came when he thought fitt to see justice done upon traytors.[88] Else the buissness was dispatcht by justices assigned to that province stiled

---

[87]Roger North visited Appleby Castle in 1676 (*Lives of the Norths*, i. 181) and would therefore not have seen the alterations carried out for the Earl of Thanet to the designs of the Revd Henry Machell in 1688.

[88]For the courts in Westminster Hall see *History of the King's Works*, ed. Colvin, i. 543–5.

coram ipso rege, and these followed the king, wherefore was added *ubicunque* &c. And tho it were the king's court and he present, yet naturall reason, and equity, gained in the law, to confine the power of judging to judges assigned. And as to comon wrangle, for *meum et tuum*, it was at the lower table in the hall, next the door, where the common pleas now is; and the servants of the hall, now called sergeants at law, were the advocates for the people; which imployment growing into liburature, and forme, it fell to churchmen, monks; as also the judges assigned out of these, which introduc't the coif to hide the tonsure. And the clerks in the courts, were those that served in the chappell, and had tithe of damages recovered, called *damna clericorum*, and late taken away, by the name of dam' cler'.[89] Thus was the king's justice administred, and the justices sat in the morning, till the officers came to prepare for dinner, and then the records and papers must be pack't up to make way for the butler. And the forme of adjournment of the common pleas at this day is *trussez justices et alles dehors*, which however saucy it seems, was the ancient language to the judges. And when the kings had occasion to conferr with their tenants, or subjects holding lands *in capite*, the meeting was in that great hall, and styled *curia regni*.

All the jurisdiction, houses, way of living, and proceedings of lords of mannors, was but aping of this. The king's house was severall fabricks under severall roofs, so the lords houses, had the hall under one roof, and kitchen under another, and perhaps parlor under a third, all distinct without composing all together as now the usage is. As the king did justice in the hall, so the lords had their courts baron, each 3 weeks, and generall courts of the tenants, for the buissness of the tenures, once, twice, or as often as occasion was in a year, which were the parlements of the manor. As the kings had their severall tables, so the lords eat upon the hearth-place, so called from the fire that was usually there, and the plowmen and other servants at other tables below. And the butler waited on, and filled the silver cup at the master's table, the porter (for the gates were shutt fast as at midnight) did the like at the table of the better servants, and had their owne meals at the side board, by intervalls of service.

And it is to be observed that the way of living in colledges at this day, hath a visage left of the ancient manner of living in noble

[89]For this perquisite of the clerks of the King's Bench and Common Pleas, commonly known as 'Damages Cleer', and abolished by statute in 1665, see W. S. Holdsworth, *History of English Law*, i (1922), 255–6.

familys. For a bell called all together, and the whole family eat in the same room, which kept order, and had done in time; and no dissoluteness but sobriety, and which pretended to piety, a portion of scripture was read at meals, in the hearing of the whole family. Wee cannot but observe how refinements have come on in succeeding times, and such solemne persons and societys retein most of the antique, and change last. The habits of orders, and magistrates, shew this, as the judges' and serjeants' robes, are airant[90] monks garb, saving the inrichment by furrs and colour. And gownes which were the habit of gentlemen, which some pictures of no very long standing demonstrate, now are devolved to orders and imployments, as a badge or forme of their profession.* Thus things followed as branches, up to the originall stem, will be found to derive from naturall singleness and simplicity.

Now to returne from this, (as to all but housing) disgression, the way of English seats from this order hath grown up to be a litle more compleat, and long stood in a posture, which one may at this day observe, mainteined a litle more or less, in most countrys of England. I speak of the generallity, particular fancys, and extravangancys, doe not much invade my theory. It is thus; first an hall, and this high, leaving off the naked roof came to be garreted, and in many with good rooms over it. Then at one end a great parlor, and a pair of stairs, called also great, and a door into the garden, and at the other end, buttery pantry kitchen, and a litle parlor, for every day eating. It is but late that servants have left their eating in the hall. This in my time was done in my father's house. But since it hath bin usuall, to find a room elswhere for them; and the master, in summer especially, leaves his litle parlor to eat there. Thus the hall is kept clean, which is not to be do[w]ne when it is the refectory of the whole family. Here ended the antique order of housing, and since the reigne of Charles II scarce any of that intention hath bin built.

The last is what they call a pile,[91] and is certeinly the corruption of building. It is so propence, for one extream to justle out another, that men seldome stop in the midway. It was an old fault to spread the housing too much, and a very commendable conduct to compose it more orderly together; that hath ledd to such compaction, that an house is

---

*The habits of Dominicans and Franciscans &c. were but the ordinary wearing habit of the founders of the orders: *North's marginal note.*

---

[90] Arrant.

[91] Or more specifically a 'double pile', on which see *The Architecture of Sir Roger Pratt*, ed. Gunther (1928), p. 24.

lay'd on an heap like a wasps-nest, and much of greatness as well as conveniences lost by it. This is the other extream. Certeinly there is a mean, which might rescind superfluous spreading of an house, and obviate the mischeifs of too strait connexion.

The inconveniences of too much spreading are the great charge of walls, and roof; for a leaf of goold not worth 1^d hath as much outside as $10\dagger$ ginnys. Then it makes long entrys and passages necessary, for passing from one part of an house to the other. And for the most part, there is no comunication but thro the open air, and weather, which is intollerable, because of the humid and turbulent constitution of our air, and in hot countrys the sun is as bad. And then it is hard upon this rambling foundation to project any elegance of disposition within or without. And lastly the rooms are single so as the lights are thro, and you cannot retire from heat and cold.

The inconveniences of a pile are, 1. all the noises of an house are heard every where; and 2., which is worse, all smells that offend, are a nusance to all the rooms, and there is no retiring from them. 3. It is hard to gaine closets and interior rooms, and never is done well without sacrifising as good room as the best to purchase them, which is needless and superflous because worse would serve. 4. You cannot modell rooms to the use, but some will be too high and some too low. For the floors lying level from side to side, the great and small rooms are all of a pitch; and if you designe high for the sake of the best apartment, your ordinary rooms are like bell-sollors.[92] If for them you pitch moderately, the best rooms that have breadth and length, look like underdeck of a ship. So that, as I observed before, it is impossible in the same order, to contrive well for large and small rooms in one house. I know they abate the height of small rooms by arching, or coving the ceiling, but that is a charge for a botch. Designe ought to be above such shifts. 5. Lastly all cold and heat are more offensive in a pile than in a spread house, being double; because the proximity of the rooms gives a tinct of the same air throout, which I could scarce have beleeved if I had not proved it.

The manner of these houses by the way of pyle, is either 2 rooms on a floor, with a closet, that is used in the citty, and is the comon forme of all late built houses.[93] The entry below is taken out of the first room, and

$\dagger$*MS indistinct*

---

[92] Bell-chambers.

[93] See the plan of a typical London house of this sort in John Summerson, *Georgian London* (1969 edn.), p. 51.

the stair-case out of the 2⟨nd⟩ and in the place of one windoe (supposing 2 are allowed) backwards on the other side from the stayres, is usually made a closet; so the room injoys but one windoe, and some make an angle chimny in the same corner; so that windoe, closet-door, and chimny are all cluttered together, which is most inconvenient. This model admitts an entrance but on one side of the house, so is not fit for the country, and is confined to cittys where divers houses stand contiguously in range. Next 4 rooms on a floor, which I may call an house of 2 ranges. The entrance is in the midle, and passeth thro, coinciding with the great staires backwards; and from thence the doors serve the rooms, and each side comunicate between the fore and back room. This model may be extended endways, by adding rooms to each range, and so is capable of very good disposition and convenience. And then the midle may be, and usually is, a sort of hall, or room of entrance. Thus an house may be extended to any porpose, and no convenience wanting in it.

The next model may be 3 ranges plaine, of which sort the largest houses of late built in the country are made, and I shall discourse of it more when I speak of such houses. The last is that of 2 rooms, and pavilions; this will be extended to the capacity of a court, as was Clarendon house, but it fell out to have great defects, as shall be spoken in its place. These are the severall sorts of moderne houses, as I have happened to see and observe them. And when I mention 2 rooms, it is depth, and not in length, which may, in sorting these fabricks, ⟨extend⟩ to any number of rooms.

1. The model of 4 rooms, or square pyle, is exemplyfied in the house of my lady Rachel Haskard, at Stoke neer Windsor,[94] and I have not seen a better; I thinck, closets are pinch't out of the 2 rooms on each end. But the stairs are to the front, and the 2d landing is over the door, which is not so well, because it makes low the view towards the door from within. And tho I have put the house in this rank of 4 rooms, I might have deferred it to the next, of 2 ranges; for the entry backwards hath the place of a room, and is used for dining. The covering is after the new way, ending the slope of the roof with a balcone and lanthorne; a gay thing without, but as was observed neither wholsome for the fabrick, nor any way worth the charge.

[94] For Baylis, or Baylies House, Stoke Poges, Bucks., the seat of the Hascard family, see Royal Commission on Historical Monuments, *Bucks.*, i. 289–90, where it is dated *c.* 1695. The existing

The house at Balmes neer London late Mr. Whitmore's,[95] and made well knowne by his hospitality, is a direct 4 room house; but being done at the beginning of this mode hath many defects, since regulated, as double garretts, and, which is intollerable, the rooms, on the right hand of the entry, are raised 4 or 5 steps, to favour the offices below. This is the result of ranging floors, for the height of the best rooms below was thought superflous for the lesser, and that a colloss[96] might be taken away to accomodate the kitchen and offices below. This modell is not often found out of townes or their suburbs, where it is proper, but very unfitt for any thing of an imployd family in the country, and no more needs be sayd of them.

2. The houses of 2 ranges are frequently found. Mountague house in London,[97] is a prince of that sort, being extended to a great length of apartments, on each side; but here is also a court, for the offices appendant to the house, which is a most judicious renovation of an obsolete mode of houses. And I should be glad to see the like imitated by others who build with full and luxurious purses, because it is the true way of composing the conveniences of a family in severall orders without fraction and indecorum, and so farr as to add, the greatest state a private person can pretend to in his house.

My lady Dacre's house at Chevening in Kent[98] is an house of 2 ranges, and well enough disposed. There is somewhat of Gothick in the finishing of the rooms, being carved with a sort of grotesque upon the wainscote in the best room below. The cheif room above is not finished, and was intended to be done with lunetts and small lights *all' Italiana*. And the whole is an Italian designe, as may be seen by the upper story 2 pair stairs, the lights of which not being so high as wide, the jaums of them are set blunt upon a fascia, without a sole conformable to the

---

attic storey is an eighteenth-century addition. This house would have been familiar to North because his father-in-law, Sir Robert Gayer, lived at the Manor House in Stoke Poges.

[95] For Balmes House, Hackney, demolished in 1853, see Priscilla Metcalf in *Architectural Review*, June 1957, pp. 445–6. It was built by Sir George Whitmore (d. 1654), Lord Mayor of London, and was an example of 'artisan mannerism'.

[96] A large space.

[97] For Montagu House, Bloomsbury, designed by Robert Hooke for the 1st Duke of Montagu, and eventually demolished to make way for the British Museum, see *Vitruvius Britannicus*, i (1715), Pls. 34–6.

[98] Chevening in Kent was begun before 1630 for the 13th Lord Dacre. Lady Dacre, his second wife, and North's aunt, died in 1698 at the age of ninety-three. For the problems connected with its architectural history see Oliver Hill and John Cornforth, *English Country Houses: Caroline* (1966), pp. 25–6, and John Newman, *West Kent and the Weald* (Buildings of England, 1976 edn.), pp. 210–12.

jaums, where they are so done. And this is that the story might seem to rise within a batlement, and so the bottom part of the windoes, forshortned away from the view by the batlement, and then your imagination must supply height to the windoes, which they realy had not in any due proportion. The designe is a room of *entrata*, where the great staires rise to the sumitt of the house, and so open to the midle room above also. On each side a room, the right hand is the withdrawing room, and the left, passing a stair downe to the kitchen, for servants. And from that by the end wall passing a litle back stair, to the comon parlor. The midle backward is a large dining room sett off with pilaster and arcuated wanscote, on the right the great, and on the left the comon parlor. The staires are too steep and height is wanting in the greater rooms below.

Bokingham house in Norfolk,[99] is a 2 range house, and if it had bin designed with a good spirit and invention, might have succeeded well, for no cost was spared. The gardens, are to a perfection. But such faults in the economy of the whole affair, as one would thinck should not happen, after so much pretension. All the rooms are too low, and that of the *entrata* scandalous, because it is made very wide. The great stayres, (answering it backwards as the way is) is noble untill you get up, and the best landing offensively neer the ceiling. No backstaires to the cheif apartments. The windoes wide, and flatt, which makes the front appear as a Chelsea cake house. But a pompous lanthorne aloft, perpetually leaky. There are on one side, very good conveniences for a family annex't; and indeed nothing is well but the servants' offices and apartments; which shews the owner had more of that than mastership in his education. I mentioned the gardens, to which I would not wish to add; the fountaines beautyfull and delicious, if they had the true nature of fountaines, perennity, which ought to be or to be supposed where they are; but there stands a deforme tower, being the structure that is for raising the water, which is to run out there. This ought to have bin hid, or no fountaines to be. For where is the curiosity of lifting water to run down againe? Another mistake was derived from hence, which was in overdoing, for he would not onely serve his offices with water, which deserved an engine, but it must goe into every room in the house, and under one of the windoe boards was cesterne, and cock, for water at all times. This made the house wett and unwholesome and that forc't them to cutt off the pipes, and prodigious charges were lost; so dear is want of

---

[99] For Buckenham House, Norfolk, see above, p. 7 n. 6.

judgment in building. The avenew is very well and the courts of entrance large and well sett off; and to say truth many circumstantiall advantages the fabrick hath, makes it pitty a better genius had not the manage of it.

The house of Sir Henry Parker in Honiton in the county of Warwick,[100] is of this sort; elegant for the decorations on all sides; courts, gardens &c.; and no less curiosity on the inside, by wainscote of forein oak, marble &c. This model is of the kind as perfect as any, the front being an hall or room of *entrata* in the midle large enough; and at one end great parlor, and at the other a lesser parlor. The great parlor and its withdrawing room, makes the end next to the garden, and the litle parlor, with a passage to the back yard, and a litle back stair, with the kitchen, makes the other end; and against the hall backwards is the great staires, but in practise all this is found imperfect, not from the ordonance of this particular, but from the fault of the mode it self, which is not capable of inner rooms and closets, without prodigious waste of the best room and lights, which aggrees not with the moderne conduct. And the pitch of the floors might have bin higher. In short all together speaks no height of spirit, tho pride enough.

I could name many other houses of this sort, it being that most followed, in regard it shews well in enterteinement, is compendious and of least expence. But I know no more to observe from them, so I pass on.

3. The other manner is the 3 ranges, which takes place with those of the best purses, being large and fair, and as much as can be practis't in a square figure. For wee must keep to thrift even in prodigality. The two cheif houses of this sort that I have met with, are Mr. Guy's at Tring, in Buckinghamshire; and Sir Jacob Ashley's, at Melton, in Norfolk.[101] The former was the invention of Sir Christopher Wren, and I thinck the onely intire house he hath done; except Winchester, which is left in a deplorable state. Mr. Guy's house is of 3 ranges; and one thing post-nate in the contrivance, at the entrance, is remarkable. The staires ascending to the first or hall floor are not without, but within a room, that serves as a portch. This was not so in the first designe, but altered. And in so large an house, where a room can be spared for the use of a porch, it is very convenient. So this porch room is in the midle, and from the landing

---

[100] For Honington Hall, Warwicks. (*c.* 1680) see H. A. Tipping, *English Homes, Period V,* i (1921), 255–80, and *Country Life,* 21–28 Sept. and 12 Oct. 1978.

[101] For these two houses, see above, pp. 9, 62. A third example of this 'triple' plan was Hugh May's Eltham Lodge, Kent.

they goe on each hand to 2 rooms on either side of it, and there are 2 litle pair of staires ascending between them. This is the first range. The second is the great hall, and stairs. The hall is from the entrance, the whole length northwards, that is towards the left, and the passage is continued strait from the door, to the back range, and there takes a withdrawing room, or great-parlor, I remember not well which. The height of the hall, are 2 full storys of the order, and the ceiling is the floor of the garrets. This is too high, and doth not conforme to the other demensions of the room. It is lighted onely at the end, and with 6 windoes, that is 3 in each story, one over the other, and in the place of the floor between them is made a balustred passage athwart that end from one side of the house to the other. These 3 windoes in breadth, take up too much of the room, and the peirs are too litle, so that the light is not easy and naturall, but constrained and hudled. At the other end of the hall is a double order of columnes which makes a screen, and carry a floor upon the entableture of the first, which is a gallery above and the entrance of the house is underneath it. The upper order goes to the ceiling, and fenceth the gallery above. This gallery is the landing of the great staires, so is a principall member of the ordonance above. The great staires make (with the hall and under this gallery that lys open to it) the midle range, and ly on the right of the entrance, and doth not run out that way so farr as the other ranges, so that the kitchen comes in there, in a low building, that fills that notch and extends outwards as much beyond the other ranges, but is no higher, than permitts fair windoes to the staires above it. This is all excellently contrived, for it doth not robb the great stairs of light and being so much without the house, prevents the annoyance to the house by smell. But when you are ris up to the best landing, which is the galary to the hall, there was a very great defect in the height; which the surveyor hath helped by sacrifising the garratt; and from the seiling a shell is lifted up, cuppulo-wise over the gallery, which looks well underneath, but above, is a monster. This proceeds from the impracticability of accomodating severall purposes in one and the same order of building as hath bin, more than once, observed.

The other house is Sir Jacob Ashley's. That is of 3 ranges, and the entrance in the midle is the lower end of the hall; but without any gallery or screen, so that the hall is too low for its length and breadth. It is lighted as well at the end as front. This is on the right. The left of that range, is an eating room, and a pantry, with a back stair downe to the yard and kitchen. Now to make somewhat of a gallery to the hall, there is a letting in over the eating room, which takes from the upper part of that about 8 or 10 foot, (and by the way quite spoiled that room,) laying it open to the hall, with benches for musick; nor is that very well, for it resembles too much a dancing scool. These places take up the first range. At the end of the hall and antagonall to the entrance, is a litle room that serves for a passage to the great parlor; and this litle room, with the great stayres, a back stair, and a chappel, (in that order,) make the midle range. The great staires open to the passage, strait from the hall door to the back range, and that strait, takes a back door to the withdrawing room, passing the great stairs on the right and the back staires on the left. The great staires are spacious and open to the garret floor; but the covetousness of those small rooms, at the end next the light, hath deprived the best light, and forc't 'em to take light downe from the rough†; for the slope of the roof on that side is abated, to open a light flat and upright above the cornish. This is light enough, but a constrained thing that doth not look easy nor proper, as ought to be in a fabrick of that import. The back staires have no light but from the great, open to which they are balustred; which is a strange contrivance, for both the privacy and quiet is deprived. There is no passage up, nor downe but is exposed to and disturbes the great staires. And in one thing more particularly; because the back staires ly to the left, the garretts on the righ⟨t⟩ of the entrance are not well served. Therefore from the first landing of the great staires, is a litle door which is to a stair breaking thro the ceiling of the litle passage room below, and so riseth out of that space to the garretts, which is an egregious nusance to the great staires. The back range of this house, is the great parlor, withdrawing room, and another square room called the litle parlor. This is a fair string of rooms, and hath one great perfection, which is, that the withdrawing room serves both great and litle parlor; a thing much to be desired in any house, and a very usefull compendium. But the entrance of the litle parlor is at a corner, from the great-stayr-passage and piercing the wall at the angle is very long, the rather, because the door must gather its bredth (like an angle chimny) into the room. This is a deformity one would strain hard to cure. Out of the litle parlor are closets, one for men the other for ladys, that looks into the chappell; which (like Mr. Guy's kitchen) concludes the midle range and sets out into the yard beyond the rest of the house. This chappell is the most ornamentall thing about the

---

†i.e. roof.

house. Now taking altogether the whole house, tho it be large, square and many windoes, yet it looks small, and doth not humour the proposition of a large country family. Above stayres, there are 4 capitall chambers, with closets and inner rooms, devided out of the breadth; but these fall out to be too long, and the closet chimnys are angle fashion next the door, which is farr from clever. All the rest of the house is garretts, which to make agreable are wainscoted and painted; and are but garrets still.

I ought not to forget to mention the noble seat of my lord Toundsend in Norfolk.[102] That is not a new house, compared with these, but otherwise may be esteemed new, being dated with the first entrance of the mode I have bin speaking of, the beginning of the reign of King Charles II. Raineham Hall was scituate anciently low, where the stables now are, and was promoted to the sumit of an hill, which makes an excellent avenue, all rising from the towne and valey, with a pomp I have not seen any where. Some things are singular in it, as the front hath no door in the midle, but on each side 2 principall doors, one passing on the right to the great staires, parlor, and withdrawing, the other to a back stair, litle parlor, and offices. Both these are screened from the hall, opening to it with 2 high arches at each end. The hall hath great prerogative of room, to the damage of the rest of the house. It is paved with marble, and riseth to the garret floor. There are in the front, 2 breaks setting a litle foreward, with gable-ends set off with slopes, and small pediments a top, which look't great when done, before the French roofs with cornishes and modilions were used. The house on that side hath no regular ornament. On the back side, towards the gardens, are a file of rooms, and one after the Italian way, of great and small windoes, with a beam-and-frett ceiling, but lumpish. Without is an Ionick order and frontone done much *alla regolare*. The connecting these rooms hath robbed both the staircases of their light, which comes not but by conducts from aloft, neither fair nor pleasant. Yet the house is noble, and pleasant, and the greatest inconvenience is, that the stables are so far off.

4. As to the great houses, having a body and pavilions, I cannot give so clear an account, because I have not viewed so many, and their forme is harder to retein in memory. That began by the late lord Conway in

---

[102]Raynham Hall, Norfolk, for which see above, p. 55. The ambiguity of North's dating may reflect his realization that the house had been built in the 1620s and 30s, but left unfinished until the beginning of Charles II's reign.

Worstershire,[103] is a pile of a vast many rooms, and was but one story high when I saw it, and if finished will be great, at least upon account of its scituation, which is high and yet of easy access; having declivitys backward. Clarendon house was one of this sort; but as I have heard, without one large or good room, as one would expect in so great a fabrick. The neighbours, Burlington and Barkly houses,[104] have their perfections beyond it, as will be manifest whoever will consider them. I am not at present sufficiently instructed to adventure upon any description. But as to these sort of howses, the space and latitude for invention is such that they admitt of much more variety, than the others, which are not capable of being much diversified. And one thing may be depended upon, which is the more they are spread (with tollerable judgment in doing it) the better they are; and the less the worse; for a good house will have elbow room.

5. After all these notes of houses, I must not omitt those as have bin not altogether new as all these are, but by way of mending old, and of this sort are most of the capitall seats of the nobility of England. And I thinck I may safely, as to truth, affirme, that there is scarce a good palace or nobleman's house in England, that is not so done. Wittness White-hall, the best, made of the worst, till the fire, one of heaven's warning peices, layd it level with the ground. And then Windsor Castle, with all its faults, was, and is, a most stately royall palace; but had bin much better, if the east part of the court had bin new built, as he desired, but royall thrift sayd nay. Burleigh House neer Stamford is an instance of this, so also the Duke of Beafort's at Badminton.[105] But this latter is built as much for oeconomy, as state, and it is so contrived that no occasion of the family or menagery is wanting, nor is there much defect in order or forme, only some of the cheif rooms are tincted with lowness in pitch, occasioned by the old ordinance taken.

I shall end this discourse of the sorts of houses with a description of my owne poor structure at Rougham. I found the house, as ancient

---

[103]For Ragley Hall in Warwicks. (not Worcs.) see *Country Life*, 1–8 May 1958, and *Archaeological Journal*, cxxviii (1971), 230–3.

[104]For Burlington House see *Survey of London*, xxxii; for Berkeley House, B. H. Johnson, *Berkeley Square to Bond Street* (1952).

[105]Whitehall Palace was destroyed by fire on 4 Jan. 1698. For the remodelling of Windsor Castle by Hugh May for King Charles II see *History of the King's Works*, ed. Colvin, v (1976). For Burleigh House see p. 63 above.

Roger North visited Badminton with his brother Francis while the latter held office as Chief Justice of Common Pleas, i.e. between 1675 and 1682 (*Lives of the Norths*, i. 169–72). The house was remodelled between 1664 and 1691 at great expense (see *Country Life*, 4 Apr. 1968).

mannor houses usually are, of severall sorts of building, and done in different ages, and for different ends. It was disposed to 3 pavilions, and a midle. I cannot say composed, for what of that kind was, fell so by accident, and the setting out at one end was not so foreward as at the other, nor was the building of one wing like the other, for west it was stone and brick 2 storys high, leaded and batlemented, and the other was timber with a gable end part, and a lower roof flanking the rest. The whole house was single, and being very ancient, had formerly a porch, next the timber wing (which was the eldest brother) and the midle, was part hall, and the rest a great parlor. And the hall went to the roof with a lanthorn, and the eves came low. Latter ages reformed this, and built a story from the hall eves, making high room over it, 13 foot, and so covered it with an high pitch't sparr and lucernes. And this new made room, from one wing to the other, was all layd into one, and called a great dining room, for the porpose of dancing. The other wing was yet elder than this reforme, and made 2 rooms below, and a great bedchamber, some say a chappell, above. And backwards at the joyning to the midle, there was a tower of stone, massy, strong, and high; but the use of it was never discovered to me, unless it was to be the priest's habitation. About the time the great dining room was made, a new stair case was clapt behind the hall to lead up to the midle of it, which was large room enough to make a very good stayr. There had bin other structures belonging to the house, which time and the needs of the family had caused to be demolished, so that the inhabitant was reduct as a farmer to the last shift of room for necessary uses. And all the offices had bin pinch't out of corners, and not onely decayed and unfitt for a family; even the kitchen was the old buttery, and a pantry was boards inclosing a peice out of the hall; which made it necessary for me to make a general reforme of the house, or build a new one, if I intended to live there.

I did much deliberate upon that point, and entering at lady day 1691, did nothing that year but thinck; and for the reasons given in these papers I resolved on the former; for which I had this encouragement, that the room over the hall was so high pitch as that with a litle charge it would make as good chambers as I could build, as the house fronted south.

I was very sollicitous about adjusting and drawing my model. I first surveyed the old house, and made an exact ground-plot of it, and then took the demensions of the front, and made its picture. And then I cast how the distribution would fall, if I had the parting it, and to make the windoes answer. The midle great chamber (as I called it)* was for shifting devided into 2 chambers and a peice of a chamber called a closet. These were 24 foot wide, strangely too bigg for lodging, and those I reduct to about 20 foot, and layd out 4 or 5 foot of the breadth backwards, for closets and conveniences to the rooms, which I cast into 2 good chambers, 20 foot square, and in the midle a passage from the great staires, to half the breadth, and the rest an antiroom;[106] which is the best way of disposing apartments by an entry in the midle first into a moderate antiroom, then to pass on each side to the apartments, lying equally to it. The old staircase lay very proper for this, because the landing and entrance was just the midle of the house. This was the encouragement, and accordingly the primier attempt. And after I had setled the devision of the rooms, plac't the windoes, and consulted with the workmen about breaking and making up the walls, I made this midle part the foundation of my whole modell and all the rest was to conforme to it. The hall underneath was 36 foot long, and 24 wide and but 11 foot high, which was a great offence to my eyes, and I strained very hard either to cure or palliate that fault. The former I could not; for then I must have lost the room above, which I could not spare; which was enough to divert such a difficult work as raising old heavy floors. The latter I might, in some measure; and that I compas't by pilaster work in the wainscote from bottom to the top, with as much procerity[107] and length as decorum of the work would admitt. And then set a row of wainscote pilaster columnes screen fashion cross the hall parting the door and passage to the great staires from the room, and breaking the course of the eye at the ceiling by a soffitt and cornish upon these columnes, which were of the same order as the pilaster of the wainscote, all in range.[108] One would not thinck how much this work disguised the lowness of the ceiling. It is most certein the room which instantly struck a disgust from the lownes now from the *vagezza*[109] of the finishing imploy'd the fancy another way, and wrought out an approbation. It so fell out that out of this long room (then 2 monstrous chambers without convenience) I could make 2 compleat chambers on each side of the antiroom, that was in the midle. For they would be 20 foot square, the

---

*In BL MS, fo. 24, North calls this room 'a great chamber for dancing, as the old way was'.

[106] See the first-floor plan.
[107] Height.
[108] See the ground-floor plan.
[109] Beauty.

windoes on the side by the door entring, the chimny in the midle of the side opposite to that of the entrance, the bedd against the side opposite to the windoes, and a door comunicating with other rooms in file, opposite to the door entring, and 2 doors to subservient places in that side where the bed was, on each side of the bed's head. Thus was the bed free from any course, or current of air in the room, farr from the windoes, and the chimny by the side, and not too near; which I have particularised more especially because such cautions are very needfull in composing a bed chamber.

The subservient places, made out of the fillet of room 4 or 5 foot wide, made a spare place to set things by in, a closet, and easment. And towards the passage into the antiroom, was gained a small lodging for a single servant, to each chamber. And however these are small, being also not of the usuall ordonance, yet serve the turne, and make the rooms practicable, which new chambers are not which are independent, and without such appendages of some sort or other.

Thus I began my model, being an improvement necessary, or at least very convenient and usefull, whatever became of the rest of the house; for this conteined hall, great parlor, staircase, and 2 very good chambers. Th'outside was also to be a litle fairer, for instead of 3 great broad windoes, of 7 or 10 foot wide, I made to each chamber 2 and to the antiroom in the middle 3, that is one of the ordinary size in the midle, and 2 half windoes on each side of it.[110] I did this in prospect of a columniated frontone, or some porch, with which such 3 windoes would best quadrate, as I shall give an account afterwards when I speak of the porch I made, persuant to this so early thought, and when I scarce thought I should have done much more than the two chambers I have spoke of.

But now I must remember what a world of deliberation I had about farther proceeding, but after all determined in a porpose of doing somewhat about my house as long as I lived, proving the truth of a trite observation, that doing injoys more than done. And being a lover of elegancys about an house, but moderatly estated out of which to supply the charge of building, I found nothing would be done in haste by me; nor must I anticipate so much as some, who make ample provisions of all things before they set to work, because I did not know, how far I should proceed, nor where I should stop; for I would have it in my power at any

---

[110]See the first-floor plan.

time to make a full stop if I so thought fitt, and what I left should not be a folly and imperfect, but improved and more usefull than I found it. I found much was to be done to compass my satisfaction; and I must proceed thus or not att all. I was blamed for not building a fabrick intirely new, which might have bin neat and elegant and not chargeable. That would not take my fancy, and it is what every attorney or shopkeeper growne a litle richer than his neighbours doth. I could not shake off the aim at somewhat above the ordinaire.* And I was also blamed for not making gardens first, that fruit might grow while the house was building, and so inhabit and injoy all together. I grant that to be a good way, but where onely the person is sure and expeditious in his buissness. For it hath happened, as at lord Craven's house att Hamstead Marshall by Newbury, elegant gardens were made and kept, but the house never finished;[111] and I have heard of some who have made gardens and never began the house. It was the house I cheifly wanted. That was the body and substance. The gardens, if any thing, might stay. And I was not well determined of the manner of the gardens till the house and homestall were fixed. I was also blamed (for I must tell my faults) for not plaistering the outside of the house to make it look like new. That I excuse, by the decay it is lyable to; wee have not hard-stone-lime nor the best of the soft, and in a few years the wett and frost will bring it off, and then it looks much worse, than old and new putt together. I farther considered that I could not make the house compleat in all things within so as to warrant a fair and perfect out side. But many things, as lowness of the hall, some beams appearing, and the unaptness of some doors, with other instances obvious to the eye, would speak the house to be old and reformed, and then it is most ingenuous to have it

---

*While still engaged in his building works North summed up his deliberation thus (BL MS, fo. 30): 'But the rules I have observed are these,
  1. To fix my designe of the whole.
  2. To reserve liberty to alter as to conveniences within and without.
  3. To doe all in prosecution of that designe, be it more or less.
  4. To keep all the old walls, as neer as I could.
  5. To direct all my contrivances to convenience of living principally, and to waive rather decorum, than that.
  6. To baulk no plenty of room, which fell comodiously within the lines, as too much, or beyond my pretensions.
  7. And lastly to be contented to make the best, where I was satisfied it was so, of my subject, which to compass I was very slow in considering and determining.'

---

[111]Destroyed by fire in 1718. The elegant gardens are shown in a plate in Kip's *Britannia Illustrata* (1714).

declared as well on the outside. I account it not any disgrace that I was not able to build as chancellors, admiralls &c., that use it to evacuate a surfet of the purse; but on the other side, I repute it creditable in making an old house habitable and elegant by force of judgment, more than cost, to doe it and be all the while screened from a caracter of vanity. And if this is to be compast, it must be by shewing less, and doing more, and not by holding forth more of pretension, than value; and such is all pomp and decoration of front. I would have the air of an house take with a spectator's eye at first glance, and he shall not soon perceive what it is that so affects him; and rather wonder it should be so well, considering the mean and ordinary materiall. If the brick were rubbed, and all coines regularly stoned, it is plain that is it. But if there be none of this but onely an outline to set it off, there shall be a tacit or secret approvall, without knowing how or why; and that elegance there is must be ascribed to the designer, and not to the materiall or workmen. The latter mony commands, *vix ea nostra voco*. Upon all these considerations, I determined to aim at plenty and convenience of room, and what beauty succeded on the outside, it should be subservient to the other, and not the principall intention, and also to consist in the designe, and neither depend on the workmen nor stuff, of which I had not choise and must make the best of what my estate and country yeilded with ease.

After I had determined to make the midle of the house usefull, I began to collate the wings and to consider how those might be made to correspond with best advantage. It fell out that the left wing, or pavilion (as I made it) was 37 foot in from,† the midle 58. Then the other wing right, must be 37, which was in all 122 foot front. I considered the midle carryed a steep Gothick-roof, being cornish't upon the 2nd floor next the garret, the room of which was lucerned. I concluded the pavilions must rise higher and cornish at the 3rd story, so that it might returne and dye upon the roof in the midle, and about the levell of the heads of the lucernes; and then the cornish of the midle would dye bluff against the pavilions. And yet the roof of the pavilions should range with the midle, but carry a short sparr, and be hipp't at the corners; and for distinction, being to the eye a lighter forme than the midle, they should carry a plaine cornish, and the midle be modilioned. And the lower windoes, should head and sole, as also the sole of the next windoes, from end to end range in a level. But the heads of the pavilion windoes above should be a foot lower, as

---

†*Sic, but evidently a slip for* front. *In the next sentence* 122 *should be* 132.

also that story, which would break no squares for the upper room,[112] was of no esteem, and steps one or two up from the midle garret floor, to the pavilion upper floor, was no eysore; and so long as all the rooms of enterteinement below and lodging above were all throout upon levell floors, all was well. And this for reasons before touch't made the front agreable and less fastidious from the length of it.

But still the setting off the door, and weathering the entry was wanting, and that I afterwards made up with a portico, of the Ionick order after the Eustyle.[113] The columnes, sett upon massy stylobates, of black flint work, coined and capt with free stone, as high as the soles of the lower windoes; and upon them bases and capitalls of free stone; which by the way are ill wrought, and neither true to the figure nor order; but few eyes find it out. The shafts of the columnes are of plaine course brick, and not good in its kind, but such as I could get made; they are strok compas to the model of the columne,[114] and filled with flint. The capitalls range neer the heads of the best windoes; so between that and the cornish is about 3 foot, which I make a plaine great flatt architrave, not being so deep as frees and architrave would have bin if regularly done. But making no such distinction, less depth serves, and being headed with a cornish, that returnes and miters with that of the midle, so shews a body that justifies the columne. For the face-cornish hath the modilions bevelled to the perpendicular gage of those underneath, in the strait; and the timpane is filled with flatt brick work. This at a distance hath a very good aspect, and neer, better than the house walls, so alltogethere is not amiss. For the stedying this columniation, I brought out the chamber floors, and so joyning to the midle of the columnes, binds all fast there, and makes a balcone covered and there is a hansom passage to it out of the antiroom.

Then coming to adjust the model for the pavilions, the west was most relived, and must be adjacent to the garden, the other was east, and must be neer the outhousing; so the former was proper for retired uses and the other for the family. Each would bear 37 foot front, which would be fairest to carry 3 windoes, which makes good the rule of making the apertures odd, that one may fall in the midst; and this distribution

---

[112]This apparently means that the third storey would not affect the proportions of the room on the principal floor beneath it.

[113]With columns set two and a half diameters apart: see Pl. 1.

[114]i.e. their diameter corresponds to the module of the column.

would allow but one chamber, and some closet, or inner room, in each pavilion towards the front, which alltogether would afford 4 compleat chambers *in filo*, so that the *visto* thro them was maintained. It might have been carryed farther, but I saw no use, but on the other side loss by it, in spoiling room, so I slighted all *visto* but of these 4 rooms, with the antiroom in the middst. In the west pavilion it was necessary to have a stair case backwards, with a passage out below. And rather than doe that by a break, I cho[o]se to fill up the whole square, from the front as farr as the back wall of the midle of the house, which was deep 40 foot. Here I gained besides the staires a good room with 2 windoes backwards, which I made my library. Below it is a private parlor. The room west of the pavilion chamber, I ordered so as to make an inner room for a servant, a closet with windoes west, and the entrance to both had the windoe on the front next the coin, and made a very good dressing room for a man, for whome this chamber was designed.

Underneath, was a withdrawing room; and a passage out to the garden, which had the windoe next the coin. And backwards, besides the staires, an eating retired parler, under the library. But in truth is a superfluous room, which I intended for my owne absolute retirement. And within that a passage to a room under the servant's room, which I made into a closet, and intend to embellish it. I covered with a compass shell, done without centers, by a gage as before is described. Towards the roof, I had 9 foot wall, and a windoe somwhat higher than wide, but the rooms being large, I thought height not enough. Therefore I sacrifised all the space within the roof to add to that height, which was done by ceiling joysts, shap't to a mitre round upon the walls of each room; and the principall sparrs were framed with vast collar beams, and not girders, which served well enough for such short sparrs. However upon the partitions wee banded in the wall plates and by this means kept the height clear in the severall rooms up to the collar-beam, which gave a slope height to the rooms more than the upright walls of neer 4 foot. And whereas advanc't roofs and garretts, especially when small, as these were, are litle worth, and the upper-rooms also but moderately high, the adding the best room out of these hollows into the chambers below, made them as good rooms as any. So this wing or pavilion was setled, and served as a model for the other, which must have the same position, shape and demensions on the out side.

I was not so hasty to setle that, for the old building served for kitchen, and comon conveniences of houskeeping, and it must be pulled downe to the ground and a new fabrick raised up on intire new foundations; which was a great work. Besides, I could not find room there for all the offices I had need of; a cellar must be dugg and vaulted; pantry, kitchen, larder, wet and dry, pastry and scullery to be provided; and if I took a litle parlor, closets, and servants' eating room in the space of the pavilion as the other was, there was no room for all these; especially considering the room must be taken out for passages, which to the comon entry of an house must not be small, for at this part must be the back door, and comunication with all the buissness abroad. And the necessary offices I mentioned, were more pressing to be done than ought else I had to doe. I could find no better scituation of these, than to double the building on the back of the hall, as farr as the staircase sett out, and to range eastward till the returne of the east pavilion met it in square, and there woud be a flat front to the east, of 3 rooms *in filo*. This work I first undertook, and was much in doubdt, how high I should carry it. I had no need of chambers, unless some very ordinary room for servants, and to raise that up to range with the rest of the house would create a superfetation of chamber-room. It came at last into my mind that a gallery, tho not much used in late fabricks, because compaction of walls allows it not, yet is very delightfull and usefull if it lys comodiously. And if I made the whole of room, from the stair case eastward, which would be about 63 long and 17 foot wide, into one room, and lay the ceiling levell with that of the midle rooms, it would be a good gallery, and ly to the house exeeding well; for a principall door from the cheif landing of the great staires served it, and standing open gave a view of the whole length, and at the farther end a door comunicated with a chamber, and about the midle with the stair case of the east pavilion when it should be done. And it was no great objection, that the view was upon back-sides and offices, and not upon a garden as regularly should be to a gallery, for it was not to have that caracter in my house, but onely ly for a family convenience, and then the more overseeing the better. So I concluded, and went to work, and compast this fabrick in one year. For melioration of view, I made the east end rise so as the cornish ranged with the pavilions, but this was litle, onely to make strait the east face; the rest carried a cornish onely to the pitch of the midle of the house, which went and compast the staires, and went on and dyed against the upright of the west pavilion backwards. The gallery had 5 windoes north, and about 6 foot peer, and 2 windoes east. About 1 half I dugg for a cellar and vaulted it. Over that I made larder and pantry. The rest below were kitchen, pastry and scullery, and the garret a lodging for the bailif and the husband men and all inferior servants.

All this while the old pavilion stood, and could not be spared till the offices in the other were ready, and then I undertook to make good the returne and finish the east pavilion, which I was now in more haste for, because I was married, and having our particular accomodation there, the house was imperfect, and scarce practicable without it. And here onely was I upon the spurr, and must now goe thro *costa-che-costa*. I brought my wife downe while the workmen were pulling downe and wee stay'd, till it was raised, and the roof sett. And I had the advantage of her inspection of what was designed for her owne use, as fast† as it was capable of being shewed. But I cannot say that she suggested any alteration but liked it as it was layed out, which I had the good fortune to doe to her intire content. I gained here a stair from top to bottom, and comunicated with the stairs of the other pavilion by an entry on the north side of the garret over the midle, and parted out that garret from the entry, and made servants' chambers. Wee had a square room of 12 or 14 foot at the entrance of the door, and from thence an entry 4 foot wide and so to the staires, which lay against the end of the old house, and had light from the sky, which having a wide open newell was enough, but over and above had a light thro the entry from a windoe opposite to the staires foot. And then the staircase room below, had a door into the kitchen, the hall, litle parlor, and a servants' dining room.

The parlor lay next the front, and had a door into the hall, another at the stairs foot opposite to the kitchen door, and the entry parted it from the servants' room. And the east corner of this pavilion, was dedicated to closets. I had one for my papers and domestique concernes, with a door out into the square room next the door, and another door into the parlor, and I carved out a peice for the bailif's closet, next the back door with a passage from mine to it; so that I could have recourse at all times to his books and papers, etct. And over against his closet door, on the other side of the litle square, was a door into the servants' room, where a part was devided out, for the better servants, for quality (forsooth) must be distinguish't. These conveniences are such ease and delight in the practise of humane life and buisness, that it compensates the charge of building, without which it is seldome to be had. Here is a family, in all their ordinary occasions lay'd together, ready at the hall, and not so neer

†*in error for* far?

as to be offensive, yet within call; every door of constant use opening into the passage from the staires to the back door, hall, kitchen, litle parlour, cellar, pantry, staires, master's and bailif's closets, servants superior and inferiour. What is above need not be described, onely our owne apartment, is a chamber over the litle parlor; over mine and the bailif's closets is my wife's, which I finish't with oak of Norway, and an angle chimny in the best manner. Then that closed opens back into a small dressing room, but most convenient, which is over the square room below, and then goes on into a litle chamber over the better servants' eating room, so into the gallery, make a string of 4 rooms (counting the closet one) at the east end of the house. There is some dark waste room next the stair case, (from which is a way into the gallery). This is served with secondary light and is wood hole, and other conveniences that shall be nameless.

Here is an account, like many given to the world, that concernes more the author's, than any else; and however insipid it may be to my posterity, who onely are like to be troubled with it, it hath a goust to me, even in the remembrance, and recapitulation of all the various doubdts and considerations I had, and the severall felicitys as well as infelicitys in the execution, which may serve to excuse the consumption of a few intervall minutes upon it. And to close all, I have onely to remember the method of conducting our water. I ever had a dislike of evesdropping, or spouting the water from the roof about an house; for it moistens the soil extraordinary, and, in brick building, filtrates thro the walls to the very roof. Besides, it hinders planting of fruits, sweets, or sallads, neer the walls. I did at first intend 2 water pipes, one at the east and the other at the west end of the house, to carry off the water. I could provide a drain for the east end; but from the west to that was a perfect flatt. However, thincking some expedient might be had for disposing that water, I made the pipes accordingly, and have cornished the whole house, and leaded them, conveyed the water, in some places upon partition walls, and in others at staircases, and waste room, into the midle of the house so as to goe out at each end. I soon found that the waste water would be an insufferable nusance; and bent my invention and spurred on the workmen, to turne the water of the west pavilion, into the main gutter that served the east pipe. And now all the water runs out and downe there, and gives us no anoyance, but all the eves are clear from dropping whatever the rain is. There are some mischeifs attend this way, but such as will follow all double roofs and guttering, that is great and extraordinary snows, and sudden thaws in winter, as also snow and melting in the sun and freezing in the shade, within the house. This brings downe water to the gutters to freese, which must be taken care of. So in summer vast innundations, as sometimes will happen to discharge upon us more water than our gutters will carry. As for snow, if it be tossed aside so that when the thaw comes there be a clear current, the water will pass. But when it lys and fills the bottom of the gutter it will make a stagnation, and the water will recoil over the dripps. Then for the freezing within, when the gutters are full of ice, as will be towards the head of them, pour downe a pail full of water, scallding hott, and the ice will come out, so as it may be carryed away. Summer waters have no remedy but keeping all clean from the filth falling from the roof, as will happen by mortar and broken tiles, and some leaves from trees, and sediment of water, which in process grows very troublesome; and it will be very seldome such harme will come. And for more caution, I made the gutters open without the house as much as I could, and within every where accessible. My lord Allington's house at Horshith hath another devise of like nature, but much more lyable to these inconveniences. It is flatt sheets upon the top of the house, lay'd with the edges turned in, and a crevice between every sheet; and under those crevices, gutters to convey the water.[115] I have heard they are troublesome but doe not imagine how they can shift in alternate freesing and thawing; if so be the gutters or rather the crevises will carry a great downefall of water. It were worth knowing how this succeeds, for it is a clever device in appearance. And, however it is performed, it must be usefull, and pleasant, that in pouring raines, the house, windoes, and prospect, is not annoyed by any falling of water round about it; and the folk may well wonder what becomes of it.

[115]See p. 40 n. 48 above.

Requisites about an house

Having spoke of severall usages in building in the generall, and given some instances of houses, fallen in my way to observe, concluding with my owne, I shall proceed and take notice, of many lesser incidents, which will occurr to a builder to thinck of, and determine, about fitting his house, before he can have his peace; and shall not pass by matters of generall importance as they occurr, respecting substance rather than method.

1. Scituation. Let it be due south if possible. I mean so as the best rooms, which are usually the front, have that prospect. The reason is obvious: there is less venom, and hurt in those winds than the opposite. And fear not heat, (which is in truth more troublesome than winds where it is extream,) for the sun fall⟨s⟩ not early in the morning nor is late in the evening in the sumer time upon that scituation, and when it comes on it is high, and shines not much into the room, especially when at the warmest pitch, noon. But in an east or west scituation the sumer sun every shining morning and evening makes the chambers furnace-hot. And in winter the south rooms hath the low sun at noon, being then comfortable, while east and west hath scarce any, but on the contrary, the east, north and of them-composed-winds, which are not easy.

2. Position. This must be governed by the place pitch't upon for an house. It was the usage in ancient times, to build low, and neer water, but that is found or thought unwholesome, and the next course is to take the other extream and build, as our age doth, upon the summit of hills, where they are intollerably exposed to weather. The mean is best, the side of an hill, a litle rising, and not farr from the bottom. Here the winds are broke, and the waters no great offence and supply may come from the hills, and the bottome serve to embellish the garden. Yet if I were to choose for a perfection, it should be such a scituation as Somerset house is: an avenew upon a level, and so come into the cheif story first, with a flat entrance, and passing to the windoes, you find yourself one, or a pair of staires high.[116] For if it could be, servants should not live above but

---

[116]Old Somerset House in the Strand, London, demolished in 1776, occupied a site sloping down to the river Thames, so that the floor of the Queen's Gallery facing the river, though raised above an arcaded basement, was level on the north side with the main courtyard through which it was approached (see plan in *History of the King's Works*, ed. Colvin, v, 1976, Fig. 22).

underneath; for all offensive things fall, rather than rise, and their noise by stirring is troublesome. And it cannot any way be compast better than this.

3. Divers countrys have their caracters, good and evil; so the choise must be as the person affects. A rising mountanous country hath the advantage in prospect and fountaines, and a disadvantage in riding, and traveling. A plain the contrary. A medium is the best, but of the two extreams I should choose the plain; for that gives more conveniences of life than the other. An hill for strangers is best, because it lays a fair landscape afore them, which being new is very diverting; but to the owner that sees it dayly, it is litle better than a dead wall. The plaines are most fertile and easy in all respects, and to the inhabitants have as pleasant views as the hills to their people. But that which is most considerable in favour of the plaines is, the air is more wholesome and the winds less troublesome and maligne than upon the hills. Charleton and Greenwich castle[117] were esteemed unwholesome, but the towne good air. The reason given was the vapours were more sublised[118] high than low; there they were watery, and not so piercing. So at Scandaroon[119] the lodging aboard is safe, but ashore death to Europeans. And tho in the plaines the winds are constant and stirring; yet they are even and not pent, as they are upon the hills, which makes the noise as well as the force of them offensive to the inhabitants. One thing is principally to be regarded in plaine countrys and that is drein of water. Some plaines are subject to innundation, as marsh countrys, and in time of drought have no water, or that which is very unwholsome; this condition of a scituation is to be avoided, as a pest, and nothing but necessity or a traduced patrimony, that a man loves for name and ancestors' sake, could incline a man to keep such a seat.—*Guai a quel uccello che in cattiva valle nasce.*[120] Some places are not marshy, but low and rich, yet offended with water, because there are not lower grounds to drein it. This is a bad choise, because a litle raised would take away that newsance, and yield all the conveniences. Wett that stands in the soil, and not to be dreined away, is a great offence to a seat, especially if it be

[117]These were well-known places on high ground above Greenwich. 'Greenwich Castle' was a Tudor tower replaced by the Royal Observatory in 1675–6.

[118]Sublimated.

[119]Iskanderon in Turkey. North would have learned of conditions there from his brother Dudley.

[120]'Woe to the bird that is born in a wretched valley': a Tuscan proverb (cf. Castiglione's *Cortegiano*, ii, 22).

of brick, or a sucking stone. For the water will filtrate from the ground to the roof, and make the walls moist, foul, and the dwelling unwholsome. Some scituations are so unhappy to have either no water, from the soil, or that which is bad or brackish. And yet for the sake of rents, or paternall love, men endure them. They are capable of a thro cure by raine banks, which gives me occasion to discourse of them, and the onely cure of bad or no water in the soil.

4. Raine water preserved is pure beyond exception. It hath a good spirit, as appears by its aptness to corrupt, and the nourishing of vegetables; but is void of all those alloms and salts which the percolated water of the soil is tainted with, as appears by the comon well and spring water, which will not mix with any thing tasting of sulfur, as soap, oyl, &c. Nay in medecine, apothecarys are accustomed to counterfet rain water, by distilling, but which is the better of the two, comon water fresh fallen, or their cold distilled waters from milk or insipid simples, I will not determine. In fine, if there were no more in the case than to collect and contein a body of water, the heavens affording it at certein times of the year, it is but the making an huge cisterne to contein it. But it so falls out that rain water standing in the air, especially in lead which heats, if it be not prevented by art, will first contract a filme, which shall grow thicker, and dilate in a sort of vegetable slime, producing continually other foulness and greens, the whole mass becoming fedid, and unfitt for any use whatsoever.

This is prevented severall ways. 1. By holding it in a large reservoir upon the soil, which wee call ponds, and in vast quantitys suceeds well, other wise not. Some soils will contein the water, others not, so this is practicable onely in the former. The cause that this keeps the water sweet, is partly the soil is cool, and partly the winds continually stirr it, which breaks the beginnings of corruption, and grouths on the surface which tend to corrupt the whole. For wee see as ponds are larger the waters in them are more defecate and limpid, and as they are lesser, and covert, they green and putrifie. But after all in extream dry years this expedient, tho the most comon, and usefull in clay countrys, hath its defects. For the best of their waters shall be repleat with animalls living and dead, which cannot be wholsome; and therefore such years about autumne are aguish and sickly, purely from the water, as I conjecture. 2. By artificiall cisternes. Those may be either above ground or under, and made either of lead or brick and tarrass.[121] If above ground, the

[121] A hard composition whose English name is a corruption of the Italian *terrazzo*.

water will soon corrupt and stinck, especially in lead, which the sun heats, and that is a perfect digestive to induce corruption. Therefore a ledd cisterne above ground serves for spring or pump water, to contein it for use; but rain will not last at all in it. A brick and lime cisterne is a litle better, but will not doe for long continuance; and such are used for soap boyling, malting, and such passing buisness well enough. So that it must be concluded that no rain cisterne will serve the intent unless it be kept under ground. And for the manner of making them, wee may best referr to the practice in divers places, where they have bin and are used.

In Venice the *cortile* of the house, is hollowed and covered with great stones and gravell, thro which all the rain water that falls from the house percolates, and so is purged of some slimyness, which is the seminall of vegetation in the body of the water. And many have for this reason put sand into cisternes, but whether it hath such effect or not I cannot resolve; I beleeve it cools and breaks the water, and so far helps it.

At Bristoll they make them under ground in their yards, but not very large. They have a very hard stone, and make lime of the same, which together hold the water very well. They use pumps to draw it out, which is not so well. Here they use it for washing and brewing, but as to the taste, they provide from springs.

In Constantinople they are made with greatest art. The water of the soil there is worse than brackish, so they can have no wells; and the aqueducts, doe not supply Pera, where the English merchants live, therefore they make for all uses, as well drinking as other occasions, subterranean receptacles for water, the method of which is this. First they secure a drein for the water without, and hollow round their cisterne for it to pass away, because there is more danger that the outward water should come into the cisterne, than that the water within should goe out. Then they build with brick or stone, and lime a square wall and volt it, leaving onely a small hole for a bucket at the top. After this they plaister the wall very well top and bottom, using this course; first they trowell it every day very hard over and over againe, so long as the plaister sweats, which will be ten or 14 days. And after the wall sweats no more, (such is the nature of it,) it falls to sucking, and draws as hard as it before put out. Then they feed it continually, that is every day, with oyl, and trowel it in like manner, untill it will suck no more, which will last as long, and upon this labour and care the goodness of the work depends. They make a litle sinking under the bucket-hole for convenience of cleaning, and erect a well frame over, and the work is done. They lett in no water of the summer-months, but of the winter, and of snow as much as they can. That is least subject to corrupt. The water will be noysome from the oyl at first, but in time that wears off. And sometimes a sort of worme breeds in it, and for destroying them, they put in small fishes taken in the Hellespont, who being more hungry than ordinary (as I suppose in that cold place) eat 'em up, and then dy and waste; for they never could find what became of them. Another great care was to take the water out with a bucket (there of copper) and not by pump. And for this, they say, the use of a bucket, by beating the surface of the water, and so hindering the inceptives of corruption, keeps the water sweet. But a pump stealing out the water silently and without concussion letts it corrupt upon the surface. When the water grew low, and needed recruit, they drew it all out and then slaves went down with mopps, and washed clean the sides and bottom, and with the aid of the hole below in the midst laded out the last drop. They sayd a plugg and drein was not so good because it would be leaky.

As to the effect, all that have lived there say there could not be cooler and sweeter water, than they had, by the means of these cisternes thus managed. And surely men are much to blame, who live in bad soyl for water, who doe not supply it from the heavens, in this, or some such manner. Men may by ingenuity meet with all inconveniences. And none is greater, than bad water, for in my judgment diseases in countrys comonly ascribed to the air, doe more often proceed from the waters than from that.

5. Among the requisites of houses, offices abroad have considerable interest to be regarded. For convenience in them is a preventive profit; for the want of them is a reall cause of much waste, and a never failing excuse for servants in being guilty of it. These are store houses, laundry, brew house, daiery, barnes, stables, neat houses, and swine stys, as also places for poultry. Of which I shall discourse a litle in their order, being things, which however despised by some fine-folks, as mean and vulgar cares, yet by the wise, who forecast the felicity of familys as well as to prevent all wants and miserys that are the sequel of vanity and supineness, are most intirely regarded. And if I have here made a larger catalogue, than every one hath to doe with, each may take his proper part, as fortune, or affection engageth, and be troubled with no more. But before I come to the particulars, I would observe, that the seat of a country gentleman, who lives as the policy of this nation, and the interest of his estate requires, with full managery in husbandry, grazing or both,

cannot be easy, unless it be a sort of a village or rather citty, with monarchick governement limited by law. That is, many sorts of persons, imployed in severall kinds of affairs, disposed and directed all to one end, the good of the master, and themselves. And that these may be all well acomodated, is the result of the master's care.

1. Laundry is an office wholly of weomen; and the men, however officious to aid their sweethearts, should not be allowed to frequent there, because all they doe, is not so much in advance, as the impertinent conversation hinders the buissness of the family. The incidents to a laundry are 1. a drying room, which is best over head, and must have a thro air; 2. a drying-yard, which must be adjacent, and with a door to it from the laundry. Hedges of prim[122] are best; thorn tears linnen, and box is slow of grouth, and not sweet. And if an easment be provided there, it credits the disposer, as much as a place of more note, for reasons apparent enough. 3. Within, copper which may be come at almost round, large dressers and good lights for smoothe upon, cisternes for holding water, soft and hard; the former for ludder,[123] and the latter to wrince. And the easier the water is lay'd in the better. Place for coals, or wood, to avoid dirt; but above all good floor and dreins, that no water may stagnate, for nothing is more noisome than stale sudds. It should stand off from the house, and yet not farr from the kitchen, because maid-servants are often imployed in the house as well as there. If soft water is not easily had, it is good to lay in rain water, which will hold sweet from week to week. It is not to be too-strait, because the dealing is with hott liquors, and they may pass about easily, and width of room makes the place more aiery and cool. It is expedient to have a frame with cords stretch't frequent upon it, to let downe from the ceiling with pullys, as bigg as the room will admitt, for drying in foul weather.

2. Store houses. These in my judgment should be alltogether in one ordinance of building, and devided so as severall sorts of materialls should be kept by themselves. And here I doe recomend such laboratorys as the master can please himself with, whether smith's, turning, or joynery work, &c. And however many are too nice for mechanick exercise, I am of opinion such are for most part either uncapable of so much ingenuity, or else are for most part more foolishly diverted. A forge is an usefull place, either for a storehouse of iron ware, or to keep downe smith's bills, by dispatching slight jobbs, either by day

---

[122]Privet.　　[123]Lather.

work, or as servants of themselves will doe many such things if they have means. Another office may be for glazing, with a storehouse for all lead and glass. Another may serve for joynery and turning, and be the storehouse for all sorts of usefull peices of wood. The glazing room, if large enough, may serve for oyl, and colours. But a main office of use is the carpenter's, one of which trade is perpetually necessary in a gentleman's house, and being ingenious will work about mills, pumps, wheeling, joynery or any thing, and keep downe bills, which are like weeds, luxuriant and destructive if not kept downe. This is a storehouse for board, timber and all grosser woods for uses of all the managery. And it is good to have a covered sawpit annex't, which must have a roof so upheld as not to hinder rolling of timber to it. I must not omitt one storehouse, as necessary as any else, and it is for all sorts of things, that are not but may posibly be needed; which is to be like a country shop, or haberdasher, which men goe to when they want any thing. Here are to be ropes, pullys, broken furniture, chaines, pitch, and all manner of odd things. The importance of this to an house time and experience will approve.

4.† Stables. These are ordinarily so well contrived because the men of best geniuses and estates delight in horses, and to be provident for them, that the less is to be observed. Onely I shall not pass by one great tho comon error found in great men's stables, and that is drawn in by pride; I mean the laying all in one long range, without breaking the file of horses by partitions, or making severall stables. This looks great, but the master's ostentation is not for the horses' health; the place is cold and noisy, nothing stirrs but the whole room is disturbed, and an horse is a watchfull creature, and hearkens after all that passeth. But when horses for coach are in one place, and sadle in another, the use of one doth not disturb the others' rest, and being of an acquaintance feed and thrive better together.

An ordinance of moderate stabling may be thus layd out: 70 foot long and 20 foot wide and 12 foot high, 2 partitions towards the ends cutting off 20 foot, which serves well 4 horses with manger at the ends, and the midle will be room for 8 horses, with the manger against the partitions, and alley between, and so stand 4 and 4 and the door against the alley, and a windoe against the flank of the horses on each side, but raised as high as their crests. Over head is proper for a granery, which will not

† *sic.*

carry up the building too high. And for repositorys of hay, and the harness, and corne chests, in order to immediate acomodation, lean-to's, or appenditious structures behind, parted also for the use of the severall stables, (thro which they may also convey the dung,) doe very well. Hay over head makes servants lazy and wastfull; they doe not shake nor lighten the hay tumbling it into the rack from above, as when they raise it from beneath. I can the better recomend this modell, having used and accordingly approved it.

For the standing of horses allow 5 foot to each; and a pendulous barr between, is better than stalls boarded up, for the horses doe not love to be recluse, but hanker after the enjoyment of their company, which is by the eye, and so they have a pleasing converse. But a post and partition at the manger is good, because it prevents snapping, and unequall feeding, as will be, if they can come at each other's meat.

5. Barnes. These are a great ease in husbandry, for one that hath a pleasure (as most have) in the fruits of their labours, cannot be content to see corne perrish, with wett and vermin, as will happen by laying abroad in uncertein times. And this is so much the worse, as the people of a country are less dexterous in stacking. In the west and north of England, the use of stacking is so constant, that the people care not for barnes but onely to thresh; and I may assigne for reasons that it is so, 1. that in the west harvest is early, and the corne is comonly good and clear, that there they have not such nice weather, as in some other places; and the cropps not being bulky they lay up much graine in small piles, the charge of doing which is better afforded, than when stacks are made very large, and the corne full of grass and weeds, out of which comes less corne; so that before a stack is made up it shall take wett, and not well quitt the cost of stacking. More northward, the harvest is backward, and the corne foul enough; and laying abroad is very wholesome, to prevent heating; and the thrift of landlords has not afforded barnes; so the people have found out ways of making up their stacks with tollerable security; and that is done by building them upon posts which they call hovells. And these are so ordered, as to prevent vermin within, as mice and ratts, as well as cattle and fouls without from doing hurt, and their corne is better ayred and kept, especially wheat and oats, which the intestine vermine love, than in barnes; and therefore the country men will not use barnes if they might have them.

Now it is in the East Angles, as Cambrigshire, &c., where barnes are so called for. The farmes are great, and cropps bulky, and there they know

nothing willingly, but clapping into the barne. And when the plenty of
the year requires them to lay abroad, they doe it on the bare ground, or
litle better, and by clumsy management sustein such manifest loss, that
it troubles their spirits very much, and they cease not to grumble till
more barn-room be provided.

The hovells in the west and north, where stone is plenty, are made by
laying rafters upon broad stones, borne by smaller uprights set in the
ground, and are not above 18 inches from the ground. In the Midlands
they make frames of wood, and lay sticks and rafts over and so lay corne
upon them, about 15 foot from the ground, and underneath they stow
carts, plows &c., where they stand dry; and next to the braces they line
the posts with brass tinsell, and by that means keep vermin from
ascending. And all thatch. By this they pretend so great convenience in
the sweetness of their corne, and preservation of it, that nothing shall
move them to doe as in the East Angles, lay all in barnes.

Now as to barnes, wee have room for much contrivance for
improvement. The comon way is a long room, about 20 foot wide; and
often the length is such, that there needs many great doors, and
threshing floors; and the roof being so much extended is often out of
order, and a great charge to maintaine. Then if it be a thatch't or tyled
roof, it is close, and keeps in the heat. This is much prevented by pantile
from Holland, which lying without mortar is as aiery as a stack. Another
way is very good which they call a wallis, or Welsh barne, and is like a
cathedrall, nave and ales. This swallows a world of timber, and hath a
vast roof, by being set upright, or sharp at the angle to cast water.
Considering all the inconveniences of each way, I have thought of a
model, for expedient, which if it may be executed is more comodious
than any other. And that is a large square, with one covering of 60 foot
wall plate. Here one great door will serve, and what lesser shall be
needfull, with one or more threshing floors, *ad libitum*. There is no
difficulty, but in framing the roof so as it may stand, which is not easy to
be done but I thinck possible, and my concept follows.

1. The strain being much at the hipps or corners, apt to thrust them
out, and so rack the frame out of square, it may be prevented to lay a
short peice cross the angle of 6 foot long, and dovetail a peice in the middle
of that, and rest it, with a stop at the angle, and into that peice lett in the
hipp-sparr, thus.

2. The sparr will run into a great length and pique at the point, too
high. That I prevent by breaking the length into 2 orders and lay the

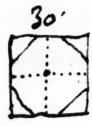

uppermost flatter; which being covered with pantile, will bear a very moderate pitch.

3. The roof will yet carry such lengths of sparr as will make it, for want of thwart propps, sway inwards. That wee prevent by making the principalls of the lower order very massiff, so as to carry their weight. And for the upper order, there may be a post at the pique pendulous, into the top of which the 4 hipps may be framed, and at lower end, strutts may issue to keep out the upper purlein.

4. The upper plate, which makes the plan wheron to pitch the upper order of sparrs, will be so long as will not keep out, but, if made of two peices in each side, strain the joynts, or belly in however unless supported. And that I propose to doe 2 ways. 1. if the length be but one peece, which will be 30 foot (a deal balker), then they may be kept out by diagonall peices, or else a strutt may be set from the midle of each side to the center post, and so keep them out.

⟨5.⟩ The thrust will be so strong on the wal-plates, that it will endanger carrying out the wall it self, unless very well abbutted, and that may be done by adding porches to the sides, which are a great inlargement of room, and comodious, for stowing particular sorts of grain, to be easily come at. And if it happens that I ever execute this designe, I shall have 2 buildings to abbutt the ends, and 2 porches at the sides, which will strengthen the walls sufficiently.

These are the difficultys that trouble the covering, which reconciled, I need not argue the forme to be both most capacious, and most convenient.

I shall not omitt to mention a barne I set up very slight, and used it before it was at its grouth, or finish't.[124] I set up a range of posts making 4 bays (5 had bin better if room had bin); they were 15 foot high, and 20 foot wide, and as much latterally. These bound at the head, and brac't well to the baulks and upper sells, ⟨were⟩† covered flatt with pantile. And this being one year's work was used as a covering to stack under; but vermin, from the openness, troubled the corne. Next year I added wings or ales to it, encompassing the ends, of 15 foot without the posts, which added a vast deal of room and inclosed all; and on one side made a porch, with the pique as high as the sell, which lett in a loaden cart. This was made of alder and deal poles, onely the posts or studds of the

---

†*MS* was

---

[124] This barn is also described by North, with a sketch, in BL Add. MS 32504, fos. 60ᵛ–61ᵛ.

outward wall were oak; the pantile were the greatest cost. The walls were of slitt deal nailed to the short studds, and this is a compleat barne.

I should not pass by an invention some are fond of, which is called a dutch barne.[125] It stands on 5 or 6 posts set in the ground, and the roof is hoisted or lett downe by a jack-winch, moved from corner to corner; and so is made to weather any thing layd under it. The fault of this is that it serves onely for hay; corne is in no respect safe in it, for it is exposed to vermin and driving rain, and snow. But the use is troublesum. The slow moving the roof up and downe, tires whom is to doe it; and they are almost layd aside. But if in any case they are usefull it is in litle and not great forme.

I had much thought about laying downe board floors to thresh on. Oak plank is very dear, tho lasting, and deal suffers by loaden carts. After divers expedients tryed, I found that deal might be layd on sand true and steddy enough to thresh on. And that I proved; for when carting time came, I took the floor up, and after harvest layd it downe againe; and so may doe 20 years together.

6. Brewhouse. That is a necessary tho cumbersome office, and formerly took up very much housing. Now of late years, things are disposed better. And I made an house 24 foot by 20, which brued 12 hogsheads and had above half the room to spare. The copper was mounted high, and was served with coal, in a by place without butts open to the room, and a cock lett goe the water and liquor from it. On one side was a ledd cisterne that held 20 hogsheads. The water was layd into that, and it rose but a foot above ground. From hence the water was pumpt into the copper. Then the mash tubb received it from the cock, and from that it sank into an underbeek,[126] from whence the pump raised it againe to the copper, and the cock lett that goe into the coolers. Those were 2; one lay over the other about 3 foot, and the lower lay 4 foot over the guile-tubb, which was set into the ground in clay. Then the cock lett goe the boyled liquor into the cooler, and from thence it past to the second and so into the guile tub.[127] And on the other side opposite to the cisterne was a place to sett what tubbs there might be occasion for, and the pump, which was managed (being copper and very heavy) by a double tackle to the top of the room, was set in it, and raysed the wort

---

[125] Such barns are known from Dutch illustrations. The posts were arranged in a circle and the moveable roof was conical in form.

[126] 'A vessel placed below the mash tub to receive the raw wort' (*OED*).

[127] A guile- or gyle-tub is one in which the wort is left to ferment.

from thence also into the copper; so all the transitions were done either by pumping or letting run. Then I convey'd the working beer from the guile tub, to the seller in pipes made square of slitt deal, and fitting each to other, to be taken away and layd by when not used.

This office and cellars have a relation and are not the least contributing to the health of the family as also to the satisfaction of it. For nothing is well without good drink at a table; and the ordinary is of more consequence than that which is more rare. There is litle to be observed of cellars but that they be vaulted, and the greater part underground; and so they cannot be ill. Air is an enimy not to be trusted to enter with any force. And if inclined to too much coolness it ought, for nice keeping liquors, especially wine, be quite shutt out. Too much chillness offends the drink and makes it vapid, and for that reason vintners gravell and not pave the floor, as warmer. Some convey drink from the brewhouse in pipes of lead; which is easy, but not so clean as (I described) by deal. For the stirring of the liquor will not soon out, and scalding is but a blind expedient. It was thought of to convey in open gutters of wood, but, least it cool the liquor too much, in a long current, and for that reason not ventured upon. If a cellar be deep, well drained, and easy to the brewhouse, there is full complement of convenience.

7. Daiery hath 3 devisions. Outward, for warm and slapping buissness, inward, for milk and cream, which must be kept very cool and clean. It is so nice, that any nastyness within[128] small will conduce to tainting sower the milk and cream. Lastly cheese chamber, which is best over both the other. There is litle nicety in the composition of these, for any sort of room capacious enough may be adapted to the use; for all the vessells and utensills are moveable, except shelves. Cool and sweet are the main points, which a north scituation, shaded by trees a litle towards the east and west compasseth; and lying comodious to the milking yard, makes all well.

8. Dovehouses. These are no less profitable to injoy than artificiall to be made, however ordinary to be met with. They thrive best in the corn champain countrys. Woodlands harbour haukes, the desperate enimys of these poor birds that inhabit with us. And it is for that reason not to pitch their houses too far from company, but in a mediocrity. If they are among too much buissness and noise, they will be frighted. If retired, the hauks will be too saucy; the passing of men to and fro frights them.

---

[128]i.e. however.

And the lovre should not be lower than the adjoyning buildings, and neerest trees; for the hauks will have an advantage to descend upon them, that cannot strike so well rising. The house must be warm and aiery, sufficient pipes for the multitude to issue at without interfering in their rise. And if a building be too large for one lovre, there should be more. And water should be at a moderate distance, and quiet; the sea is a great advantage to a dovehouse, because they love, grow, and thrive with salt water. But after all nothing encourages them more than the sweep of a good corne farmeyard; for food is the temptation that brings all fether'd birds together.

As to the particularitys of a dovehouse, concerning the building and accomodating of it, I cannot find a better method of declaring my opinion of them, than by giving the model of one I built for my self.[129]

It was of an octangular forme equilaterall, raised upon a very strong foundation. And at the floor height I set up a center pole, and wrought the inside exactly circular. And after the wall rose about 3 foot high, I sett in the door, $4\frac{1}{2}$ foot high (enough for entrance, and more had robbed the walls of holes). Upon the table on the outside, which was 2 or 3 courses above the head of the door, I foundationed 8 angle-pilastres of brick's length on each returne, and so carryed up the pilastres with angle brick made to the forme, and sett the walls in from them 2 inches, pannell wise; by which the pannells shewed the base, and the pilastres were in the upright of the sub-base of the building, butt battering in all the while to the top. Here I erred; for the base of the building should have stood a course at least or two setting off 2 inches each without the upright of the pilastres; and then the base had carryed 2 setting off courses round the fabrick and 3 in the pannell, which had given a great strength and security to the fabrick.

But the other way, as the walls were fortified underground, were stout enough; tho those settings off had spread the base, and shewed a strength which is allwais beautyfull in building. The walls were above 2 foot, neer $2\frac{1}{2}$ at the angles, thick, and the pannells in the midle but thin, for so the compass sweep ordered it, and together made a great abuttment, for the point of each angle had the force of an abbutress, and the whole being of a peice from the door head without any apperture, thinness in the places proper for appertures did not weaken the walls. At 15 foot high, I closed the walls with 3 courses overhanging the pannells, and ranging with the

[129]This building still survives at Rougham.

faces of the pilastres, which as a corona bound the whole together. Upon the levell of the walls the building was above 30 foot from angle to angle without, and above 28 within.

It was no easy task to contrive a covering for this. A small fabrick will hold the thrust of the roof, by the strength of the walls, or some bracing in the frame. But this had so great a bredth, that without some art in the frame the thrust would drive out the walls; for considering the freedome to be for flight of doves, and that winged vermin might have no means to fly out, if once ventured in, wee could not have any cross-girders, and if any they must bind in each angle, or else better none. And if so, the meeting in the center would be so thick, as to be an hindrance in many respects.

I considered that the frame must be projected upon the angles, with 8 principall hip sparrs, which standing all was safe; and the plates being short, about 12 foot, would bear their part if the angles stood firme. I considered also that, if the angles were so bound as that they could not part in the joynt, then the thrust of every hipp bore against each other; for one could not stirr unless the whole frame of the plates gave way. Therefore I ordered the joynts at the angles to be framed in this manner, vizt.: mortois the plates at the joynt; then lett in a brace upon the plates of about 8 foot long; and after that take a knotty peice of 8 inches wide and sufficient length, and laying it upon the work as in the draught, and scribe the wood underneath, by which cut clefts to take all in, so as the solid goes downe every where at each end and between; by this driven hard downe the angle is so bound together, to be as, if not stronger than, one solid peice of timber so large. Then upon this overlayd peice, pitch the hip sparr, lett in with a dovetail, and shouldring, which stands as upon a rock, and gives no partiall strain to the walls, as might be made apper if I shewed all the hold and band that this cleft peice made, but that is obvious enough. I onely add that the cleft peice was of the best oak, and such as had the toughest knotts. For in clear wood the cleft is apt to rive off, and loose hold all at once. This done at all the 8 angles, hath approved it self for strength in severall great stormes of wind.

At about 16 foot length of the hipps, there was a lesser octagon frame, received by the angles upon them, of 10 foot from the corner to corner. Upon each angle, stood a 4 foot post, which carryed an octagon roof covered with board, fether edged and painted, with a cornish, and lead eves. And a slitt of 6 inches was left next the foundation of this superfabrick for the doves to enter, and above that glass windoes round.

profile
a the plate
b the brace
c the cleft piece
d the truss

The covering was reed, making good the slope next the lover with board, which made a convenient stage round for the doves to sit on. The margin hath some faint representation of the whole projected on a panell. This roof was secured from twisting by porlaines[130] about the midle of the sparrs, and braces sett from the joints of them to the opposite sparr. And the lover was braced within, to secure it from racking, and bound at the root mortoises with iron holdfasts, to keep it from rising out. The bracing of the frame was in this manner, and that of the lover as followeth in profile; which because of the meeting of 8 peices in the midle was troublesome, but inch boards edgwise, with the braces lett into the wood, fixt all very well.

As for the descent to the house from the lover, it was thus contrived: a, b, c, d, the foundation frame of the lover, was cros't with 2 timbers square, from 4 sides opposite, as a, c and d, b. Then a plank was lett in upon each which should angle and dye at the midle points of the other 4 sides, e, f, g, h, which devided the plan into 4 exact squares, which were the holes, by which the doves were to descend, the rest was covering for the doves to walk upon.

On the inside is intended, (for it is not done,) to make an altar[131] of holes round, and upon the center pitch an axis, which shall turne upon that and the midle cross peices of the lover. This axis is to carry 2 ladders, within 8 inches of the walls, and to be opposite to each other, so as 2 persons may search the house at once, with the same movements. The holes are to be raised from the ground a course or 2 with brick, the rest with moulded clay, which, they say, pigeons love most of any thing. And the holes rising above the level walls, will gain a yard in height, which matters are touch't in the draught sett in the margin.

The covering is of reed, which well layd and bound, (for binding is the strength of all that thatch,) is a most durable roof. And here the thickness of the reed standing off makes a slope platforme, (as I sayd,) to be made good with board, for doves to light upon, and being painted, as all the lover being wood must be, will weather tollerably; and the lover rising, as seems, out of that platforme, looks *all' Italiana*;

[130]Purlins.
[131]The 'altar' is the base supporting the pole to which the two ladders were fixed.

Further Writings by
Roger North
on architectural topics

I

On Gothic Architecture

BL MS, fos. 73–4: from 'Architecture', *c.* 1690

First they had no manner of regard to the externall figure of a structure, but fall it as it will, so the humour within was kept, and generally the abuttments stood at distance and received the weight by a comunicating arch and it looks as if shores were set up to prevent the downefall of a lofty building, than which nothing is uglyer. For the art is always to be hidden, and the substance should shew it self sufficient; otherwise a defect is exposed. And the supply never mends the matter, for wee cannot so well trust the contrivance, which may easily be short to resist the great force of a decaying structure. And generally all art is an objection, as of doubdtfull success. The same is to be sayd of all the extraordinary projected studys from walls which are wrought with strong counterpoises to make them stand, which for the foregoing reasons are errors in architecture, wherein you are to judge of your owne security, and not to trust to art.

In the next place, they observ'd no order, but would place the pillars of one story upon the keys of the arches of an other, and carry up such prodigious uprights without any breakings or settings off that, to speak freely, every one must doubt the strength unless time hath establish't the opinion of firmeness. Then the pillars are not onely too small to answere the imployment they have, but by the drawing the weight on to seeming threads, and so led downe to the bases, they seem less strong than they are, and the peers between vast windoes are to the eye inconsiderable, tho in truth the great depth to the out of every buttress makes amends for the want of breadth, but that is not discerned; and which is worst of all, to exalt their roofs, they would depress the floor, and lay it under ground, a fault now unpardonable.

Then for their enrichments, as I say'd, they are all meer caprice, the tabernacle work paultry, consisting of narrow cells set as close as could be, without any due distances to give law to the walls, and running up in ragges spiks, ⟨as⟩ tho intended to resemble campania tents[132] or

---

[132]Tents used in military campaigns.

pavilions, which is an imperfect shift of it self, but in truth more like a hop garden in June. The rest of the enriching was for the most part threds running upright. If any figures or sculptures are set, it is for the most part improper, as to suport some spring of an arch, too great a weight for a figure of a man or beast to bear, and of no good handling, so much better spared.

The windo work is pretty, especially that which humors the rose, usuall⟨y⟩ set to fill the great fenestral apertures in gable ends, but it looks very weak and slight. In the whole the Gothick manner looks great at first and the more you are acquainted with it the more you despise it, for it looseth by acquaintance.

fos. 70–1

It is an universall rule in building, that nothing is handsome which doth not appear to the eye strong.

This is the result of all the experience of the refin'd ages and countrys, which exposeth the barbarity of the Goths, or rather their infancy in arts, (for I must prefer their morality to the Greeks and Romans,) who, out of a childish fancy that ostentation of art was beautyfull, introduc't such a fashion of building as they have left us in our cathedral and other great churches, wherein the drift of the architect is for the most part to make his structure great and the support seem small, so that you may wonder how it stands, when such massy roofs are upheld by such threds of stone as they seem by the contrivance within, and the true support, and abbutment, which is also pincht as much as might be, is hidden. And in old castles, you shall find many odd projected windoes and closets, which seem to stand upon a point, and the country people admire the builder's art, having no true *gusto* of beauty.

In the mean time I must, to doe those good men that built our churches right, profess that in the ordinance of walls and abbutment they have done as much as is possible, to make the stone and lime work its utmost, an⟨d⟩ that now wee have not any that will venture to set such weight upon so small support, and I question whether they are able, or have the skill they had, to calculate those propositions. To give one instance, there is the cathedrall of Salisbury, and the tower in particular, stand upon very small support and the abbutment but moderate. There is nothing in appearance to support the tower but the 4 uprights, and the weight is prodigious. But observing it with some curiosity, I found abbutments wrought very cuningly in the walls 8 severall ways by 2 half arches, the uppermost resting upon the 2nd pillar from the tower, and the undermost upon the next to it. These two arching abuttments appear in crossing the windoes next to the tower, so that at seting on, the tower hath a very broad support, otherwise it were impossible it should stand.

Kings Colledge chappel in Cambridge is wonderfully thought, and executed, the abuttment being small, and the roof broad and massy. I beleeve that there is no coar, or filling in the buttresses, but it is all made up with squar'd stone, which adds much to the strength.

I never saw any thing neater than some of their monachal cloysters are, that at Glouster especially, and for such order of rooffing, I thinck they exceed the regular much; for in that they ⟨are⟩ either flat or concha[133] — and have not (that I have seen) any good way of cross arching, which in the Gothick is admirably pretty; for they follow the fashion of a chokle,[134] which meet in the key, and fill the interstices with a rose, or some other network fancy, that none can dislike it. The regular ornaments of soffits of arches, which are alwais circular, either plaine or sphericall or choncha, are onely squares and roses, deminishing in the sphericall with the figure; and that in great domes, is noble and august, but in lesser works I thinck the Gothick prettyer.

fos. 31–36ᵛ: from 'Of Building' *c.* 1696

It is usuall for dablers in this art (as I am,) as well as the adept, to pretend to skill in all sorts of fabricks, publik as well as private; therefore wrighters will run thro all branches of the art, tho their skill ly's but in some, the rest, as rime, for forme sake. And if I have any knowledge of building, I must owne it to ly in the reforming part. I doe not pretend either to great publik designes, nor new models of great howses. It requires an extraordinary genius, to exceed what is now common in the world; and builders, as poets, should blush at mediocrity as well as faults. But notwithstanding this, like my fellow dablers, I will venture my bolt, in somewhat more intire, and new than what I have profest; and first of publick buildings.

The distinction now of building in the world, is reducible to Gothick

---

[133] In the form of a shell: see Palladio, *I quattro libri dell' architettura*, i, chap. xxiv, for this and other forms of vault.

[134] A cockle-shell. North is thinking of the way in which the striations of such a shell converge at the base.

and Regular. The former was a mode introduc't by a barbarous sort of people, that first distres't, then dissolved the Roman Empire. These fell into a new way of great buildings, which was mixt of their owne invention, and what they found, and had for the most part destroyed among the Greekes and Romans. And this manner is most eminent in our cathedrall churches. But Westminster Hall, one of the best fabriks not dedicated to sacred uses of that time in the world, is purely Gothick.

It is no unpleasant thing to observe the course of proceeding, in that sort of building, which prevailed in our nation, till almost King James the first. For the elder are more rude, heavy and speak the clumsyness of their contrivers, and came finer, and I thinck ceast, in Henry VII's Chappell at Westminster, which was all that Gothick witt could doe. Now I give three periods, exemplified in the building of the respective times. The first is the antidiluvian of the Danes, who to England were worse than the deluge to the world, which sent all to peace, they held the nation in dismall torment severall ages. This I suppose to be seen in the church of Durham, and is the most antique of any. The order is round upright lumps for columnes, with perfect semi-circular arches, as rudely  expres't in the margin. This church hath had the fortune not to be much ruined, as the more southerne were by the frequent inundations of the infamous Danes, so remaines more intire in its old order, than others are, tho first built neer the same time, which was, as I take it, when the Saxon kings took to an humour of cloystering themselves, and thought there was no composition with heaven, for their infinite wickedness, but at the price of a church or monastery.

There are severall other cathedrall churches, which have some foot steps of this antiquity, as Glouster, and at Norwich. And indeed most have some, many are composed of divers sorts according to the severall ages wherein they happned to be repaired, which I have bin much enterteined to observe, and I allwais concluded this order of round and compass to be the oldest. And one would wonder what should guide the fancys of men to a different order of pillar, and arching more remote from naturall beauty, which may consist in easy and reasonable composition, rather than in regulating this, which would have at last brought it to the condition of that which is called regular, which consists in adjusting the proportions of weight and support, agreeing with the previous opinions of the spectators, who are apt to pronounce what is enough, and what too much or too litle, and so determine naturall beauty. Which method, with much study, art, canvassing and experience in Grece, produc't the laws of the 5 orders, and the (now) knowne method of Regular building, which I shall consider in another place.

But to proceed in the consideration of the Gothick, (which now is apply'd to all that is not Regular). The next step was to make the arches angular or as half a birds eye and the supports quadrat diagonall and thredded, as Westminster Abbey, and is roughly exprest in the margin. And this manner hath come downe to our time, when first the regular way hath bin used in publik buildings, being introduc't by Inigo Jones in repairing St Pauls London. And most of our parochiall churches are of this order, but some more fine than others, as the ages, or persons happened to affect.

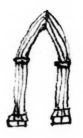

I must owne to preferr much the former, being the round way, which I conceive was derived from the Greek and Roman regular columnes, but for want of art, and learning in the reason of it, so rudely executed as wee see. But devious from the right as it is, none can deny but, it bears not onely an air of grandure, but hath a strength and reasonableness beyond the other; and is such as an extrordinary high spirited judicious barbarian might be supposed originally to invent, and leave to his posterity to refine upon as a subject capable of being improved to the greatest perfection. And I must needs excuse their grossness of support, as also in latter times, from the want of materialls. It may be they had not the art, nor had found quarrys for raising and leading of massy stones such as are necessary to strengthen finer works, for wee observe all is put together of small stones, and so small as makes it strange how they could make the work hang with them, having not the aid of iron cramps, which are now used in the best works.

Then considering that it is seldome, that men vary for the better, tho often in degrees of greater nicety, and seeming fineness, whatever the true reason and judgment happens to be, not often better, but worse than those who went before; so here to be finer, they fell into the birdsey way of arching; and at length, so great a rarity was art, that shewing that, or rather an empty shaddow of it, was allow'd to be the best ornament a magnifick structure was capable of. And this brought in that way of thredding the inward work, as I noted, to make the art wondred at, as if all that weight of roof stood on those thredds. If one may guess what ledd to this, I may set out these conjectures.

First the old way seemed clumsey, and dark, because the supports were great and the apertures small. Therefore they might pretend to correct those excesses, and in so doing fall into a worse; as, if they judg'd the lights too small, this carry'd on a conceit that light was good, and consequently that there could not be enough of it. So whole sides of churches, all that was possible to be gained by pinching the support, was turned into windoe, according to the rule, *stulti dum vitant vitia in contraria currunt.*[135] For the same reason, when they observed the supports or pillars took up too much room, they would mend the fault, by making them so small, that one could not imagine them capable to sustein the rooffe. And being sensible, that their light was too much, and offensive, as really it is, they came to darken the windoes with painted glass, which could not be so studiously, and generally used, if reason had not ledd to it. And without they were driven to strange deformity of propps (as I observed) to make good the support, at the same time concealing it within; as if the same persons were never to see both sides. And as to the windoes, they were driven to a great puzle to hang their glass in such vast breadths, which brought in that variety of frame, and rose work in the windoes, as wee see in Westminster Abbey, and King's Colledge chappell at Cambridge, which I propose as the 2 best peices of the Gothick work in England.

But to proceed, this round work lasted to the inroads of the Danes, the next order was the birdsey arch and diagonall collumne, which I propose lasted to the Edwards time, and then a still finer sort of building came in, which is exemplified in the Cathedrall of New Sarum, which church, for the area of it, I beleeve stands upon the least support of any in the world. It is all of one order, and in stead of the diagonall thredded columne, it is composed of rounds, whereof one is the midle, and four about it much smaller, upon which the thredds of the arches fall, and are therefore diagonall to the range. This conceipt is taken from the Temple Church in London, which is more ancient, but its columnes are four rounds consolidated, as in the margin. It hath bin thought, both these and Salsbury were made and not quarr-stons, but it is not clear, nor whence they had them.[136] These are the 3 periods of the Gothic building, which is now expired in the world, and the Regular taken from old ruins and books succeeds it.

But before I leave the subject, I will observe 2 manners which are inviolably observed, 1. The single range, which is for chappells, and the

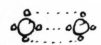

---

[135]'Fools in avoiding one fault only fall into another': Horace, *Satires* i. 2. 24.

[136]It was, no doubt, the numerous columns of Purbeck Marble in Salisbury Cathedral and the Temple Church whose composition puzzled North and others.

treble range, which wee call the nave and two iles, or the shipp, as the words import, and two wings, but more properly the body. This hath bin affirmed by the cheif architect of this age,[137] to have bin the manner of the Greek and Roman courts of justice, used in latter time, of which some account is in Vitruvius; but I suppose after the translation of the Empire to Greece, which was long after his time, those fabricks were most cultivated, and was coevall with the Christians beginning to build churches; whether there ⟨are⟩ any *basilike* yet remaning I know not, scarce thinck any; if att all, they must be converted to churches. All other fabricks [by] one rage or other, of warr or frenzie, hath demolisht, and allmost all monuments of antiquity about Greece are lost; even the people, however of old brave learned and free, now are like as abject and illiterate slaves. It was peculiar to these *basilike* to have 2 iles or wings, devided from the main fabrick by columnes, because they were to conteine and keep dry as well as cool vast multitudes of people; and it was hard to cover such a breadth any other way, which should contein such numbers. Therefore the columnes are in the place of upright supports to the maine weight of the roof, and the wings as abuttments to the outward thrust of it, so as the whole stands firme, and founded on the likeness of a man, and his two armes, or any thing reasonably attended, as a great person leaning on 2 pages: one great pile with smaller neer, which with regard to uniformity and strength, are the best and most universally approved order of things, and may be introduc't in all sorts of finishing work, as well as fabrick, which lay'd out thus in almost any proportion will be well. If this were so used for courts of justice, as the word *basiliche* imports, it was onely strait ranges, with the justice seat at the upper end. But that which wee call the cuppolo, dome or tower in the midle, with the cross iles, and east end, those were introduc't in the forme of a cross by the Christians and are peculiar to their churches, which [are], from the manner whence they were derived, are still in the antiq languages called *basiliche*, and with us means a capitall or cathedrall church. There has bin much alteration in the mide part, which generally was a Gothick tower square upon 4 uprights, and abbutted 8 ways upon the 8 walls centring in it. But the elder times, I mean not with respect to the primitive, but our owne, when building in Greece and Italy began to draw towards Regular, and the Goths themselves to be reformed, there was a way of volting this midle

---

[137]Presumably Sir Christopher Wren.

introduc't whereof the Santa Sofia in Constantinople is a glorious example. And these were the use if not the invention of that time, for I doe not find in the wrighters of Antiquitys any arches made like half sphears or half ovalls, as the use then, and since has bin. And because in Italy the great churches were called *Il domo*, and were of this manner, the manner itself is now called a dome, and is in my judgment a greater perfection in architecture than the ancients knew or made use of, for they ordinarly covered with timber, and seldome made arches, but architraves, unless in latter times the triumphall arches for spear men to pass throo*. But volts of this magnitude, as in those Greek fabriks, and Roman now, particularly St. Peter's at Rome, and as I hope to see in St. Paul's London, are types of art, never enough to be admired and encouraged. And even the barbarous Turks are in this glorious, who cover stupendious fabricks with hemisphere volts and open the four sides, as well as abutt the whole with 4 quarter spheres, which is a figure of so great perfection, I wonder it is not introduc't with us, who so much love room, and lofty coverings. A rude outline of this figure is in the margin, than which nature scarce admits a more perfect for churches.

And in this state wee must leave the Gothick, which being arrived to its ultimate refinement must submitt to the course of changing the world was allwais given to, and lett in the old formes apply'd to our fancys; and that will be in perpetuall change, and new modes come in fashion, but probably will not so easily truckle to mutability, as the Gothick hath done, which goes off all at once.

*The Rotunda and some smaller round temples may be volted: *North's marginal note*.

II

The origin and development of Regular Architecture

BL MS, fos. 74ᵛ–80ᵛ

Let us now venture upon that which is knowne by the name of Regular, in the Italian and Greek manner.

A building hath two uses of the side walls, that is support of the roof and defence from heat, and weather. The roof, as I observ'd before, ought for that end also to overhang, else the wett will come to the apertures and the foundation. The overhanging will need some more support than the walls, otherwise the weight of the roof looks too heavy; this makes pillars needfull, and I take it to be the onely ground for the use of them, and consequently of the ornament. Thus it is that wee see the antique temples portico'd round, and where it makes not a portico, the pillars support the entablement of the roof, which could not stand so foreward had it not the aid of columnes. And in my opinion, pillars without this entablement, usually styled the architrave, freeze and cornish, supposed to be the contignation[138] of a roof, would be as improper as pillars supporting nothing; for where there is no weight but in the upright, there walls, without the superaddition of columnes, are sufficient. It is a usuall thing to turne arches upon single pillars, but, for the foregoing reasons and what follows, in my sence not decorous nor proper. For first, they are too weak for the imployment, secondly the arches are onely apertures in the wall, and therefore what is left besides the aperture shoud be part of the wall, and then all appears firme an⟨d⟩ good. Those are called peers or pilasters, and are set off with a small cornish, for adorning the arch where it setts on, and that is called the imposts of the arches. Now if you will have pillars, you must superinduce them upon these peers and carry an entableture strait upon the keys of the arches; then will the whole seem firme and fair. Whereas wall and arches upon single pillars is as if it hung in the air, or, as the comon people often say, by geometry, and hath not due suport, the pillars seeming weaker than what lys upon them.

[138]Timber structure.

This puts me in mind to reproove another error very frequent in great structures otherwise well designed, and that is breaking the entableture, so as it shall project more forewards upon the columnes than between them, all which breaks are a defect and should be shunned if possible; for the entableture is supposed a frame of a roof and nothing else, therefore ought to be strait. Much less can I endure when the architrave and freese dy in the upright of the columne, as if they were sunk into the wall, and the cornish onely is continued, which is the fault of Pauls as it is now designed,[139] wherein the Surveyor hath bin in my opinion most opiniatrely improvident in concealing the designe till it appear'd in the execution, for no eye that hath bin acquainted with good designes but would have relucted at that, and the universall consent would have oblidg'd him to conforme, as now it doth to repent. I must confess in structures so great, where by reason of windoes and doors the intercolumniations are so large that to carry the entableture strait would be difficult, and not practicable without vast stones or massy counterpoises, it may be tollerable to break the tableture, as the case is of the Banquetting house, but to doe it in joynery is nonsence.

It is another error to place the orders of architecture on the inside of rooms. For I thinck they look too gross, and seem useless, because the annoyance of wether, against which they are contrived, comes not there, and whatever is useless is ugly. Sometimes in halls where there are galleries, supporting pillars doe well, the like in churches; but roomes should be uncumber'd and easy distributed onely into decorous compartiments. Thus much for the use and introduction of collumnes, which, being so proper for the porpose, fall in with every one's fancy, therefore must be agreable and handsome. All the rest is but judgment of too long and too short, which by the critiscisme of ages is setled in the proportions of the knowne orders, upon the foundation I have already layd downe, of strength betwixt the two evils of too much and too litle. The like may be sayd of the entableture upon it, which is adjusted to our hands in the same manner.

As for the bases, capitals and other ornaments of the orders so much pleaded for and so religiously executed, I cannot ascribe such necessity to them; but all the world must agree they are beautyfull, having past censure of times, and nothing since found out of equall request. So that I

[139]The elision that North complains of occurs in the interior of the Cathedral, where the architrave and frieze of the main order are interrupted by the intervening arches.

must allow an ingenious architect to vary in those particulars as his judgment prompts; but let him take heed, few in the world have ventured but have succeeded ill, and there is no excuse for going out of the way, when that very thing is a fault in the opinion of most, and to follow the patterne is right, the sence of all; which to mee seems a great consolation to the men of designe, that they are sure to please, if they are not capricious.

In most cases mankind seek beauty as a positive thing, which for the most part rests wholly in opinion without any reall ground in nature, and in truth is no more than not deformed. This is much in the buissness of architecture, wherein fashions change in every country, and all countrys have somewhat distinct that is esteemed good not used by others, which demonstrates the assertion. Therefore a man is weak that in building or finishing doth not follow the fashion of his time and his country. It is most true that things which change seldomest are those that are seldomest renew'd. For cloths that are renew'd quarterly change the fashion almost as often, so beds that are renew'd once in 10 years change in about that period; houses are not renew'd in less then 100 years, therefore the fashion is permanent accordingly; finishing somewhat oftner, but no man need fear outliving his house, at least he will be so old to have outlived his curiosity tho his malice encreaseth, which will dispose him to opiniastre upon old fashion against all the world, and thinck to mortifie his enimise, the youth, by dispising their ways.

There is some reason that inclines to affect fashions, and it is that wee are partly acquaneted, and not satiated; and as a thing intirely new is not of a suddaine understood, so carrys no enterteinement at first, so a thing that is vulgar is knowne as well without seing, as with it, and there is neither desire nor enterteinment about a thing that wee have had too much of. A mixture of these pleaseth; as when upon an old approv'd ground a new contrivance is superinduc't, and old orders are newly apply'd, and disposed, the mind runs instantly into contemplation of it, and is pleas'd. Besides, that which follows great caracters, is thought great and brave, for it is like what such a one hath, for whose greatness and wisdome wee have a reverence and are proud of any thing like him. And after all every particular man hath somewhat singular, and will like this or that by accident or caprice without any account to be given, which leads fashions. These matters occuring my pen drops them, tho they be of a nature too metaphisicall for the instruction of a builder who deals in solids, and also must deal somewhat with humors too or shall have small imployment.

For this reason I will not goe about to give a rationall of all the ornaments, which I hold but a mode or fashion, and are alterable *ad libitum* without deforming a designe, provided the mode allows it; altho somwhat might be sayd towards it, and yet not upon that exellent basis of man's symmetry, of which I have no sort of opinion. But take the bases, capitalls, ovolys, triglifs, fretts, and other enrichments of the orders, they have bin so much considered, that they are not in any thing absurd, and of all the innovations that ever I saw, they have bin much for the worse. In the transition between the Gothick, and the Regular, which was about King James time or somewhat sooner, they made very bold with the orders, and put stockins on to the pillars, and wringled them, breaking the measures very much in the intableture, making odd crotesque ornaments every where, all which are most fulsome; a speciall instance of this is in the Scools at Oxford, where over one of the avenues within are the 5 orders plac't in proper degrees, but so ill handled, that it is a shame; tho I must confess the designe was very suitable for an academy. For these reasons lett an architect have a care of variing, for if he doth it well he is at mercy, and it is great odds but he will doe ill; at most it is his buissness not more to excell, than to avoid blame and the handles to it.

Having discours't of the generall reason of beauty in architecture, which in my judgment consists cheifly in judgment of sufficiency, tho likewise very much in fashion, I will subjoyne my thoughts of some particulars as they occurr to my fancy, shewing as neer as I can guess the occasion of the use of them, and then the use will justifie it self.

First as for pillars in generall, I take it that the nature of wood was the cause and originall of them.[140] For wood is so firmely knitt in the graine length-wise that, resting upon the ends, it will bear not onely itself but a great weight in the midle, unless drawne to an overlength, and is not apt to snap or crack, as stone and all other materialls of building; but is tough and springy, yeilding to its weight before it breaks. Besides this, as a further convenience, I must observe that it grows in the shape it is used, and is universall easily got, and easily wrought. Whereas stone is not easily gott, the making and working of brick and mortar, a trade and much imbroyle attends the use of such materialls, which makes them not

---

[140]That the ornaments of the Orders originated in timber construction was already noted in antiquity by Vitruvius.

taken, but where the trade, and imployments of a people are subservient to it, and the materialls are ready for the workman before he is ready for them. From whence it seems that wood dispos⟨ed⟩ in the manner of columnes was the first building, and the ingenious refined upon that, which plainely ledd to the orders of columnes.

Thus the mode of building, or fashion, to give it a more apt terme, being setled by the use of wood, and afterwards stone, brick and mortar coming to be used also, by reason of the strength and duration of such materials, it is naturall that they should ape the building in fashion, and make their shapes as that of wood. All which may plainely be trac't in the economy of the five orders; for besides the columne consider the other members as the architrabe, freeze, and cornish.

My worthy and curious freind at Stambole[141] hath informed me of the method of building in the Easterne parts, which in this theory is cheifly to be regarded, because the 5 orders are fetch't or derived from thence, and not our way, which is farr different from that, and therefore may make the deduction seem more strange. Wee frame all our timber houses, letting one stick into another, securing it by wooden pinns; which they never doe, but lay one peice upon another, nailing all together with long spikes.

As for example the wall of an house is a row of upright trees, the next thing is a long beam nailed downe to each of them, which I call the architrabe,[142] thereby answering the purport of the word. But I must not forget, that upon every tree they lay first a transverse peice, as in the figure, before the architrabe comes on, which adds strength to the frame, and was the beginning of the capital, which is a distinct peice put upon every columne cut into severall shapes, of which the Ionick comes neerest to the naturall. After this, to make a flat ceiling to the room, trees were layd upon the architraves transverse the building, whose ends appeared on two sides, and length on 2 sides. Therefore, to make all alike, they tackt a peice onto those ends, then there was a perfect freeze, which to this day in the Ionick order is half round, and therein still nearer to the naturall. The next and last course was a peice over the freeze, and then the rafters, which for shooting raine and better bearing the weight of covering were raised, having their feet over hanging the freese, and made the cornish. So that the method and economy of the orders or Regular building are originally derived from wood, which in

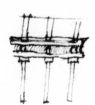

[141] His brother Dudley (above, p. xi).
[142] Architrave means 'chief beam'.

very truth by reason of the straitness, and shape is most butyfull, by rendring all more polite and fancifull, as the ingenious and ignorant together have bin pleased to vary the methods in their different ways.

That which I had in my thoughts during the insertion of a few of the last lines to reflect upon, is that which wee call a strait arch, much used in Regular building, and absolutely necessary, because the entableture must be strait, but is the great defect of Regular building, especially in great proportions, wherein, by reason that vast materialls cannot be had, and then scarce manageable and at last the weight overcome⟨s⟩ its owne strength, it is almost impracticable. Therefore architects fall into those mean shifts of breaking the orders or heiths into two or more, whereas in no height ought there to be above one columne. And then also they break the entableture, to rest it upon the wall, because they cannot secure it streight. And yet after all these devices they are forc't to cramp all with lead and iron, so that such works are not so much masonry, as blacksmiths work, and not courses of stone but frames of iron. In short such is the mortality of a flat arch, that I have seen few of any considerable width but have gaped, and for the most part failed. The best in the world I beleeve will be in Pauls, especially over the doors of the north and south iles, in which I very well know, what iron and lead, besides the vast work of perforating the stones, hath bin imployed to the fixing of them.[143]

Yet after all I must needs allow that the flatt arch is the most beautyfull part of Regular building and cannot but lament the imperfection of it, that as it is derived from the strait lying of wood, which is corruptible, it is not as easily effected in all demensions, in the most durable stone.

It is manifest that all the members of the order, (I mean the great and not the minute,) are derived from wood building; for, besides the particulars spoke of, the metops and triglifs in the Dorick order seeme to convince in this, that they are the ends of the joyce in freese which are cut and shap't into long strokes downewards and beast's heads and so might have bin into any other shapes, if the humour at first had so hapned. It is a rule that those members must be equidistant, and so

---

[143] A reference to the secret arches employed by Wren at St. Paul's Cathedral to carry classical lintels and architraves across openings too wide for a single stone beam. By 'the north and south iles' he means the north and south transepts. A drawing reproduced in *Wren Society*, iii, Pl. xi, shows one of the secret arches in the entablature of the south transept portico, and the 'chaines, cramps, lewises & trussing barrs' by means of which the architrave was suspended from such arches are mentioned in the building accounts (*Wren Society*, xiv. 36).

much as the height, to leave a perfect square between triglif and triglif, which is certeinly the most naturall and obvious disposition for beauty in the ends of the joyce.

Now I have mentioned the Dorick, it will be fit to observe, that the sacrifices were the occasion of adorning freezes with dead heads, for the orders were used cheifly about their temples, (house⟨s⟩ in ancient ages of all countrys were litle regarded,) where perhaps were strew'd many bones and remaines of their sanguinary, or rather gulous,[144] worship, which they pick't up, and hung upon a border round the temple (then of wood) for a shew. Nothing more naturall to a plaine people, besides the ostentation of it, that they spent more meat than their neighbours.

No wonder that the aping stone cutters followed the humour, and this adorning the frees with the representations of what the building was used for was so comon that there are ruines this day that shew the whole order of the sacrifice, and the very tools used by the butcherly priests are hung up, which is but an improvement of the actuall affixing those things upon their wooden temples when the roof was scarce out of their reach. These humours, when past and mended thro many ages, have got an authority safe to follow, when it is not safe to invent.

[144] Gluttonous.

III

On planning a country house

BL MS, fos. 46ᵛ–68ᵛ

Now to come to what is stationary and unalterable, in the art of building, for the judging the disposition of rooms, (for what regards the fashion and humour of living perpetually mutable, has bin treated). I must propose another distinction; and that is by the country and scituation. And as introductory to this I may consider first generall rules, that square with all places, then the clime, and particularly that of England, where wee must live, and breath, till wee surrender all our living concernes, to succeeding ages, who are to censure us, as wee our ancestors.

And 1. it is an inviolable rule, to raise the first floor, and vault the foundation-room, for cellar and stores, that will endure moist lodging; for this is wholsome for the inhabitants, being as it were a draine to the whole.

2. To have the *entrata* in the midle, because that position serves the whole better than if it be at one end, which must steal much room for entrys. And it is also uniforme without. But this must not be the common passage for all things, in regard your freinds and persons of esteem should pass without being annoyed with the sight of foull persons, and things, which must and will be moving in some part of a large and well inhabited dwelling. Therefore, for such occasions there must be a back-entrata. And as you lay your principall entry so as most conveniently may serve the enterteining part of your house, the back way must be lay'd to serve your offices, and be out of the sight of the other. I know that which wee call a back door, is not convenient for good economy, because many escapes will fall by that vent undiscovered by the master. But in the disposition of greatness, the master is supposed to act in such small cares by servants, and not himself; as a prince, tho the fountaine of justice, doth not himself often sitt in judgment. I shall not forgett a relation I heard the Duke of Beaufort make of the advice his country-man, the Chief Justice Hales, gave him when he was building at Badmanton, to have but one door to his house, and that in the ey of his ordinary dining room, or study where he past his

time.[145] This shews how all men measure things by their owne education and circumstances, and expect others should governe their actions accordingly, tho farr from the like engagements, and what morosity this breeds in the elder, nay the wisest old men.

3. The like is to be sayd of stayres. For the cheif must not be annoyed with disagreeable objects, but be releived of them by a back-inferior staircase. And the principall must fall in your ey at your first entry, to any place of repose in the house, that there may be no occasion of asking which is the way up staires, but those to be as conspicuous and inviting as is possible. And because stayres at best are but an expedient to a defect, because the perfection of room is by laying all upon one and the same floor, they should be made as easy, delightfull, and inviting as is possible; or in short, as deceiving as may be, to perswade there is no such inconvenience as staires, by bribing and enterteining all the sences with better objects.

4. I should before have spoke of the avenew, which is now much sought, to be embellish't, and contrived, for setting off the view of an house to the most advantage. I shall at present onely touch that which concernes the house itself immediately, and leave the more distant disposition to a properer place.

Now to speak a litle in generall about the conduct of a new designe for a dwelling either of the topp or midle quality, I have these remarks to propose, which point out to the most considerable faults ordinarly found in new designes, and the means to correct them.

It is the use now, to carry all storys thro in the same levell between floor and ceiling. So was Clarendon house, Sir Jacob Ashley, lord Allington's,[146] and many, I might say most, of the new and more elegant fabricks of this latter age. The consequence is thatt all rooms in the same story, are equally high pitch't; the inconvenience is, that if you have any great rooms with fitt height your lesser rooms are all like steeples. And this fault is not helped by the comon way of covering the ceilings and lowering the cornish of the wainscote; for either room must be lost by a double ceiling or the rooms will be too high. On the other side, if you make the pitch to accomodate the comon or square rooms, your oblong and larger rooms will be low to an offence, as is apparent at Sir Jacob

---

[145] Sir Matthew Hale (1609–76), Chief Justice of the King's Bench. For Badminton, see above, p. 77.

[146] For these houses, see above, pp. 9, 40, 61.

Ashley's; and that was the reason that Clarendon house could not have a great room.

Many have thought to cure this fault, by laying two storys into one, as is done at Mr Guy's house, at Tring, built by Sir Christopher Wren;[147] by which means an high hall is made, with 6 lights at the end, in an upper and lower range, having a balcon† corridor from side to side upon the level of the chamber floors. The faults here are, the lights are too staring, because there are 2 rows, and there is very litle peer between them; and the room is very much too high for the width, and that hurts the other rooms and is no great beauty of it self. The lord Alington's house in Cambridgshire hath cured this deffect better, for the hall is in the midle and, as I remember, lighted from the sky, and balconed round, with 4 compleat apartments at the corners; but as I remember, it is somewhat dark.

Another fault is when principall, or rooms of parade, are made over one and other, which cannot be well. Nor is it convenient to goe up stairs for the parade, but to have it upon your first landing, because it is most easy an⟨d⟩ grateffull in the access. And then if any thing considerable be above, it is such a climing proposition to goe to it by reason of the height, that it is scarce civil to ask any to walk up. So that there is no true adjustment of this matter, but to sett all the grandeur of the house on the first floor, and leave the rest to servile, and inferior occasions. And thus is Sir Robert Daver's house at Rougham in Suffolk contrived; and also the lord Jeffress house neer Uxbridge, [148] but the fault I mentioned follows all of them: the great rooms are too low, and the small ones too high, and will follow all designes that are restrained to thro storys in the same levell, which I propose to artists to be amended by some other way of proceeding.

And that, in my conceit, may be done by composing a fabrick of different orders, whereof the larger shall be dedicated to parade and the lesser to comon, family use. And I make no question, but this may be done; I have attempted some designes towards it,[149] which if I have leisure

†*This word ends illegibly.*

---

[147]For Tring, see above, p. 62.

[148]Rougham Hall, Suffolk, built by Sir Robert Davers, Bt., *c.* 1684–8, was rebuilt about 1818, and no record of its appearance is known. Bulstrode Park, Bucks., was acquired by George Jeffreys, James II's notorious Chief Justice, in about 1676 and remodelled by him. There is an engraving in Rocque and Badeslade, *Vitruvius Brittanicus*, iv (1739). Jeffreys was created a Baron in 1685.

[149]For North's surviving drawings, which include several designs for houses, see pp. 153–5.

to exemplifie the draughts, I may represent, to shew the feasibility of the project; but it is in vaine otherwise to pretend to demonstrate any thing of this nature. And it is obvious how this way all occasions of any family may be supplyd without loss of room.

Now as to the decorum of roomes, one would inquire, what is the sourse of beauty in them. Wee are very apt to pronounce, as wee fancy, and say too great, too litle, too high, too low, too wide, too narrow and the like, and litle consider from what principle wee draw that sentence. Therefore in the consideration of this, I must introduce the same measures, as arbiters of all decorum within as well as without, vizt, reason, and usefullness. For it is hard to say that any proportion is naturally beautyfull, because all are allow'd of in fitt circumstances; as great height, in a hall is a beauty, or (which is the greatest affectation of height) domes in churches which rise above the fabrick into a cuppolo, as if there were to be no end of aspiring. But a room or closet so high is offensive, and appears most like a sollar in a steeple. In like manner any length in a gallery, is beautyfull, which in a chamber is deformed. Therefore the judgment of proportion must be regulated by the principles I mention'd, and for that end I am coming to note a few particulars. But first it is to be observed, that this sort of beauty is mutable, and not universall alltogether, for the severall ways that men affect to live doe much alter the propositions wee have to regard; and in this respect fashion is not a meer caprice of fancy, but a solid reason, which oblidgeth all dispositions in a habitation to conforme. And therefore beauty is not onely relative to the severall conditions of men, but also to the severall modes of living which different ages and countrys affect. As for instance in the ancient or Gothick times it was the mode for numerous familys to eat in the same room at severall tables and have few waiters; the butler for serving the master's table, and the porter the others (for the gates were all closed at that time) was sufficient. And this was not onely the use of England, and other nations the Greeks and Romans called barbarous, but by Homer* wee may observe the like method in the Grecian countrys. And the Romans use to eat in the porticos next the streets, shewing to the people (whom ambitious warrs kept poor enough) that their senators were content with a spare dyet. But that way of a comon eating room made great halls open to the roof, with a lanthorne, to lett out smoak and stench, a laudable fashion, and consequently an indication of great dignity and plenty, and excuseth the

*Odiss' (i.e. Odyssey): *North's marginal note.*

unclenlyness of it; but at present the way of the world is chang'd, and the eating is devided, many servants wait, and take their repast after the master, who is served at a table in a room layd out for that porpose. Therefore those wide halls are layd aside, and in the room of them comes the *grand salle*, which is a place to entertein persons coming to the house, and therefore ought to be well adorned, and neat. For the affectation of cleanness hath introduc't much variety of rooms, which the ancients had no occasion for, who cared not for exquisite neatness. And for the same reason wee at the entrance of an house have a moderate sized room, which the French (from the Latin) call a *vestibule*, supposed usefull for strangers to adjust their habits in, before they entered the *grand sall*, in forme. The ancients had a porch too, but that was more to weather the door, and cover waiters, and beggars, from weather when the door was shutt, than for the reason I produc't. And a man who had such an hall as this, with a bell to call the family to dinner, was a thane or lord.[150] And a room to withdraw into, was a finess taken from the Continent, as wee take up French and Italian fashions; and this I conceive was a Norman addittion, because of the name *parloir*, or a place to discourse in. And this custome wee have caracterised to us by the usage in colledges at this day; for it is a notorious thing that formall men retein and not invent fashions. As for instance gownes were the comon habits of gentlemen, as wee see by pictures, and these not very ancient; and when began to be layd aside, the graver and elder men reteined them somewhat longer, and at length rested with magistrates, and are become not onely a garb, but an ensigne of profession and authority. So that way of eating in society in colledges, was the common mode of great familys, and reteined there.

Thus a great hall, and a great kitchen, and afterwards a parlour, was the establisht grandure of the English gentry. And for convenience, a chamber over the kitchen, and another over the parlor, were large accomodations; for servants used truckle bedds, or out houses to lodge in. From this ordonnance the mode grew up, and, by the wars and intestine troubles that followed about the time of the baron's warrs, was disposed for strength as well as somewhat more of ornament and accomodation, but altogether castle fashion. And a house was not esteemed great, without a tower at the gate, and a moat, defence enough against any sudden assault. And this held out till neer the Scotch union.

---

[150]North may have been familiar with the eleventh-century text, printed by Lambarde in 1576 and by Spelman in his *Glossarium*, 1664, in which the possession of a 'bell-house' is one of the attributes of thegnly status (Stubbs, *Select Charters*, ed. Davis, 1929, p. 88).

For wee see most ancient seats to be batlemented, towred, and moated. The statlyest tower I have seen is at Oxbro in Norfolk, built by the ancestor of Sir H. Beddingfeild, when lieutenant of the Tower in the time of Queen Mary.[151] And that at the lord North's seat at Kirtling, was of elder time, but not much, and a very strong fabrick, vaulted underneath as for a prison; wherein is an admirable compass windoe upon the front projected from the wall in 2 storys over the gate.[152] This was to shew a great pensile load, to make the ignorant wonder, as the mode of those times were. After the Scotch union, when pease was establish't, and not before, did building in England come to be reformed, after the Italian and French examples, but more especially the former, as the best, most studdyed, and free from Gothick excursions. But the humor then being much after jollity, and dauncing, the gentry affected to have one great room (as I observed all windoe), which they called a dining room, and so severall chambers for company, but independant rooms without subservient accomodations, and back staires, which now are become essentiall.

And in this matter, I must differ from the comon practise in England, which is to keep company from the fore-court, and decking it like a garden, using the same curiosity of planting, mowing, weeding, rolling, as if there were to be no other. And for this reason it is kept close shutt, least doggs, horses, &c. happen to come in and contaminate the neatness of it; so that a stranger who is to come to the house, seeing the front, which is a notorious direction to the entry, goes on but finds all close, and then is to seek and must enquire which is the way in to that house. I doe not see what greater absurdity can be contrived, and neatness it self, however amiable, doth not justifie it. And it is much better not to carry neatness beyond the nature and condition of the place, than to loose the use of the best avenue. And to say truth, neatness is good, but that, as all other ingredients of a fair dwelling, is relative to the condition of the places. No one would be so neat in his stable yard as he is in his flower garden, and yet there is a sort of neatness proper to thatt also. The forecourt is of a midle nature, which calls for an higher pitch of neatness than a stable yard, and yet not such as you afford your garden. Therefore in my judgment it is fitt the forecourt should be so layd out as to endure comon using, according to the intent of it. And if it happens to

---

[151]For Oxburgh Hall, Norfolk, see Garner and Stratton, *Domestic Architecture in England during the Tudor Period* (1929).
[152]For Kirtling see above, p. 54.

be fouled or disordered, it is well worth the care to clean continually, and returne it to that reasonable decorum it is capable of. And many times, the seeing a place used, and yet clean, and in order, is more agreeable than when it is altogether lock't up, and, tho made for use, sequestred to be of no use, but to ly exquisitely neat. For that hath too much of affectation, the other is naturall. And it is a thing of course, which prevailes as a law to the whole world, that works are done and returne. Even the garden will be so, from the variety of seasons, which sometimes bring foullness, and againe flowers. Then why should we grutch comon paines upon our access to the house, for the direction and ease of strangers, in keeping the decorum by frequent restoring it, which is reasonable and expected, consistent with the true use of it.

But now having spoke of the access to a mansion house, it may not be amiss to touch the other parts of that subject. And first I would not have it understood that I mean (as in that jocular story of Hales)[153] that the house should have but one access, or entry, and that the cheif. For as in all animalls there is a mouth, and a vent, so a house ought to have a back entrance, as well for the comon servile part of the family, and buissness to make constant use of, as also for the master (who I doe not suppose to be above economy) at ordinary times to pass at, whereby the dilligence and performances of his servants will fall under his eye, and also he can transact with them, and other mean persons, without concerning his guest, or anoying the principall, and enterteining part of his house. Therefore this back entrance should not be like that of a vault, hollow and dark, altogether unpleasant, as I have seen some, but somewhat cheerfull, and aiery, which the best of family at private times may with comfort make use of. And I would have it made with these conveniences: first that it be neer to the kitchens, private parler, and back stayres, as comodiously posted respecting all these as may be; but the plainest direction to be to the eating parlour, so that persons coming in that way may be soon clear of the moving inferioritys of your family, if they please.

2. I would have it so that a coach may come close up to it, that persons may light, and take coach perfectly dry; because it may be thought convenient to fence out some part before the cheif entrance, for a sort of state, as often is done; then upon great raine, this back convenience serves for an expedient.

---

[153]See above, p. 122.

3. That there be an easy comunication between the forecourt, and the back entrance, that persons may goe from one to the other as they thinck fitt, and that coaches and carts also may pass from one to the other; for I am not against using the forecourt for comon passage of servants, but on the one side onely, and not in the principall walk. It is no unseemly object to an English gentleman (for such I propose) to see his servants and buissness passing at ordinary times.

But now to returne where wee parted, at the staires, which was proposed to fall in the stranger's eye, as soon as he hath leisure to look about him, that is upon his entrance into the *grand sall*, or as wee English use to terme it, the hall. If the house be of very great state, the vestibule is the first place within the door, which is not to be large, nor curious, but plaine, and neat; and the ornaments most proper to it are niches, and statues. In Mr. Guy's house at Tring,[154] the hall being at one end of the midle range, for the house hath 3, the vestibule was that part of the front range, that lay betwixt the door and the midle, or hall. And at first the ascent was all without, with a broad paved landing before the cheif door. But by I know not what critiscisme, that was not thought convenient. Perhaps courtiers could not venture to mount so high in wett weather. However it was, at length those staires were disbanded, and the poor vestibule, which I thought the cheif ornament to the avenew, was condemned to a stair raised all within the door, which was neither proper nor beautyfull in my eye.

This vestibule is no other than a porch, but with this advantage, that a porch, being without, is not shutt up, but left exposed to all the uncleaness which beggars, doggs &c. may leave there. Therefore if there be such a thing, it is not amiss to take it within the fabrick, rather than hold it without, unless it be very well sett off with colomne, or pilaster work, after the Italian manner, than which nothing is more stately.

And this leads me to speak of those portico rooms, which the Italians call the *loggia*, and are with them seldome omitted. The Queen's house at Greenwich hath one, and Serjeant Maynard's house at Gonnersbury by Braintford another.[155] And I cannot but grant, it is most agreable to view, and, at many times of the year, use; but withall I must hold that it is not generally recomendable to us, because the same reasons doe not hold here, as in Italy, the climats being so vastly different with respect to weather. There it is of use to fend the sun from their cheif rooms and to

---

[154]See above, p. 62.   [155]See above, p. 62.

darken them in some measure. And the raines, and snows are not so furious, frequent, and driving as here; nor is the heat so furious. But wee have walks abroad, in ordinary shades, which serve our turne. And here wee cannot endure a canopy over our windoes to robb the light as the loggia doth. Wittness Serjeant Mainard's house, where the cheif room is most unpleasant, because it hath no light but from that covered walk. But if it can be so contrived in some recess, for it cannot be in the front, that it shall respect the south, and not trench any considerable light, but be weather-tight, it is convenient enough with us. Yet considering our frequent raines, windes, &c., all will agree a close gallery to answer the use of walking better than that, and here doubdtless it is so in all respects but that of pomp and state.

I am a great freind to portico walks abroad, and should recomend them more earnestly, did not the charge avert the designe from the condition of an English gentleman, which I treat; I must confess it is of use to every individuall person of the family, who hath a title to pass time in a degree of idleness. And therefore great familys, who for parade maintein many such, ought to provide such *promenoirs* for them, that they may be so well diverted at home, as not to seek their pastime abroad, and so add debauchery to idleness. And I know no place so calculated for this end as Audely-End,[156] which hath (as I remember) 2 courts portico'd round. And it is a reasonable ambition, in a less model than that, to propose somewhat of like nature, but I would not have it connected to the house, so as to hurt the lights of any considerable part, but rather advise it may be by way of pent-house, or appendix to the walls of the forecourt, with tollerably decent supports, columne- or pilaster-wise, which I thinck may be done, and covered with gutter tile,[157] without any excessive charge, and be an extraordinary convenience to a dwelling. Because the master and his family and freinds may walk, and air in all seasons and weather and less† very furious indeed; who else must keep to their walls, and be content to turne in the most capacious rooms, which is les pleasant and less conducing to health, than the other more aiery promenade abroad.

Now at length to consider the lower rooms within. After the hall or grand sall, there is no more expected than a great parlor, withdrawing

†Unless.

---

[156]See above, p. 63.
[157]A gutter-tile is a tile with one end turned up to form a trough.

room, closet and back passage. The greatest as well as the least demands thus much, and few affect more. The common dining parlor is usually at the other end of the house, which is dedicated to the service of the family. For I sayd all entrances should be in the midle to be indifferently subservient to the whole. One way from the entrance is what I have mentioned, the other apperteins to the family. And if both could be so composed that the withdrawing room, and closets should be equally serving the private as the great parlor, it would be an usefull compendium and worthy a private person's contrivance who would make a good appearance for a moderate charge.

It is usuall in great and noble appartments, to have an ordonnance beyond the withdrawing room, which is a state bedchamber, and inner rooms suitable to it. And in that case it is very proper, as also for the master, to have his appartment and conveniences neer his eating room. But in the case of a private gentleman I should rather have him propose to imploy his upper rooms to that use, unless his designe be to bring all the best room of the house upon one and the same floor.

Now for the art of composing a fabrick for these, or any worthy porposes, so as to maintaine order, and accomodation within and state and uniformity without, with a generall decorum of the whole, avoiding all manner of defects, and impropper excesses, wee must referr to the practice of the skillfull, it not being my porpose here to present modells but to make generall observations. Onely I would recomend one thing, which is to err rather on the side of plenty, than straitness of room. The latter is often, but the other seldome reported of. Wee know not our occasions till wee come to use, and then it's too late. Wee are, in designing, apt to regard most the principall things, and to goe on refining them, without consideration of the many litle things, which will be called for, in the use of a dwelling, and then wee are inclined to make additions, to supply defects, which is patching and never look⟨s⟩ well. So lay out at first room enough, and then, after that main designe is under execution, and perhaps covered, you have continuall liberty of disposing your room according to the occasion or humour of your self and family.

But to proceed, wee have done below-staires, for if the first floor be not the whole, as in some designes as I hinted, wee must reserve a great part of the cheif rooms for the 2nd floor, wherein the grand difficulty ly's in composing the fabrick so that you mount not too high, because it takes mightily off from the beauty, to endure a fatigue in the access. Mr.

Windham's house at Fellbrigg in Norfolk[158] hath this fault; for a new apartment is layd to the old, so as the upper floor might range with that over the hall, which is 16 or 18 foot. And their stair case, however pompous and costly in the frame and finishing, doth not stupifie the sence, so as to make the paines of mounting 3 or 4 stretching flights insensible. Therefore it is incident to an apartment of state above, that the ascent be easy, else the state is lost, and it were better never to seek it there at the cost of many stepps.

But being once mounted, I thinck the *ordonnance* requires the entry to be fair from the staires into an antiroom capable of being adorned and made very diverting. Then 2 apartments from that, either way, ranging in a line, so as the doors make one *visto* from end to end, is the perfection which one would desire, and, if understood, easily obteined, because it fitts the humor of a front, whereof the midle windoes may serve the anti room, and on either side the chambers. The antiroom is fitt for many uses, and need not have a chimny, because it is for passage, short attendance, or diversion. Musick is very proper in it. And it is scarce knowne what a life it gives to the upper part of an house, when it is conveniently layd out, and adorned. It must not be large, for that kills the rest of your rooms, and makes them seem less. The plan of the ceiling may be the same height as the rest and for ornament a shell or volt may be raised upon it, to be painted or adorned with art, than which nothing of ornament is more pleasing. And for the occasion of subservient rooms for convenience for the chambers, this antiroom may not take the whole bredth from the staires, but part be layd into a passage, which, if the contrivance be open and lofty, rather setts off than hurts the entry, and serves to contract the antiroom into what compass you shall thinck fitt.

The chambers are next to be considered, which, being layd out for good beds, and lodging the best quality, should be as perfect as is possible to be contrived. And this may be had, observing these rules: 1. that the chimny fall in the midle of the side opposite to the door of first entrance, that the decoration of it may instantly take the eye, and the finishing on either side, whether wainscote, painting, or portraits, may admitt an uniforme disposition, which is an elegance scarce otherwise to be had. And observe once for all, that where things are single, there is no way to dispose them ornamentally but by middling them, with pairs plac't on either side as they may be well ordered, to make a pleasing

---

[158] See above, p. 57 n. 69.

figure. Then, 2. the side where the bed is to stand, must be opposite to the windoes, to the end the air of them may not offend. And the room should be of that depth, that the feet of the bedd should not come so foreward in the room, as to cover the chimny jamb, but that must stand clear and free to be view'd.

It may not be amiss here to speak of an alcove, which some affect in bedchambers, which is an agreeable view, but in my opinion not so convenient, nor desirable as a fair room, with a bedd well plac't, unless it be where a room is of a deforme length, and in that respect unfitt for a bedchamber; then I confess an alcove to take off that undue length doth well. The faults I find with it are, that it darkens the bedd, and looseth much of the beauty of it. And if a room be large, it seems too much aired and colder, than when a bed stands in it. And lastly I have bin informed that an alcove is extream cold of it self, because there must be, or usually there is, litle back avenews to and from it within, which keep it very cold, however it is out of the sight and air of any fire.

Then for the windoes, I would never have more nor less than 2 with a peer in the midle for a glass, and 2 peers on each side the windoes equall, so as the light and dark may be uniforme. This is seldome regarded, but I thinck it very materiall to the beauty of a room, and cannot but reluct when I see a windoe nearer the coigne on one side, than on the other, and sometimes almost close to it, which to me is a meer shift and deformity. I know it is the flattery of a fair outside which makes men say *con-licentia* on this point to their rooms within, it being not easy in a regular work to compose all the parts within and without in true uniformity. But still that is a defect, and the less of it the better, and when none, best of all; which an artist should fly at, and never be satisfied till he finds it.

As for doors, lett this rule be observed in the placing of them, not to lett a strait course from either one to another, or the chimny, ly thro the bedd, but lett the air that comes into the room, which is apt to find a way to the chimny, shoot clear of the bedd, and so there is more security of warmth and consequently health to them that lodge there. A bedchamber cannot well be without 4 doors, for serving the accomodations I am about to mention, and those I would place thus: 2 on each side next the windoes, and the other 2 on the same side with the bedd's head; and so this point is gained as much as may be done.

Now for the conveniences to a bedchamber. I doe not know that building hath received a greater improvement in any respect than this. Not long since it was thought enough, if a fair room for a bed were carved out, tho lighted round, and but one door for all things to enter, and issue at; and scarce a dark hole for an easment, or disposition of the less clean and sightly utensils belonging to the persons of them that are to lodge there. But now ease and convenience is made the rule; wee demand these accomodations: first a passage to a back stair, for the servants in their comon offices to pass by; next, a room for a servant to be within call, and lastly for a closet, where the person, who is supposed of quality, to retire for devotion, or study, whilst the chamber is cleaned, or company present.

These are necessary, and indispensable; and the placing an easment is at liberty to be done any where, as the places shall happen to invite, with least annoyance to the best room. But in more state and plenty, one would add to this a dressing room, nay more, one for a man, and another for a woman, with chambers for the servant of each to lodge to be within call; so that at rising each may retire apart, and have severall accomodations compleat. This I say is the perfection that one would expect in the seat of a prince or nobleman, but is too much for a private gentleman, who seldome enterteines guests of that nicety. And it is enough if this convenience with him be single, and that is required; but, if latitude of room will permitt, he is at liberty to enlarge towards more of that sort of convenience as he shall see fitt. And I may propose it as a compendium, that if there be room of an inferiour order, fitt for these occasions, that the rooms for common persons be layd so that, upon occasion they may be used as inner rooms to your great appartments; for there must be small as well as great, and thus the former are an accomplishment to the other, if the use calls for it.

Now to place the doors, to serve these accomodations, I will touch the use of each of them: the first is the entrance; that opposite, a passage to the cheif room of some other appartment; then on one side of the bedd may be a passage to the back stairs, and servant's room, with the easment, and on the other side of the bedd to the closet and dressing room. And if the conveniences be male and female, one door serves one, and the other the other.

But of late, whether from the straitness of appartments at court, or of London houses, I know not, the mode hath indulged the retrenching the dressing room, or rather delegated it to the use of the man, who most needs it, because of the roughness of his service and dressing, and the lady keeps the possession of the bedchamber, and is served with a litle table brought in, with her glass and toilett, and doth not affect a different room for dressing, as formerly. It may be, the ladys, who love to have all their finery about them, and nothing of that kind runs higher than the furniture of a bedchamber, are pleased to pass their time more in the injoyment of it by receiving company there, as well drest as dressing.

Then for the lights of these rooms and passages, there is more liberty, and any disposition is tollerable, because not on the cour of parade, and seen by servants or as belonging to such. But yet an artist will gaine much upon a clumsy builder in making the best of things, and will find out expedients and accomodate for convenience beyond the imagination of those that are unacquainted with the joys a happy builder knows.

Now I have done with the cheiff appartments usually required as necessary to gentile living in England. That is the hall, great parlor[s] with its appendices, staires, antiroom, and bedchambers, and their subservients. All the rest of the house is family convenience, wherein an artist may help to contrive, by suggesting, and assisting to the invention and applycation of the master, but the judgment lys upon him, who knows his owne occasions, and therefore, if not very dull, must be the best architect, as to what he is to use personally himself. My good freind Mr. Hugh May,[159] who reformed Windsor, used to say, that in every house there was to be one appartment of state, wherein all perfection, and the rest was but convenience, which every man must contrive for himself. However I shall touch even those inferior ordinances of an house, for wee seldome meet with that elegance in the disposition of them as might have bin if artificially treated. But first I shall discourse somewhat of that noble accomplishment to an house, a gallery.

This is a room, for no other use but pastime and health, so farr as the gentle moving usuall within the walls of an house may concerne it. And in generall it is to have these propertys: 1. that it be easy of access, and for that reason should be upon the first floor; but there is so much occasion for room, that it cannot be spared so liberally to afford a gallery, unless it be by way of covered walk as I noted before. But higher than the next floor it must not be, for such as are in garretts, as I have often seen, are useless, because none will purchase the use of them with the paines of mounting. And for the same reason, promenades on the topps of houses are useless, and cuppolo closetts, and the like, because it is irksome even to thinck of climing so high.

Then, 2. it is to be considered whether the gallery be taken into the

---

[159]Hugh May (1621–84), Comptroller of the Royal Works. May and North had been fellow executors of the will of Sir Peter Lely (d. 1680).

parade of the house, or be kept for the private divertion of the master and to be seen as such, and not as a capitall room. If the former, as is to be desired if the model will contein it, then it must be layd in the most joyous, and diverting part of the house without any offence to the ey or otherwise from any services about the house; but all fronting the garden, and viewing it in the best place. For this place, intended to entertein and divert the best company, cannot be too much composed to that designe. And therefore the finishing should be accordingly, either carv'd, painted, or sett off with pictures. 3. And I thinck it is a great complement to a gallery to have some breaks, in the nature of bow-windoes, not such as are Gothick, and used in old houses, but squares setting out one large in the midle, and the others at each end some what less. And if great curtaines are hung in the strait range, and drawne up with great bobbs, it hath a strange aspect of grandure. But these recesses are for select companys to converse in, and vary the prospect by side lights, being as small withdrawing rooms to the grand tour of the gallery. But this supposeth the state of a prince, whereof I know but one compleat example, and that is Audley-Inn. At Cyrencester there is one, which next to the other is the best I have seen.[160] At Beavoir Castle there is one, but not so stately, with respect to the greatness of the pyle.[161] But Audley Inn-gallery is in all respects as one would have it, unless it may want those recesses, which I doe not remember. But I cannot but reiterate the recomendation of them, because they doe not onely accomplish the gallery within, but are a beauty without, being projected according to art, and with all convenience below and above, for many porposes, not so consistent with a dead flatt range.

If the proposition of a gallery be onely for the convenience of the master, then less regard is to be had to these decorums, for as the other is to ly next his cheif appartments, and be accessible with ease from them, this is to have the like regard to his private family appartments, and to be detach't from the others, and not apperteining to them. And also, it need not be so carefully removed from the domestick offices, but ⟨if it⟩ be plac't so as that the master may in his promenade there see to the acting of his servants, it is by so much the better. And as in the other case, it must be pompous and large to answer the grandur⟨e⟩ of the apartments to which it belongs, else it is a trifle, and a disgrace rather than a beauty.

[160]For an engraving of Cirencester House before it was rebuilt in the eighteenth century see Kip, *Britannia Illustrata*, ii (1716).
[161]Belvoir Castle, Leicestershire.

Here it need not be so great, but as holding due proportion to the appartments to which it is layd, and the use it is intended for.

These are the extreams of these two porposes, regarding the 2 very different states of mankind, a prince or great potentate, and a private economist. But as the state of a gentleman, or at least his company, may be of a midle condition, or he desires by his enterteinement to raise them above their order, which is allwais pleasing, I should propose a gallery of a midle sort, not wholly dedicated to parade, nor to private use, but such as may serve reasonably to both porposes, and not pretend to the height of grandure, as usually is expected. And I doe not know any superfluity in an house more desirable than this, for it pleaseth all, and is usefull to all, and being tollerable scituated serves as well as the best, few minding nice matters. And therefore this should be placed with indifference so as to serve both the ordinary, and reserved appartments of the house. And a sort of moderation may be allow'd as to the decoration, and position of it, with respect to the offices of the family, being supposed for the use of the master and his family, and his indulgent freinds onely, and not for proud and ambitious enterteinements of grandure.

But now to come downe staires, (tho the back way,) to view the state of the family apartments below; I find 3 ordonnances: 1. the master's comon parlor; 2. the servants' ordinary eating room, and place of attendance; 3. the kitchen and the appendices. As for the cellars, wee must suppose them to be provided for either under the first floor, as supposing it raised, or else by sinking downe vaults in proper places, of which I shall discourse afterwards.

1. For the comon parlor, this for economy sake must be layd neer the offices, and back entrance, but yet I would not have it ly remote from the hall, or downe staires, or to be come at thro windings and turnings, as I have seen many, but to have an immediate door from the hall, for the principall entrance, and a back way to the comon servants' passage door, and also another door, that leads partly clear of both towards the back staires. For if wee consult convenience, wee must have severall avenews, and bolting holes, for such as are in the family and undrest, or for any other reason, to decline passing by company posted about by accident. This doth not seem to be of any great moment, but in the course of living will be found wanting, and be much desired. For it is unpleasant to be forc't to cross people, when one has not a mind to it, either for avoiding ceremony or any other reason.

This room must not be great, but neat and pleasant, and posted so as to view the front and back avenew to the house; for, being the place of generall pastime, it is not amiss from it to see all the movements that happen neer the house. And if the walls can be brought to allow it, nothing is more usefull here than closets, cupboards, and presses, for the laying by books, swords, cloaks, and other things, which may be of quotidian use and should to avoid lumbring the room have places to lay them b[u]y in.

2. As for servants, I know it is usuall to clutter them all into a kitchen, partly to save fire, and partly for want of room; but that is not consistent with good economy, because not onely the waste of meat and drink from the petulance of idle fellows who will be spunging, but also it hinders the passage and management of the servants assigned to the kitchen imployments; and I have had complaints, that they could not pass for the fullness of people, which will happen, when all come together, and perhapps many labourers, and hang-bys besides. Therefore I thinck it is a good imployment for a room, if onely to keep the servants from the kitchen, at unfitt times.

It remaines a question if this room should have a door from the kitchen or not. It is certeinly best to have it contiguous to the kitchen, but I would have a distinct door, but very neer to the kitchen door, for the convenience of passing and repassing of dishes. But by no means must it be contiguous to the parlor, for the noises will be insupportable, and yet it must not be farr removed, that the servants may be in awe; an entry betwixt is enough.

Here I have to propose one convenience, which, if it can be brought into the model, will pay for the room it takes up; and that is a small room of about 12 foot square just within the back-door, and from that passage to the hall, kitchen, and litle parlor. And out of this litle room or porch, I would have 2 closets one within the other, and a door from the parlor to the 2nd and perhaps both open into the porch-room.

My reasons for this are that it is not convenient to have all passage from the back door inwards; for, if any person comes within the door, and stays in expectation of any thing, there is no room to repose, till an answer comes, and it is troublesome passing to and againe by them. But such a litle room, may have a bench or forme or two, and be compleat for that porpose.

Then next, persons that come to treat with the master about any buissnes, to make payments, or accounts, to receive mony, or relate any thing that is not to be publik, he may take them into his closet and dispatch them, and till he comes, they may wait with convenience. Then the other closet I appropriate to the bailiff, steward, or accountant of the managery, where the books of entrys may be allwais open, and files of papers disposed, so as ready recourse is had to them. The master takes the bailif into his closet, or comes into the bailif's, without notice of the family, and conferrs about divers emergencys, sees to the continuall ord'ring the accounts and memorandums of buissness. There the bailiff (him I call the cheif accountant and manager) may have his cash-chest; and is to receive and pay all, his books being ready to make entrys; and take his customers in and dispatch them, without kitchening every fellow that comes to an house. All which is an extraordinary usefull ordonnance, and must needs make a man's domestick affairs both pleasing, and thriffty; and atho this fitts a very great managery, such as would imploy an account or clerk all the year, yet in less buissness it is not amiss, and will pay for a litle cheap room, such as that takes up, for any one who breaks the imployment of his time, as part to books, part to law concernes and part to accounts, and were these heads multiplyed, or made still more by subdevisions, as Accounts, 1. Domestick, 2. Trust, and the like, he will find a great use in dispersing them in-to severall stations in his house proper for them. I knew one who had a great trust for a minor peer upon him, to which belonged many books, papers and accounts, and he assigned one whole room of his house onely to the buissness of that trust, and sayd he had great ease by it; for he no sooner came into the room, but the traine of thoughts brought the proper buissness into his head. But if they had bin all blended with his other concernes, there had bin not onely a confusion without a carefull method of economising his materialls, but also an unsteddyness of thought, which the objects apperteining to different concernes brought into his mind. I confess that so few of our gentry thinck of buissness, that it's no wonder there is so litle invention and care taken to accomodate it, where most needfull, in the country, and consequently so many familys decay for want of it, but there wants no accomodation for their pleasures. Now I would have buissness a pleasure, and the fittness of its accomodation in an house declare, that the master thinck it so.

3. The last ordonnance below staires which is of necessity is that of the kitchen, to which belongs a scullery, pastry, wett larder, dry larder, and repository, which may be also a stillhouse, or closet for the houskeeper.

There is not much to be discours't upon these articles, because they may be disposed *ad libitum* to the content of the owner, who is the best architect of such rooms. Onely they must remember that largeness is good, and if space be any where throwne away, it should be here, for: first, the kitchen will be, in spight of order, the *rendezvous* of all the servants and such as have to doe with them; then for air, which will keep it sweet, as also cool; for much fire in a small room torments those that work in it, and such must be on every occasion of dressing large meat. And such coolness conduceth also to the health of your servants, for which reason a kitchen may be plact north or east, because the sun is not troublesome in that situation at the time of working in a kitchen. There is also much of repository, as for bright utensills and dryed flesh, which must hang where there is air and some fire, all which argue for room. The wett larder calls for a north scituation, air and room, than which nothing more conduceth to the keeping of unsalted flesh from corruption. Heat and wett, the latter especially, set corruption a going immediately, and gives life to the spawn of flys. And for this reason, if I might advise, the wett larder should be over the volt of the cellar, which would maintaine drought and coolness; for both must be north, and the vault would drein all moisture, which is apt to setle it self downeward. The pavement must be of pamant[162] or hard brick; wee seldome get stone hard enough which will not suck moisture, and that is ill, because it will in time contract a stench, and stink makes things corrupt strangely; even pictures will suffer and be spoiled with the extremity of it. Therefore ill sents are very much to be avoided in all places about a dwelling house, especially the conservatorys.

A scullery is necessary, and must be next to the kitchen; it is for disposing crocky utensills, and washing dishes, and plates, therefore must have a drein, and should be easily supply'd with water.

I have had a conceipt for serving a scullery with plenty of water, that may also be drawne off for many uses which require soft-water; and I intend to putt it in execution in my small dwelling. And it is in short the drawing all the rain water of the house into a cisterne over it. This cisterne must be of lead, 3 sides whereof shall be flatt to the wall, the other side at about 3 foot distance, fenc't with timber. The largeness of this cisterne shall keep the water sweet, especially if no sun comes att it, and if need be a water fann with a string may be made to keep it so by

---

[162] A term in common use in East Anglia for bricks specially made for paving. They were often half the thickness and double the width of ordinary bricks.

stirring it sometimes. And be the cisterne never so large raine will fill it, and each brewing or washing be served from it. This is gained by laying a floor of joysts about the midle of the scullery room, about 6 foot high. There needs no greater height for the movement of a servant in buissness, and heavy utensills are not raised so high. Then supposing the pitch to be 12 high which is the least one would allow a kitchen, there will be near 4 for the cisterne and 2 above it for a servant to goe in and clean it. From this may be conveyed pipes and cocks for all occasions proper to such water, and thus ease the servants in drawing, pumping or horse carriage of water, and imploy them to other services of advantage.

The pastry must be next the kitchen, and needs not be large. A boulter, kneading trough, meal-chest, and table, must be stowed in it; and it should ly so as there may be an oven, whose tunnell should be conveyed into the chimny-stack of the kitchen. And there may also be a small tunnell for the use of broyling. It is most usuall for the smell of meat to annoy dwelling houses, especially such as are compack't, as the mode now is. This hath made some make a kitchen in a detach't isolar fabrick connected by a corridor, as at Burlington, and Barkely houses in London. And at Mr Guy's house at Tring, it is sett out (being in the midle range, devided from the hall by the great staires) beyond the house a litle, to give it vent, and no rooms over it, but that wall reserved above the kitchen to light the great staires. Such paines are taken to avoid so great a nusance as this is. But I conceive it may also be avoided, by using large tunnells to give vent to the smoak of the kitchen, and to keep broyling under tunnells fitt for it. But if any rooms be above, they must be guarded either by arches, or a double ceiling of loam between, and lime and hair underneath the joyst⟨s.⟩

Lastly a drylarder is a very usefull office, and serves also for the houskeeper's repository of spice, and all manner of necessarys, consistent with the preservation of cold meats such as use to be stowed there. As for destilling, which is usefull in any family, I should advise that convenience may be made for it either in the kitchen, pastry or both. For so the houskeeper, whose ey should be abroad, is not withdrawne from her attendance, by waiting upon the stills, which must be continually look't after.

In the disposition of these offices, there is room for infinite thought to improve convenience, but wee attend so much the masterly rooms, that for the most part the offices are but meanly disposed.

IV

Criticism of modernized houses

BL MS, fos. 5ᵛ–6ᵛ.

Many, in the supplying defects in old houses, are very intent upon some one proposition, and oversee hundreds. They thinck to add a convenience or beauty in one place, which is the sooner done but that perhaps proves a deformity, or else discovers some greater than were before imagined. Old houses will vary from moderne in some particular or other, and purchasers or yong heirs, must needs be mending, and doing it without a full collation of the whole, and mature deliberation upon it, and then either they pull downe what was done, or somewhat else, and so continually, and never arrive at satisfaction. I heard of a lord,* who was not contented his hall should be low, and therefore raised the ceiling to a competent height, but then the parlor next to it was abominably low also, which was well before his hall was altered; and that made him pull downe all.[163]

But the greatest instance of this error is Euston in Suffolk, which was a nobleman's house with wings of single order.[164] This fell into a profuse courtier's hands, who must needs make the place fitt to entertein his master the King, to whom court was made by treats, and administring pleasure. But to be frugally profuse, he did not take downe the house, and build another with the aid of the old materialls, but would compass his designe by altering and vamping the old. This first produc't a *grand sale*, staircase, and royall apartment, in the cheif part of the house. The *sale* was brought into order by raising the ceiling floor, which lost the rooms over head. And the King's apartment was accomodated by volting the rooff into the garrett room, which was totally absorpt by it.

---

*Lord Mountague at Boughton: *North's marginal note*

[163]Ralph, Lord Montagu, created 1st Duke of Montagu in 1705, rebuilt Boughton House, Northants, *c.* 1685 onwards. Roger North was misinformed, for the lofty roof of the Tudor great hall remains above Montagu's plaster ceiling painted by Chéron (J. A. Gotch, *The Old Halls and Manor-Houses of Northants.*, 1936, p. 47).

[164]Euston Hall, Suffolk, was rebuilt by Henry Bennet, Earl of Arlington, *c.* 1667, remodelled in the 1750s, damaged by fire in 1902, and reduced in size in 1950. Illustrations of the original house, showing the pavilions referred to by North, will be found in *Architectural History*, vii (1964), Pls. 30–1 and in *Country Life*, 10 Jan. 1957, Figs. 3 and 6.

The order of windoes were litle more than square in this upper story, because the eves allow'd them not to rise higher, and consequently the upright of the wall within could not be high; the rest of the height was in volt, but sett off richly with cornishes and painting by Signor Vario.[165] Opposite to this apartment, cross the great staires, was a long gallery, of the same order, but not volted so high. Now the incurable disease of all this is the lowness of the cheif appartments, smallness of the windoes, and consequently darkness of the ceilings, as also of the rooms in generall; and all the decoration bestowed upon them, was but smoothing of wrinkles, or painting on a bad draught. Nothing could cure these defects; and insted of the more worship, there is more contempt for all the cost. So that it had bin much better to have bin contented with the plainess of the old designe, than to vamp it to no porpose.

And farther, in this example, to shew the vanity, of aiming at perfection, in a defective model; this lord once shewed an embassador his house, and coming downe by the avenew from the park, ask't him how he lik't his house. The embassador answered with a question, whether the wings (whose single-lighted ends pointed towards them) were not too narrow. No more was sayd, but immediately order was given to double them by clapping 4 pavilions at the four grand corners of the fabrick, of vast charge. Thus running on, adding and contriving for the receipt of the Court, the house is become a towne; and the grand defect is in the principall part, the royall appartment: one would expect in a house of that receipt and pretension, that there should be one appartment princely and magnifik, in the order of the house, but this is mean, and litle other than a garret well drest.

If this noble lord had intended at first the same end he drove at towards the latter end of his buissness, he had never let the old walls stand. *Immedicabile vulnus* &c.[166] At least he would have made his cheif apartments new and reserved the old fabrick for secondary and inferior uses.

fos. 26–28ᵛ

I touch't before upon Arlington house at Euston, as an example of an old house vamp't; and considering the charge, and pretension to greatness, it is the worst I ever saw. But no more of that. The next or rather the

---

[165]Antonio Verrio (*c*. 1639–1707).
[166]'An irremediable fault'.

cheif instance of this kind is Windsor, which is so well knowne as need not be described. The great fault there is the narrowness of the gardchamber, and first room layd out for the presence chamber, are too narrow; but antiquity, and its incorrigible walls must be accused for that, and not the architect, who in all that was in his power acquitted himself well. In some things he would have done better, but the King would not permitt, as pulling downe all the east side of the court next the park, which is patch't, repair'd bevil, lower floor'd, and very imperfect. [167]

An other repaired and reformed old house is Ham, upon Thames, done by the Duke and Duchess of Lauderdale, and is the best of the kind I have seen.[168] It was what vulgarly is called an H, but the wings not long, being rather pavilion fashion, the midle single, and the windoes large, as the use of the time was when built. This house is, in its time, esteemed one of the most beautyfull and compleat seats in the kingdome, and all ariseth out of the skill and dexterity in managing the alterations, which in my opinion are the best I have seen. For I doe not perceive any part of the old fabrick is taken downe, but the wings stand as they were first sett, onely behind next the garden they are joyned with a strait range intirely new. And there are all the rooms of parade, exquisitely plac'd. And taking in the wings, as addittions, which at the end next the lesser garden serves for one good roome, with closetts etc., joyned to the new in range, and at the other end the wing constitutes part of the family quarter. So the visto is compleat from end to end, with a noble roome of entry in the midle, which is used as a dining room. The deformity (as now it is esteem'd) of compass windoes, is so disguised either with the furniture within, which reduceth all to a square, or else by bird-cages, and such conceits without, or else serve in the greater and less elegant places, as hall, chappell, and gallery, that it appears to no offence. Then the plantations about it give a great complement and gardens (made with unlimited cost and excelent invention) perfection to the whole.

There are other houses, which have bin reformed or rather renewed, as Badmanton by the Duke of Beaufort, Beavoir by the Earl of Rutland, Burleigh neer Stamford by the Earl of Exeter, which to critiscise upon,

[167]For Hugh May's remodelling of Windsor Castle for Charles II see *History of the King's Works*, ed. Colvin, v (1976).

[168]For the remodelling of Ham House, Petersham, Surrey, for the Duke and Duchess of Lauderdale see J. G. Dunbar in *Archaeological Journal*, cxxxii (1975). Roger North and his brothers 'were not seldom entertained at the great house at Ham, and had the freedom of the gardens and library' (*Lives of the Norths*, i. 232).

would imploy more witt and paper than I have to spare;[169] besides they are large and great works, wherewith I am not very well acquainted; and cannot give any account of the reasons that moved to the respective alterations and additions; but in generall I may observe, that they are so much altered as may well pass for new, and I must needs say, in my opinion, that is a fault. And it is rather an advantage than otherwise to have the old fabrick appear, especially in the avenue. Vanity is not arrived to that degre, as to forbid the using patch't houses, as well as cloath. Hitherto that seeming parsimony is not a shame but rather a credit, and speaks the owner to have care and providence, which is seen in nothing more than mending of housing. Besides when the new appears upon the entry to the principall quarters of enterteinement, it is surprising, and accepted with extraordinary satisfaction. And nothing is so bad, as a promising outside, and deceiptfull disposition within, such as shall give an idea of somewhat very fine to be expected and no whitt of it to be found; which error the English gentry are very apt to fall into. Lett my garb, and frontispeice be serious, stately, and not husty like a *braggadoccio*; and lett my sence and usefullness take my freinds and company when they expect litle.

This is so agreeable to all the common maxims, I need not enlarge in it. Therefore lett none depend on a fair face as a beauty, if the inward composition doth not excell it. But it is still usefull to shew the old fabrick at first, to cover the faults that will stick to old walls, and cannot be wholly wash't out. Nay, it shall excuse such as either mistake, inadvertence, or the restraint caused by the old, shall happen in that which is new and added. For none expects that perfection in what is reformed of old, as in fabricks intirely new. If the latter be not perfect, there is a want declared, either of mony or skill. But all will allow old buildings to want of moderne perfections, and that they cannot by any art be reduct to it. Therefore where the new is first and the old comes after, it is odious, as in my neighbour Colonel Woodhous (to mention a small one), for the front and one or two rooms are promising, but within where the family resides is downe staires as into a cellar and there to paper walls, low roofs, and all the litleness imaginable.[170] But where the

---

[169]For Badminton, Glos., Belvoir, Leics., and Burleigh, Northants., see above, pp.63, 77, 136.

[170]East Lexham Hall, Norfolk, rebuilt in the eighteenth century. According to Blomefield, Edmund Wodehouse of East Lexham became colonel of the Norfolk militia in 1696. If this is so, it provides further corroboration of that year as the date of North's writing the British Library essay.

old comes first and the new suceeds, as at Ham, the contrary effect appears.

Therefore it should be avoided, that an old reformed house should appear as if it were new, as Badmanton doth. For the lowness of the cheif rooms within (a constant fault that cleaves to most old houses) doth not agree with the expectation rais'd from the front without. Whereas the truth knowne (as I have found best in all things as well of ornament as conduct of life) would have excused that defect.

V

Description of the Sector devised by Roger North

BL Add. MS, 32506, 'Of me', fo. 60ᵛ

I also caused to be made an architectonicall sector, whereby one might draw any order after Paladio, to the minutest parts without help of any book or memoriall but what was there. And this consisted in

1. a scale from the center, and next a table of the 5 orders upon the reverse. For the scale, I observed from the *Paralell*, that the model of a columne was devided into 60 and the half into 30 and each of them into 4. So the account of the parts often stood thus, $3.5.\frac{1}{2}$ or $\frac{1}{4}$ and no lower, that is 3 half models, 5. 30 parts and an half or quarter. Now I first devided each part into twelve, then an half was 6 and a quarter 3, so I could note thus: 3 mo — 5 parts — 6 minutes or 4, which came to a greater nicety. And in this method the half diameter past for the model = 30 parts. Then next I considered that if an order were to be composed, the first thing was to take the whole height and from that find the model (*ex Hercule pedem*) and then mechanically to make a scale to it, which not being done very carefully would make error in our designe. Therefore I thought that if a scale for this porpose were put up on the sector, the model found, and the sector set to it, there was a scale to any model could be proposed, therefore I had it done. And the line was cutt first into 10. 20. 30. then each $\frac{1}{10}$ subdevided into 12 minutes. I have a scale thus made which will project to any model not exceeding 4 feet. For the line is $1\frac{1}{2}$ foot long, and the sector opens well 2 foot wide. The reverse of this sector is dedicated to a table of the 5 orders. This is broke in to the usuall parts, vizt., cornish, frize, architrave, capitall, columne, base and pedestall. And so stand as titles to the tables of minutes under-neath. Then follows downewards 10 columnes, which are five, for the 5 orders, and 5 lesser, for describing the shape of the member annext to each.

fo. 61ᵛ

Tuscan		Dorick		Ionic		Corinthian		Composite		
				Cornish						And the height and projecture of each member, with its form[171] is noted in the manner following vizt. in 30ths and 12ths and degrees and minutes.
										Title of the devision underneath.
43	6	38	o	46	o	47	6	50	o	The height of the whole cornish.
3.6		2.3		2.6		2.3		2.6		Height of the first member, flatt.
66.0		76.0		72.0		74.0		78.0		Projecture of the same from the center.
10.0		6.9		7.0		6.4		8.0		Height of the cymatium and shape. The projection is from one to the other.
2.0		0.9		1.0		0.8		1.0		Height of the next.
54.3		68.0		64.0		66.6		70.0		Projecture of the same flatt.
10.0		3.3		3.6		3.0		3.9		Height ⎫ Projecture ⎬ and forme.
52.3										
1.6		6.0		3.0		8.0		2.6		Height ⎫ Projecture ⎬ and forme.
32.0		39.6		55.0		62.0				

fo. 62

This may serve for a running description of the table, which is intended to preserve the memory of the height, projecture, and forme of all the minute parts or members of each grand devision of every order so that with a litle acquaintance with the shapes and manner of the parts, one may with the help of this sector, a square, and a compas sett downe, describe, or make a patterne for workmen, without recourse to a book, which no man can otherwise undertake for.

[171] North's indication of profiles in the narrow columns of his table is so sketchy that it cannot be reproduced.

fo. 62ᵛ

But for the exactness of this table as also of the sector, and other instruments I shall describe, I must referr to the things, or exact delineations of them. For these are but course descriptions. I did intend, and had begun to forme a like table, to all the authors of the *Paralell*, but buissness coming upon me, hindered it. However if I have leisure, and want of company (which with me produceth much fruit of time), I shall perfect and annex it, together with such icones, as shall be neat and expressive.

VI

Project for rebuilding Whitehall Palace

BL Add. MS 32504, fo. 54

Jan. 4th 1697/8 at 4 p.m. fire took in Whitehall, and by 6 ⟨a.⟩ m. it consumed the whole court, except the Banquetting House, and some remote lodgings.

Project of Rebuilding in generall.

1. Lay all open to the Thames from Northumberland House to Westminster and make a key, as now at the Queen's lodgings.
2. Let the Banquetting House, have place of one wing, build its fellow at due distance on the north side of the Gate, in the same rang.
3. Set up a gate between both which shall topp all, and beautyfully as well as magnificently front the Thames.
4. Turne all the Court inwards towards the Park, and let the way be upon the key.
5. From the Midle Gate carry a covered way to the water staires, by the guide of the lower order of the Banquetting House, which underneath, be for a walk ⟨and⟩ hath 4 rows of supports. vzt. the outward, imposts and arches, and within, 2 rows of Tuscan collumnes, and above, let the walk goe strait as a gallery embract with an order as below of the Banquetting House continued. This may be set off with breaks S.A.[172]

[172] *Secundum artem*, i.e. according to established architectural usage.

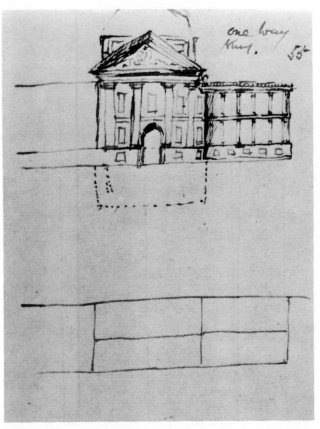

Roger North's
architectural drawings

Roger North's architectural drawings

Architectural drawings by Roger North survive in the British Library and at Rougham Hall. The drawings in the British Library form part of Add. MS 23005, which was not among the North manuscripts acquired in 1885, but was bought at the sale of the library of the Norfolk antiquary Dawson Turner in 1859. It had evidently belonged to Roger's son the Revd Montagu North, for included in it is a plan of his rectory at Sternfield in Suffolk. This must have been drawn after 1767, the year in which he was presented to that living, but all the other drawings in the volume, fourteen in number, are in the hand of Roger North, and are listed below, together with six drawings that remain at Rougham. They show that North was a competent rather than an elegant draughtsman, well able to envisage a complicated building in all its dimensions, but (despite the regular use of colour) unable to avoid a certain clumsiness which betrays the hand of the amateur.

Drawings in British Library, Add. MS 23005

1 (fo. 2). Plans, elevations, and sections of a villa-like house (Pl. 6).

2 (fo. 3). Plan and four sections of a similar house.

3 (fo. 4). Plan and four sections of a square house (Pl. 7).

4 (fo. 5). Plans, elevations, and one section of a house with a pedimented centre (Pl. 8).

5 (fo. 6). Roof plan and four elevations of a square house (Pl. 9).

6 (fo. 7). First-floor plan of Wroxton Abbey, Oxfordshire, showing proposed south wing, and corresponding to Rougham Hall drawing no. 2 below. Drawn c. 1681–5. (Pl. 5).

7 (fo. 8). Plan of an old house, identifiable as Rougham Hall, Norfolk, before remodelling by Roger North in 1692–4, but apparently showing projected alterations not carried out (Pl. 4). See also no. 14, where the pantry enclosure establishes the identity of the house.

8 (fo. 9). Plans, sections, and main elevation of a two-storey addition to a three-storey building, perhaps connected with the Middle Temple (Pl. 10).

9 (fo. 10). Plan of a floor and section of a roof.

10 (fo. 11). Axonometric drawing of the ground floor of the house shown in no. 11. Endorsed in Roger North's hand (see below) (Pl. 12).

11 (fo. 12). Plan and six internal elevations of the house shown in no. 10. Endorsed in Roger North's hand (see below) (Pl. 13).

12 (fo. 13). Plans and front elevation of a house endorsed 'Model of a citty hows lying backwards', with annotations in Roger North's hand (Pl. 11).

13 (fo. 14). Rear elevation and details of the stable at the rear of the town house shown in no. 12, with annotations in Roger North's hand.

14 (fo. 15). Sketch-plan of an old house identifiable as Rougham Hall, Norfolk, before remodelling by Roger North in 1692–4. This plan corresponds to no. 7, but also shows the position of the pantry made of boards 'inclosing a peice out of the hall' mentioned in the text (above, p. 78).

Drawings at Rougham Hall

1. Elevation of the Middle Temple Gateway, showing a different treatment of the basement from that adopted; drawn by Roger North *c*. 1683 (Pl. 2).

2. Ground-floor plan of Wroxton Abbey, Oxfordshire, showing proposed south wing, and corresponding to BL drawing no. 6 above, drawn *c*. 1681–5.

3. Ground-floor plan of Wroxton Abbey, Oxfordshire, showing proposed south wing, but with different internal arrangements from no. 2 above; drawn *c*. 1681–5 and annotated in Roger North's hand (Pl. 5).

4. A sheet showing four plans of small symmetrical houses, with dimensions, etc. in Roger North's hand (Pl. 14).

5. Perspective elevation of a house inscribed in pencil 'Garden front Hunstanton', and showing the west side of Hunstanton Hall, Norfolk, that was destroyed by fire in 1853. A drawing contemporary with Roger North, but probably not in his hand.

6. Elevation of a doorway set in a pedimented wall with brick coins, etc., carefully detailed, endorsed 'Plans drawn by the Honourable Roger North' and evidently used as a wrapper for nos. 1–5.

Endorsements

BL No. 10 is endorsed as follows:

> The faults

This perspective is drawn upon the former model, and so carrys all the faults of that and besides

The stayres to the entrance are too gross and spreading, besides not drawne exactly by the rule.

The stayres of ordinary use are not expres't.

The small back staires are done by guess, and not by the rule, so appear not well.

BL No. 11 is endorsed as follows:

> The faults of this designe

The doors plac't so that the pannells on each side are not equall.

Doors should be from each stair to the steps descending without.

The great stayrs are to be ordered without turning.

Great parlor door from the skreen stands askew.

The withdrawing room, and parlour, too long, but may be better above, making an entry behind for convenience.

Wants back staires to serve the great apartment conveniences.

Index

Index

Index

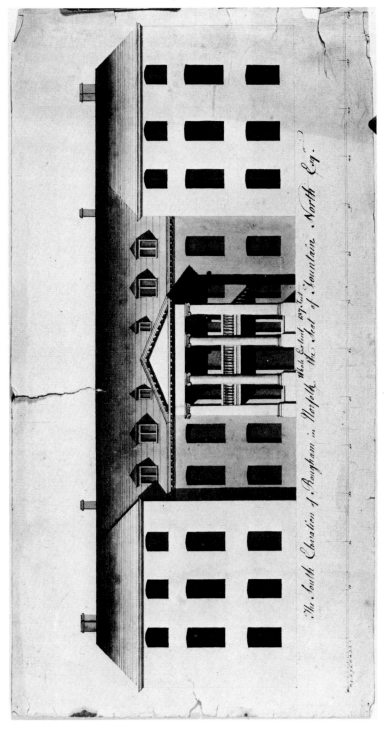

The South Elevation of Rougham in Norfolk, the seat of Fountaine North Esq.
Whole Extent 87 feet

1. Rougham Hall, Norfolk, the south front as remodelled by Roger North in 1692-4

2. A design for the Middle Temple Gateway in Roger North's hand

3. The Middle Temple Gateway in the Strand, London, built to Roger North's design in 1683-4

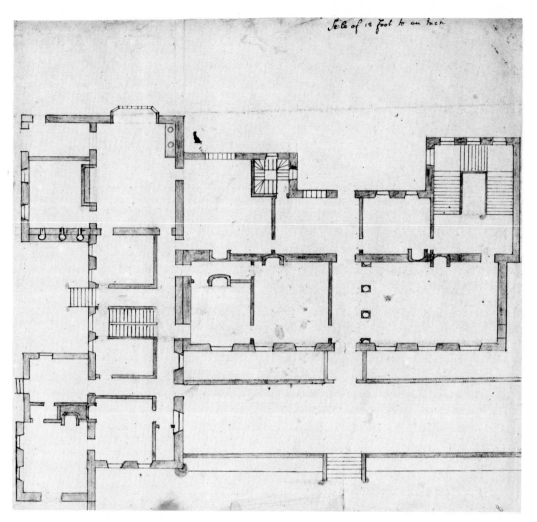

Scale of 12 foot to an inch

4. Plan of old Rougham Hall by Roger North, showing projected alterations

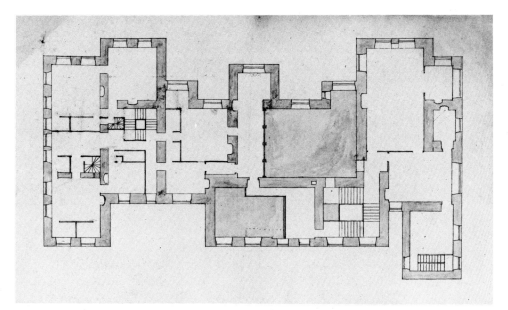

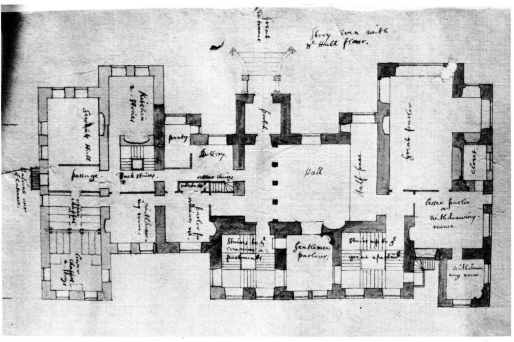

5. Plans of Wroxton Abbey, Oxon., by Roger North, showing proposed alterations

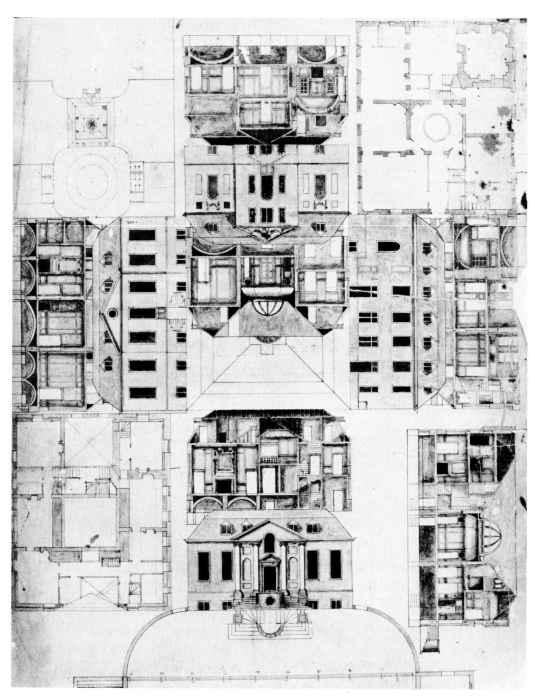

6. A design by Roger North for a villa-like house

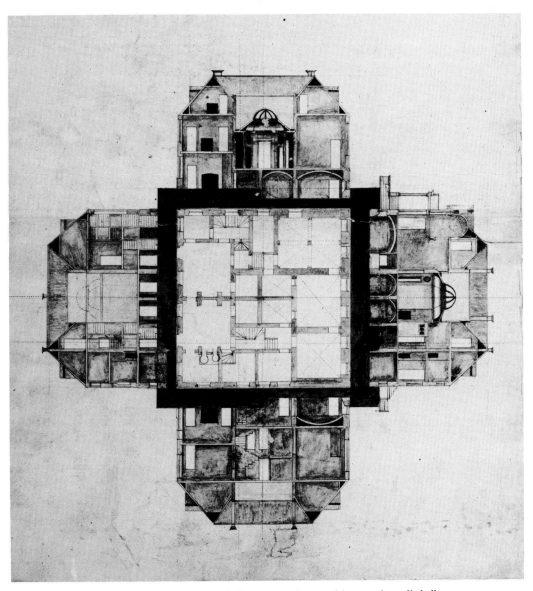

7. A design by Roger North for a square house with central top-lit hall

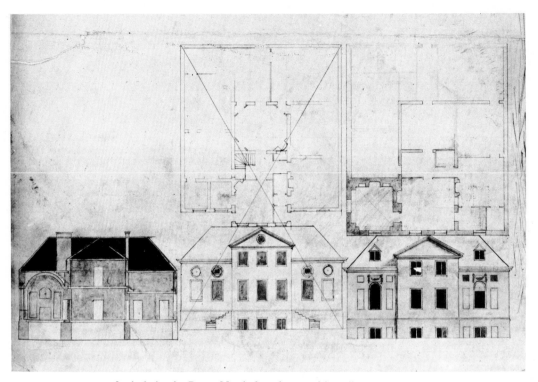

8. A design by Roger North for a house with pedimented centre

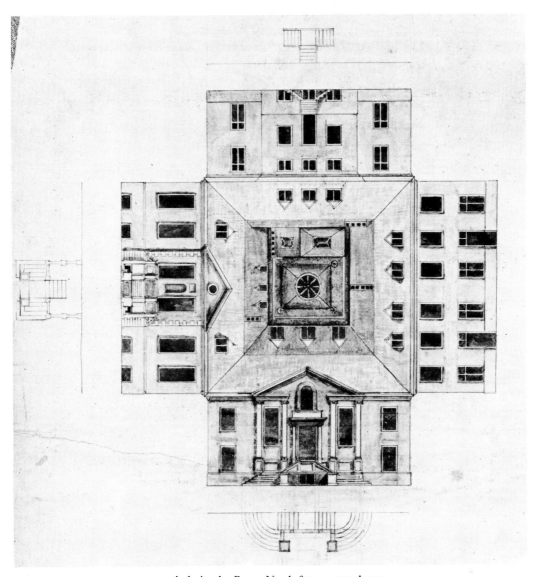

9. A design by Roger North for a square house

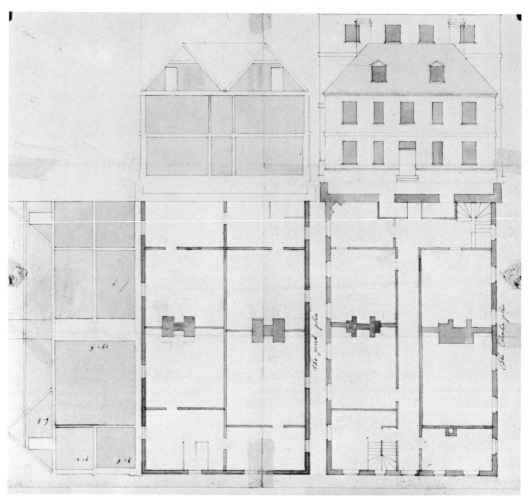

10. A design by Roger North for a two-storey addition to a three-storey building, perhaps connected with the Middle Temple.

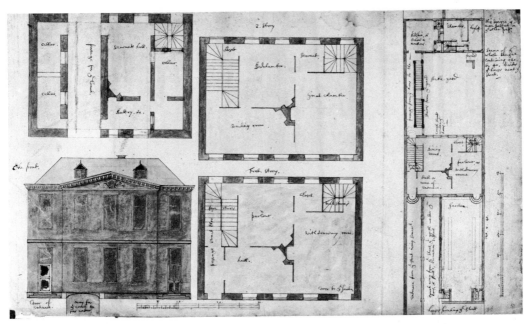

11. Design by Roger North for 'a citty hows lying backwards'

12. Axonometric drawing by Roger North of the ground floor of the house shown in Plate 13

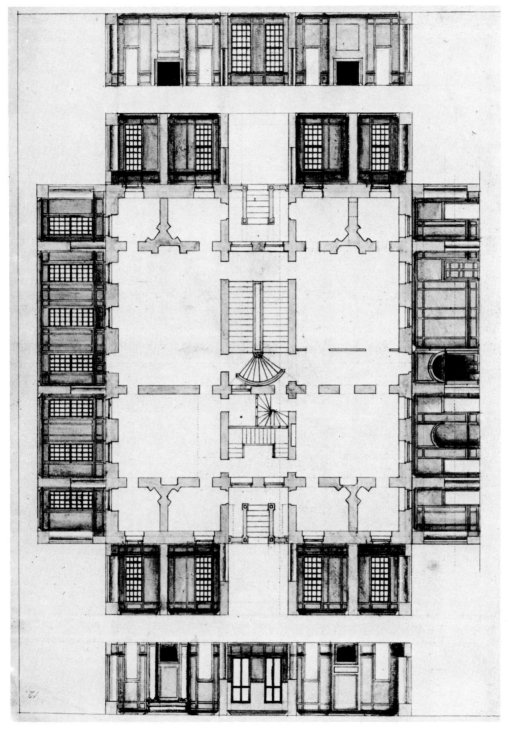

13. Plan and internal elevations by Roger North of the house shown in Plate 12.

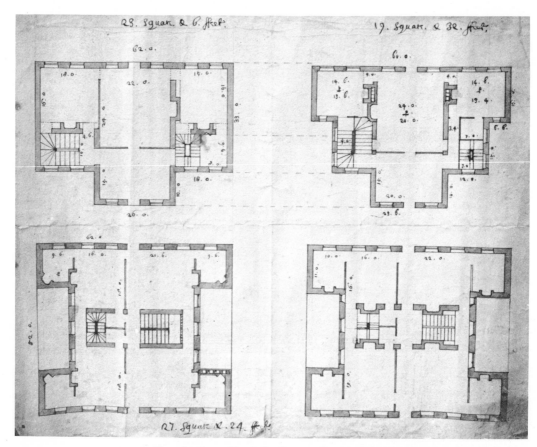

14. Plans by Roger North for four small symmetrical houses

15. Rougham Hall: the surviving capital and base of one of the columns of the portico, converted into a sundial